PAT CONROY

ALSO BY BERNIE SCHEIN

PAT CONROY

Our Lifelong Friendship

BERNIE SCHEIN

WITH A NEW FOREWORD
BY RICK BRAGG

ARCADE PUBLISHING · NEW YORK

First Paperback Edition 2024

Arcade Publishing books may be purchased in bulk at special discounts for sales promotion, corporate gifts, fund-raising, or educational purposes. Special editions can also be created to specifications. For details, contact the Special Sales Department, Arcade Publishing, 307 West 36th Street, 11th Floor, New York, NY 10018 or arcade@skyhorsepublishing.com.

Arcade Publishing® is a registered trademark of Skyhorse Publishing, Inc.®, a Delaware corporation.

Visit our website at www.arcadepub.com.
Visit the author's site at bernieschein.com.

10 9 8 7 6 5 4 3 2 1

Library of Congress Cataloging-in-Publication Data

Names: Schein, Bernie, 1944–author.
Title: Pat Conroy : our lifelong friendship / Bernie Schein.
Description: New York, NY : Arcade Publishing, an Imprint of Skyhorse Publishing, 2019.
Identifiers: LCCN 2019020658 (print) | LCCN 2019980221 (ebook) |
ISBN 978-1-64821-089-1 (paperback) | ISBN 978-1-948924-15-3 (ebook)
Subjects: LCSH: Conroy, Pat—Friends and associates. | Schein, Bernie, 1944—Friends
    and associates. | Authors, American—20th Century—Biography.
Classification: LCC PS3553.O5198 Z83 2019 (print) | LCC PS3553.O5198 (ebook) |
    DDC 813/.54 [B]—dc23
LC record available at https://lccn.loc.gov/2019020658
LC ebook record available at https://lccn.loc.gov/2019980221

Cover design by Erin Seaward-Hiatt
Cover photo: © Associated Press

Printed in the United States of America

FOR MARTHA,

*the prettiest, the most perceptive, the most loving in the whole world,
my wife and best friend, always and forever*

CONTENTS

A photo insert is located between pages 132 and 133.

FOREWORD
by RICK BRAGG

Pat Conroy had a lot of gifts.

Most of us only get one, or just a little bit of one. Pat had dozens of them.

He was a fair writer, I am told. I don't know for sure because I rarely got through a page without crying, or being struck dumb at the wonder of it, or just sitting there with a goofy smile on my face.

He had courage, and generosity. You need that in a world so thick with injustice. He had a gift for rubbing selfish and pretentious and ignorant people raw, and then rubbing salt into them.

He was, I am told, a fine dribbler. Which is an excellent gift to have if you cannot shoot or jump.

I hear he made a fine crab cake.

But maybe Pat Conroy's greatest gift, maybe even on par with his incredible writing, was his ability to grow a friendship, a thing so deep and wide that you cannot swing a dead cat in the world of literature—and beyond—without hitting a person whose life was affected by him.

I thought, once, I was one of a special few he championed, but as the years passed I would come to understand that this is what Pat did. He collected friends the way I do pocket knives. Every now and then he would realize that he not reacquainted himself with them in a while, and he would take them out of some cluttered drawer, wipe the dust off, and admire them.

I could go months and even years without hearing from him, and then one day my phone would ring and he would start talking without preamble, like we had talked a few minutes ago and been interrupted by the UPS man.

"Ours could have been a father-son relationship, but you rejected me to go associate with the Yankee bigshots in New York," he would say, like it was me who had disappeared, like it was all my damn fault.

We would talk for hours, about words.

And then he would have to go, and tell me he loved my work, and loved me, and loved my momma, and the phone would go dead.

I guess it didn't matter that I was one of hundreds, or thousands.

Some of us have written about him, now that he is gone. A lot of us have. I guess that is just one small way that we can keep him with us. His words are truly immortal. It is the rascal behind them I miss so much.

But the truth is, hell, we didn't really know him. We just knew the grace in him.

It occurred to me, just the other day, that we had never had a fight, He was always with me. He kidded me, and chided me, but he was with me.

He was my friend and my champion, but I didn't truly know him.

You have to be somebody's blood, or share their name, to know them. Or maybe just their buddy. Someone you knock down, then help them up. Someone you know across a lifetime, or at least a whole lot of years.

This book, written by Pat's buddy, Bernie Schein, is about that.

They were friends across decades, if you don't count the sixteen or so years when they didn't speak to each other. They fought and carped and just mightily disagreed, about important things and foolish things, but somehow their friendship survived until Pat left this world. I am almost certain Pat had the last word.

There is no namby-pamby punch-pulling here. Their friendship was too genuine for that, and that is what this book is, a deeper look than most of us were allowed. This book is the journey of that friendship, from the Lowcountry to the wide world beyond.

Pat's wife, Sandra, who is from the same part of the world as me, has written—beautifully—from her own broken heart. She said it was okay for me to want to know more, and like it.

Bernie loved his friend, warts and all. I think we all would have, if we had come to know him better. And that is, in an odd way, the great sadness in his passing. How odd, to envy someone the briars, the stickers, of a friendship.

I am at the age where just about everybody I have ever loved is gone. Some people I refuse to remember, because it hurts so awful much. But I have permission now, for at least one of them.

PAT CONROY

I

FAMOUS ALWAYS, WHEREVER HE WAS

Pat Conroy, even as a child, long before he became a world-renowned writer and public figure, was either blessed or cursed, depending on how you looked at it, with a greater-than-life, love-your-ass, break-your-balls personality. As he himself so cheerfully noted, it was "fabulous." It was.

He was unremittingly open-hearted and hospitable, especially when he didn't mean it. Of all the actors—Jon Voight, Michael O'Keefe, David Keith, Nick Nolte—who ended up playing his character in the movies based on his novels, none had his charisma, his outsize capacity for joy, for love, for hatred, for tragedy, to say nothing of his sense of humor. His personality was simply too much for them to grab hold of and contain, to internalize, to take on, even though they were just pretending, as he often did, which no doubt complicated their understanding of him even more. Throw in his false modesty and sanctimony, his Irish mischief, and his warrior-like mentality, and the cup really overfloweth.

No matter how much he tried to deflect attention elsewhere, it managed to open Pat's front door, invite itself in, grab a chair, and make itself at home. Why? Paradoxically, because Pat invited it in, people he'd barely met, some whom he'd *never* met, considered themselves his intimate. Pat loved people even more than he hated them, which meant he could see into your heart and soul like no other, expanding both your world and his, inspiring you to heights you might never have otherwise imagined—unless, of course, his world got in the way of yours.

Long before he became a celebrated writer and public figure, as far back as our teenage years in Beaufort, South Carolina, he was the type of person you heard about, were curious about, before you actually met him. He was famous, wherever he was, before he was famous all over the world.

Then when you actually did meet him, he was so gregarious that he made you feel as if *you* were that person, that, hell, he'd heard all about *you*. Even if he had. That's right. Even if he had.

Like most people, both before and after he became famous, I too heard about Pat before I met him, in study hall in Beaufort High School, where in the fall of 1961 I was the self-appointed teacher of a small group of my classmates at a privileged, secluded table *For Seniors Only* in a remote corner of the cafetorium. Our small, discreet group gathered at that particular table because it was strategically out of earshot of the study hall monitor. Senior privilege, Beaufort High's public recognition of our growth and maturity during our school years, afforded us our table's status and preferred location. The title of the course I taught: How to Successfully Cheat without Guilt and Remorse.

The purpose: graduation, namely mine.

Though I am a Jew, I was famously dumb, and my mother was all over my ass about my grades. And since a few of my classmates were beginning to express moral scruples about The Easiest Way to Get Ahead, I took it upon myself to absolve them of that unnecessary baggage, which probably, in retrospect, consumed more of my time and energy than actually studying for tests and paying attention in class, which was boring.

School sucked, but I did need to graduate and get into college. I didn't want to end up, as Mom so frequently warned me, as a homeless derelict knifed to death in my sleep under some anonymous bridge or overpass for my "ratty old overcoat" that probably smelled even worse than my assailant. So copying test papers and homework, and plagiarizing research papers, despite my lifelong friends' and classmates' misgivings, were becoming more and more a priority.

My credo at the time was: Never do for yourself what others can do for you.

What they did for me was get me a diploma and therefore into college, for which I am forever grateful. Years later, when I went to graduate school at Harvard, they took full credit. "Without us, you would never have gotten out of high school," they said, and it was true.

As their self-appointed instructor, that course in study hall was my first foray into teaching, which eventually would blossom into a lifelong career and, early on, get Pat and me out of the draft.

But that was years later. When I first met Pat, he was new to Beaufort and Beaufort High, his dad, Colonel Don Conroy, having been transferred to the United States Marine Corps base at Parris Island, Beaufort's local military base. Beaufort, my home town, then redneck rather than resort, was as unknown to the world as Colonel Conroy's eventual *nom de roman*, the Great Santini.

As I say, I heard of Pat long before I met him. Two really pretty girls, Gretchen Maas and Kathleen Kennedy, who sat at our *For Seniors Only* table, were themselves military brats and couldn't shut up about him. Pat Conroy this . . . Pat Conroy that. "Oh, he's so funny . . . Oh, he's so cute, so nice and friendly." And he wasn't even a senior! Just some snot-nosed junior wannabee.

This was a guy to be reckoned with, I thought, as I copied Billy Canaday's math homework.

When they got too loud, naturally I reprimanded them. "Jesus, can you shut the fuck up? I'm trying to get some work done here." Cheating, I informed them, is a serious business. The need for concentration, focus, as in any serious endeavor, could not be overestimated. This was as much a part of the course as anything else, as far as I was concerned.

I was tough, I admit, but they'd thank me for it later, I promised them.

Boy, were they pretty.

The first actual contact between Pat and me was when the basketball came my way in one of those pickup games in the gym involving what seemed like a thousand players on each team. Talk about threading the needle. The ball floated toward me through a byzantine maze of players—I didn't even know at the time who had passed it. I'd been jogging lazily toward the basket, hoping maybe for a loose ball or an easy rebound bouncing my way, and there the ball was, floating softly into my open palms and, at the cost not even of a dribble rising upward, glancing off the backboard into the basket.

A soft pass, intended to lead me toward the pot of gold, the hoop. No unnecessary spin, easily handed, clean, thrown not only with stealth but with astonishing foresight, especially for a madhouse pickup game.

The guy who'd passed it, who would become the greatest basketball player ever to graduate from Beaufort High, an all-state player and Citadel point guard known for having eyes in the back of his head, introduced himself to me that afternoon. His gregarious smile, his bright blue Irish eyes, his body so hard and taut that when he drove to the basket, he drove undeterred, opponents just bouncing off him.

"Pat Conroy," he said, offering his hand. "You've got a great shot. I was watching you. That's rare."

Already he was thinking about who, in the future, he was going to throw the ball to.

He was a military brat. I knew that. They were more worldly than locals like me, having lived all over the place. They were more cosmopolitan, knew geography and how to get around. On senior trips, they knew how to take the subway in New York. They almost always made good grades, which was the only thing I didn't much like about them. How anyone could truly enjoy school was an enigma to me.

Since Beaufort was a military town, it was economically dependent on the military, giving military brats like Pat somewhat of an honored position, even though he, like most of them, talked like a Yankee.

"Gretchen and Kathleen talk about you all the time," he told me. "They can't get enough of you. They think you're hilarious."

I must have been pretty easy, because that's all it took, though when he found out about my cheating course he hated it. He found it "disgusting," "unethical," "immoral," "cowardly," and "dishonest," but what did he know? He was only a junior.

Geez, man. He was lucky I was even deigning to speak to him, particularly with people watching.

Actually, I think he was oddly intrigued.

"The outrageousness of it!" he loved to proclaim.

He was as bored with school as I was but just too eager to please, too Dudley Do-Right to admit it. We both loved to read, though, and we both loved sports, and popular though we were, we were nevertheless different from our friends and classmates in that he attended Mass and I attended synagogue.

More important than any of that was the fact that, unlike the Gentile boys in town, we couldn't *do* anything. Like me, and all the Jewish men in town—except for the few who hunted, fished, drank beer, played poker with the boys, and were capable of going through a crisis without a change of expression—Pat was a hysteric and on seriously less than congenial terms with the toolbox, the fuse box, the hammer, and the nail, drag pipes, hubcaps, automobile engines, carburetors, and Evinrudes. All of which were, at that time in the South, Gentile specialties, like barbecue pits and pep rallies.

Daddy was a terrific businessman, great with numbers—he did Pat's taxes once Pat got old enough to pay them—but if a light bulb needed changing or an electrical cord needed plugging in, he hired a handyman, and while the handyman was doing his work in the house, Daddy gathered the entire family together in the front yard waiting in case the house blew up.

When Pat entered Beaufort High his junior year, my senior year, Beaufort was pretty much just like any other small Southern community in the Bible Belt. Back then, long before Beaufort went from a town suspicious of strangers to a resort that courted them, long before anyone in town had even heard of soccer, much less soccer moms, the good Christians of Beaufort worshipped God and praised Jesus on Sunday mornings and worshipped football, basketball, and baseball and prayed for victory for the Beaufort High School Tidal Wave on Friday evenings. With the exception *perhaps* of Jesus, nothing was bigger than the Friday night football games during the football season or the basketball games during the basketball season, not even everybody's favorite verbal sport, gossip. All the whispering about the mayor's black Cadillac wedged among the camellias and azaleas in the school librarian's backyard at 3:00 a.m., about the bounced checks on display in the front windows of downtown stores, about the pretty little thing left at the altar on her wedding day all stopped abruptly when Richard Drawdy hit Paul Barber with that perfect spiral in the end zone, when Butch Epps silenced the opposition with a grand slam, and when Pat Conroy took to the basketball court.

And no one was more jealous of him than Richard and Paul and Butch. They were seniors. This was supposed to be their time. And Pat would have usurped their time in football if he hadn't gotten hurt at the beginning of the season.

Senior athletes were the most popular boys in the school, socially formidable. As soon as his football prowess entered their sights, they shot him down at every opportunity, jeering, ridiculing, going after him in practice. He was quick and fast, so derisively and sarcastically they called him "Jethawk."

Pat had an advantage in football and basketball. He'd played with black kids on the fields and playgrounds in Washington. Before he got hurt, which was in the fall of his junior year, Beaufort High's football team, naturally led by the seniors, pissed him off so much he gathered a ragtag group of military brats from his neighborhood where most of them were quartered, put together a team that he quarterbacked, challenged the entire Beaufort High football team to a scrimmage, a team that without him would go on to win the Lower State Championship of South Carolina, and almost beat them.

With greater respect came even greater fear and envy, especially when basketball season began and he was once again healthy. Pat would have to deal with jealousy and envy, those classic adolescent sneers, all his life. That was his curse, that was his blessing. He was always a star.

What added to his difficulties with the natives—the seniors, that is—in high school was that he was so friendly and gregarious, not only a star athlete but, among his fellow juniors as well as the sophomores and freshman, he was a *social* star, immediately, as soon as he walked through the door. So this made him even more of a threat. Not only was he a junior, not only was he new, he was already popular.

For my entire life, except when he was pissed off at me, Pat would tell everyone in the world that I had invited him to his first party, which I did after hearing Gretchen and Kathy talking about him that day in study hall. His first party? At *seventeen*?

And why did it mean so much to him?

It meant so much to him, I realized later, because, like many military brats, until he moved to Beaufort he'd moved every year, entering a new school, never getting to know people well enough to really be included in parties that their classmates had attended all their lives, from birthday parties when they were younger to teenage parties when they were older. More importantly, an enduring relationship was just about impossible. Upon arriving, they knew they would be leaving, and so did everyone else. They were military brats, nomads roaming from military base to military base, following their fathers to wherever the government sent them. It was only when I began teaching that I learned just how traumatic moving and relocating could be for kids, not only for those who weren't that social but for kids like Pat, who were.

But just as athletics would become the social lubricant that would later ease the process of integration, so would it now, in high school, ease Pat's integration into the social life of not only the entire school but that of the seniors. He became not only the most popular kid in the school but president of his class.

And what made him different from most of the popular kids was that he didn't have a snobby bone in his body. He was *grateful* for your friendship, no matter who you were. He *thanked* you for it. As far as I was concerned, that was odd. I'd never heard anybody do that before. He didn't care in the slightest about what you wore. Or for that matter, what he wore. And when you were with him, for some mysterious reason, you didn't either. Gant shirts? Bass Weejuns? Alligator belts? To be among the cool kids, which was all I aspired to, that was the ticket. What you wore was who you were. Clothes made the man. That just never seemed to enter his mind. He was uncommonly interested, it seemed, in you, in the person himself. I'd never heard of such a thing.

Also, because Beaufort was new to him, it was as if he was seeing it for the first time, which led me to discover that I, who had lived there all my life, had never seen it at all. I'd never once thought of it as lovely, romantic, beautiful. I don't know whether it was because, as a native, I just took it for granted or, as a Jew, I was at two with nature. My grandparents had been Russian-Polish émigrés. According to the Russian-Jewish writer Isaac Babel, lost forever in Stalin's Purge, there's only one word in Hebrew for *all* the birds in the world, and that's the Hebrew word for "bird," and only two words in Hebrew for all the flowers in the world, the Hebrew words for "flower" and "rose." In Babel's Odessa, Jewish kids were expected to read, study, and play the violin. Babel had to get a Gentile to teach him how to swim.

One Saturday afternoon we were walking on the bay when Pat stopped, gazing out over the Beaufort River. It was a bright, shimmering blue in sunlight, hosting the usual sailboats and sea birds and the occasional barge, and because it was low tide, the hood of an old taxicab peering out of the water close to the shore. It'd been there since I was a kid. The only cab driver in town was a drunk, nobody bothered to fish it out, and we kids swam down in there for treasure. Frankly, at the time, that's all I noticed, remembering how back then we'd play baseball in the streets and just naturally back off onto the nearest front lawn when Ol' Dacus—that was the cab driver's name—came careening down the road. Now that was an adventure. It was like watching a bumper car going awry. Daddy said anybody short-circuited enough to be on the road when that guy was coming probably ought to be run over.

Pat paused on the riverbank, breathing in the smell of pluff mud. "Damn," he said, throwing out his arms, embracing all in front of us, the river, the boats, the light, the flower and fauna and gargantuan oak trees on the riverbank. "This is so fucking beautiful. Isn't it? Don't you think so, Bernie? I mean, God. Lovely. Just lovely."

All I'd seen was a memory, an old taxi jutting out of the marsh in which was the forever-elusive X marking the spot where the treasure was sure to be.

I looked as if for the first time, and I saw, I believe, what Pat saw, after which I could never stop looking, every day, it was so stunning, so unimaginably lovely and beautiful, so inspiring. It brought me to tears, right then. The beauty of my home town, long before it became a haven for tourists and retirees, seeing it, smelling it, hearing it, would make me forget about the treasure for the rest of my life.

Until then, the river had been a place in which to swim, over which to sail majestically out on the rope swing, the thousand-year oak the perfect support for it, a place to fish and to ski with the Gentiles. Trees for shade in the dog days of August. Flowering shrubs obstacle courses through which to maneuver your bike, flower gardens to sneak into on your hands and knees to retrieve baseballs, grass soft and welcoming to bare feet in the summer. The woods for camping or to shoot BB guns with Gentile friends.

I never thought of any of this as something to look at.

I was so unattuned to nature in every respect that, unlike the Gentiles I knew, I could not have named one flower, one bird, or one tree other than an oak. A great blue heron was just a big duck to me. All seabirds looked alike to me.

Pat reveled in my ignorance. We'd be showing off for our dates, cruising around Beaufort. "Tree," he'd say. "Repeat after me, Bernie: tree."

"Sky," he'd say. "Repeat after me, Bernie: sky."

If we were parking, right when I'd make my move, "Moon," he'd say. "Moon."

What a hoot.

Pat graduated Beaufort High on his own. I did so with a little help from my friends. As he so vividly recounts in *The Lords of Discipline*, he was miserable at the Citadel, the military college in Charleston, South Carolina, while I went to Newberry College in upstate South Carolina, where partying was everything, so cheating was the norm, at least in my social world. Unlike Pat at the Citadel, I couldn't have been happier, no doubt because I couldn't have been more superficial. Ignorance, for a brief period in one's life, indeed can be bliss. However, upon completing the required courses, I was so inspired and stimulated by a course centered around the Holocaust and racial prejudice in the American South I actually became such a serious student that professors would stop me in the hallway to ask, "What happened?"

What happened was until that particular course, in which flashed before my eyes my Jewish past and Southern present, I was thoughtless, the statistic of the "six million" Jewish dead in the Holocaust distant and remote, the institutionalized racism in my home town if not relatively benign, "normal." Now, however, in a course taught by a man with a distinctly German name, in slides, film, photographs, through diaries, lectures, texts, and personal narratives, images from the Holocaust took on a startling life of their own, one after another after another of Jewish men, women, and children just like me, I was realizing, just like my parents, my brothers, my cousins and aunts and uncles, and the Jewish families I had known all my life in the congregation of Beaufort's Beth Israel Synagogue, *my* congregation—the Farbsteins, the Liptons, the Levines, Bobby Hirsch who sold me my Keds, Hymie Lipsitz who pulled my teeth, Sol Neidich who brought me into this world, his wife Evelyn who organized the Oneg Shabbats—had *less than twenty years ago* been herded into ghettos, then into cattle cars, then into either abject servitude and slave labor or into the gas chambers and crematoriums. The photographs were haunting: a mother hiding her child behind her skirt before a firing squad—that could have been, had her parents not emigrated, my mother. The shoes, always the shoes: the shoes of my grandfather and grandmother, of my father, had they remained in the Pale of Settlement? Jewish lampshades, Jewish soap—made from whose mother, father, children? Where did their names go? Jewish gold teeth as Nazi currency? Truckloads of mangled, emaciated corpses? Dr. Mengele's sadistic experiments on Jewish twins?

No wonder, I realized, the Jewish community of Beaufort held its children so close, doted on us, smothered us with affection, considered us as so "special." If your singing voice sounded like a blue jay's, you were still "little Eddie Cantor." If you made straight *A*s, no standing on your feet all day waiting on customers, absolutely not, "not for this little one"—you were going to be a doctor or lawyer or, without the slightest tilt toward modesty, Albert Einstein. If you were secretary of your home room class, nothing less than the presidency of the United States, though there was a bit of trepidation here because if you screwed up, who would be blamed? Right?

Of course we were special. There just weren't that many of us left. The demand was high, I realized, because the supply had so dramatically diminished. And here I'd always thought all those beaming maternal smiles and hardy paternal pats on the back were because we were "chosen," something I'd never hesitated pointing out to my friends in high school, just about all of them fervent Christians, particularly when they tried to convert me.

"As a member in good standing of the Chosen People, *I'm* the one with the inside track to the Lord, thank you. Fork over your lunch money, and I'll put in a good word for you."

And what I had taken for granted in my home town! What was the difference between No Jews Allowed signs on Munich storefronts and No Negroes Allowed in Beaufort restaurants and hotels, between the slums of Beaufort and the ghettoes of Europe, between putting the Jews in their place in Germany and keeping the "coloreds"—people I knew and had loved as a child in my father's neighborhood grocery store, *their* neighborhood grocery store—in their place in Beaufort.

Yes, I had been thoughtless, downright blind in my ignorance and insensitivity, but this course, this course taught by a professor with a distinctly German name who was in and out of my life in a semester, began opening my eyes.

Pat was not thoughtless. His eyes had long ago been opened by his own personal "Holocaust," as he would characterize it, perpetrated by a brutal, tyrannical father that took place throughout his childhood in his own home, which he would later expose to the world in *The Great Santini*. His mother told him when he was very young in the midst of their own terrifying travails that if there was another Holocaust like there'd been in Germany, she wanted children brave enough "to hide Jews." Those who have suffered can either deny it or be drawn to it. Like his mother Peg, who'd been poor and abandoned and knew hunger as a child in rural Alabama, Pat was compelled by it. He always would be, and when he saw how obsessed I was with the Holocaust, he showered me with books ranging from Leon Uris's *Exodus* and *Mila 18* to more serious writers like Rabbi Rubenstein, who after the Holocaust proclaimed that God was Dead, Primo Levi, and later Elie Wiesel.

That course at Newberry College was personal—the material in and of itself made it so—and it taught me too that just about all of my courses should be, that to be personal was to be relevant, universal, as the poets teach us, in the absence of which my schooling up until that point had failed me. So "getting personal" became not only my credo as a student but mine and Pat's as teachers. To Pat, it came naturally.

After graduating from college, Pat and I both returned to Beaufort to dodge the draft and to teach, in that order. Pat taught in Beaufort High, the returning prodigy, and I was the teaching-principal of Yemassee Elementary and Junior High in tiny Yemassee, South Carolina, twenty-six miles up the road in neighboring Hampton County.

Yemassee was so small, in fact, so barren of anything but a few churches and a business district less than a block long, so desperate in their first year of desegregation to find any principal, qualified or not, who wasn't a racist, that they ended up hiring me. All the teachers were veterans, all female. The school had pretty much run itself before. Now, however, with the black kids coming in, they figured they needed a man, a real man, at the helm, and that man was me, Bernie Schein. I was a Jew, they figured, so I couldn't possibly be a racist, and I was a known product; they all knew my family. Besides, one board member told me, if I couldn't find anything to do, I could always jump on the riding lawn mower and cut the grass.

I can't tell you how bored I was in Yemassee. Young people left for jobs in bigger towns and cities as soon as they graduated. Everybody else was much older than me, all settled in with families, their lives centered around hunting, fishing, and the church.

I lived in a motel room in the only motel in Yemassee, but every afternoon after school I'd jump in my car and head to Beaufort to see Pat and our friends Mike Jones, George Garbade, and Tim Belk. Mike and George, old friends with whom I'd grown up, were both teaching with Pat at Beaufort High; George also a guidance counselor. Tim was teaching literature at the University of South Carolina in Beaufort.

Tim rented a small house on the Point, the old, aristocratic section of Beaufort which by that time had seen its better days, and down the street Pat rented a tiny cottage on the property of an antebellum home on the Beaufort River. Mike and George lived together in a more modest neighborhood only a few minutes away in the part of Beaufort known as Pigeon Point.

In Beaufort back then, everybody and everything was only a few minutes away. It was what I called an eight-minute town: you could drive from one end to the other in eight minutes or less.

I'd drive by Schein's Grocery to chat with Dad for a bit, then drop my laundry off at the house where I'd brag to Mom, to her amusement, about what a hit I was in Yemassee, then head over to Tim's or Mike and George's to meet them and Pat.

There we'd drink and argue entirely uncorked with each other.

"Each night," Pat wrote in *The Water Is Wide*, "I joined my best friends, George Garbade, Mike Jones, and Bernie Schein in front of the television for the evening news. . . . After the news we held disorganized, vehement debates. The four of us argued until the late hours of night, exposing half-hidden prejudices. We mercilessly pounced on the member of the group who dared utter a belief without foundation or rational credibility. Those gatherings were group confessions of guilt, of cynicism, of rudderless idealism, and ultimately of hope."

As Pat also wrote, "The war in Vietnam ate people on film. The seven o'clock news smoked with napalm and bodies."

And Beaufort, the town we so loved, was not only a conservative, military, pro-war town but a depository of institutionalized racism at war with desegregation.

II

THE WAR AT HOME, THE WAR ABROAD

It was in my second year as teaching-principal of Yemassee Elementary and Junior High that not only did I betray my country, I exploited, however discreetly, Beaufort's black community, for whose cause Pat and I, along with Mike, George, and Tim, had begun in our own small ways to advocate.

Pat and I were both looking for ways to incorporate black history into the curricula at our respective schools. Of course, first we had to study it, which we were doing, but once we had learned enough to at least introduce it to our students, we found ourselves learning right alongside them.

George, who was tall, athletic, easy, and good-natured, was known back then as a real "ladies' man," so we admired and envied him. We wanted to be "ladies' men," too, but weren't up to snuff. In his role as guidance counselor, George had black kids coming to his office for help. He was questioning the racist attitudes with which he'd been brought up in nearby Ridgeland, particularly with Pat and George and me so adamantly arguing against them.

Mike had taken off a year from divinity school to teach in his home town. A popular, well-respected liberal Episcopal priest in the St. Helena Episcopal Church, in which Mike had grown up and was still very involved, suggested "discreetly"—Mike's word—that he form a "study group," which Mike "interpreted"—again, his word—to mean a biracial group of progressive activists who were pro–civil rights and against the Vietnam war. As a native and a progressive, Mike had the necessary connections. Mike gave a guest sermon at the church, whose congregation was not only all white but adamantly pro–Vietnam war, the last line of which was that, yes, people were being killed in Vietnam, but "on both sides."

Afterwards, over at his and George's place, Mike was pretty smug about this, grinning with pride, which Pat couldn't help but tease him about. With an entirely straight face, he asked us all to raise our glasses of Old Crow and toasted Mike.

"To Mike," he said, "to courage and untold bravery."

We were all amused, no one more than Mike.

"And to the line 'people are being killed on both sides'" that I personally predict will end the war. And why?" he concluded. "Because words are more powerful than guns."

At which point we were all pretty much convulsing with laughter.

"Thank you, Pat," offered Mike, "for giving credit where it's due. One small step for Jones, one huge step for mankind." He raised his glass, taking us all in. "Thank you all. I couldn't have done it without your support."

George, sitting there with his trademark lopsided grin, said, "You're welcome, Mike." George probably meant it too. He'd grown up thirty minutes west of Beaufort in Jasper County, in what would become known nationally as "the Corridor of Shame" for its neglect of black children in Jasper County schools.

And in retrospect, despite Pat's teasing, what Mike said in perhaps the most white, aristocratic, conservative church in all of Beaufort was pretty far out there. *Vietnamese* lives? Who in that church in that time in Beaufort, South Carolina, had even considered them?

Black kids at Beaufort High were beginning to seek out Pat, Mike, and George to talk with, which they often did in small groups as well as in their classes. In one of Mike's classes a white kid, Purvis K., used the word "nigger," not with disdain as you might expect but only because that's what he was brought up with, common usage in his home. According to Mike, he just didn't know not to. Tabitha L., a black girl in the class who was quite fond of him, as was just about everyone, looked at him like he was crazy. Back then "Negro" was the acceptable term. "Negro," Tabitha tells him.

He's confused, taken aback, but he likes her, Mike told me, you could tell.

She points to her knee. "Knee," she tells him. "The knee, like every other part of the body, 'grows.' So," she concludes, "Knee-grow. Nee-gro. Negro!"

Meanwhile, twenty-six miles up the road in Yemassee, a cluster of fifth-grade white boys in protest of a black classmate taking a "number two" on the toilet are refusing to use the bathroom. Waiting them out, needless to say, is not an option. What exactly is the difference, I ask them, between you and him? He's a nigger, they say. Our maid doesn't use the bathroom in our house. What exactly is a nigger? I ask. He's "colored." Aren't we all, I think to myself, but I've gone that route before and it led nowhere.

So he's different only because of the color of his skin? You're humiliating him for that? Does he have feelings that can be hurt, like you do? When have you had your feelings hurt? Felt left out? Like you were a nobody? And don't tell me you never have because I've seen you do it to each other if for no other reason just to be "cool," popular, at each other's expense. Raise your hands if this has happened to you, leaving you feeling lonely and isolated, looking for someone to hang around with. I'm in the lunchroom every day. I'm on the playground every day. Ricky, your hand's not raised. Do you want me to remind you when I saw it happening to you less than a week ago? Right. Thank you. How did you feel? How did all of you feel when this kind of thing happened to you?

When they actually sincerely apologized to their black classmate, he just couldn't help it: he collapsed into tears, which made his classmates even nicer to him, so much so that he gave me a discreet smile.

And the white eighth-grade girl who lures her black classmate into a nearby wooded area across the street at recess only afterwards to accuse him of trying to rape her. Her father storming into my office raging about the "niggers." We almost got into a fistfight right there in my office, but I got scared and backed down, telling him instead that if he ever used that word again anywhere on the school grounds or in the school building I would call the police and have him thrown out.

Boy, did he hate me. For some reason, it felt right—that is, until soon afterwards, when purely out of curiosity, I went to a Klan meeting, just to see what it was like. It was in an enormous open field out in the country somewhere between Yemassee and Hampton, the county seat. There must have been a thousand people there. What a spectacle. A sensational cross, all lit up, looming taller than a scrub pine. The outdoor stage, the Klan members all robed and hooded. Was my eighth-grade student's father one of them? The Grand Dragon at the microphone.

I stood at the back, probably the only guy there in a suit, when out of the mouth of the Grand Dragon I heard the phrase: "Niggers, Catholics, and the liberal Jewish principal from Yemassee . . ."

"The liberal Jewish principal from Yemassee?" I got out of there so fast I probably left my shadow behind.

Pat's mom had inoculated him against racism. George was learning, challenging himself. And when an outsider whistleblower named Dr. Gatch let the public know that black children in Beaufort County had worms, Mike's dad, a respectable doctor, dismissed it with, "Of course they have worms." What?! Mike protested, disgusted, the apple having fallen far from the tree.

I'd grown up in my dad's store in the middle of the black community. My granddad had adopted an abandoned black baby in Beaufort in 1896. Almost all my dad's customers, except for a few white shoplifters, were black, some middle-class but most of them poor. His customers were so reliable he referred to them as his "regulars." People supported each other in that neighborhood. About the shoplifters, Daddy was pretty philosophical: "I make more than I lose." If customers couldn't pay, well, they couldn't, Daddy felt, but they still had to eat, and feeding people, over the long haul, he explained to me, was good business.

He was the only one in town to anticipate the war rationing that was to come during the Second World War. He'd been renting the rooms above the grocery store, where he and Mom had lived before moving into their house, to noncommissioned officers. Once America entered the war, naturally those rooms were empty. Daddy filled every room, every nook and cranny, even the hallway, with everything from onions and black-eyed peas to canned goods to bags of flour and sugar to kerosene to brooms and mops and cleaning supplies. Once the war rationing was in place, food was everywhere in Daddy's little grocery and hardly anywhere else in town. Suddenly, the "bigwigs," as they were referred to back then, who generally shopped downtown at the A&P or Piggly Wiggly—places frequented by people well off enough to own automobiles and who wouldn't deign to bother themselves with neighborhood grocery stores—began showing up, of all places, in Schein's Grocery, naturally all hail-fellow-well-met. "Hey Morris, how's the world treatin' you? Yes, sir. Lookin' good, lookin' good."

Daddy eyed the sacks of flour, as they did, the canned goods, the onions and lima beans and black-eyed peas spilling off the shelves stacked all the way to the ceiling, spilling out of the vegetable bins.

"Sorry, boys," he told them. "All this . . . all this is for my customers, my 'regulars.'"

The Jewish cemetery happened to be in that neighborhood, and on the day of Dad's funeral in the spring of 1979, black kids strolled by the cemetery dressed in their Sunday best even though it was a Saturday, their black patent leather shoes, which had taps on the soles, oddly slung over their shoulders so they wouldn't go "clickety-clack" down the sidewalk, "out of respect for Mr. Schein," their parents had told them, so as not to disturb him "at rest."

In fact, it was in this neighborhood, as I so frequently boasted to Pat and anybody else who would listen, that I whipped Joe Frazier's ass. Yep, Joe Frazier, the late great nemesis of Muhammad Ali. Joe and I were both about five then, two skinny little kids. He lived just down the street from Daddy's store, and he would come in Saturday mornings for a Coke and a Milky Way. We were playing outside behind the store, and we got in a little tussle over one of those Milky Ways—I was trying to get him to "half" it with me, after which, defeated and humiliated, he stood up, looked directly in my eyes—I'll never forget it—pointed his finger at me, and said: "You better watch out, Bernie Schein, because one of these days I'm going to be the heavyweight champion of the world."

Sure enough, he was, and sure enough, Pat never believed me. Others might have been skeptical, but Pat was just totally dismissive.

To this day, I have no idea why.

In any case, while Smokin' Joe was now twenty years later brawling with Ali, the draft board was breathing down my neck. Not only mine but Pat's and that of every teacher in the Lowcountry. We were worried as hell. None of us wanted to go to Vietnam. At that time, in the winter of 1967, most of us didn't even know where it was. I was a coward, I told Pat. Shouldn't that qualify me for a deferment?

"It's true," he said. "You are a coward—but no, it won't."

I was summoned to appear before Beaufort's draft board, where not only did I shamelessly hurl to the winds the cause for which Pat and I and our entire small group of activists were fighting, I was so convincing that I got myself and every other teacher in Beaufort County exempted from the draft. All, including me, had been destined for military service before my appearance. So, entirely inadvertently, since anyone else's life, as you can no doubt surmise by now, was the furthest thing from my mind, I probably saved lives. I really wasn't that fearful of losing my own life. I was too young, too naive, at the time. The glory of battle was still a fantasy for me, Hemingway inspired. That nurse in *A Farewell to Arms*. It was a great way, it seemed to me at the time, to get a girlfriend.

No, it was a matter of inconvenience. I'd spent a year at a military school, Broward Military School in Branning, South Carolina. Mom thought it might scare me into making good grades. It did scare me but not into making good grades, because nobody there cared about good grades. They didn't beat you for making bad grades. Prestige was in rank, as elusive to me as good grades. What they were obsessive about was, in their words "making a man out of you." Hey, no problem, right? I'd been bar mitzvahed. That's when it occurred to me that if I were indeed a man, it was only in Jewish eyes.

In Gentile eyes, I was not a bang but a whimper.

God, was it agony! Taking a rifle apart and putting it back together again, while being timed, with some insane sergeant screaming at the top of his lungs in your ear. Doing all those crazy rifle gymnastics while in formation. Eyes right, eyes left, about face, present arms, right-shoulder arms, forward march . . . all day, every day, staring at the back of the guy's neck in front of you. Getting your ass beat. Your only solace, sleep.

Desperate not to go through anything even remotely resembling military life again, I was unwilling to give up my life for my country. Well, I was at least unwilling to give up my life for another country.

Even Pat was unwilling to give up his life for that particular country. Despite LBJ's warnings, Pat scoffed at the idea that the fall of South Vietnam to the Communist North Vietnam was a threat to the United States. "Vietnamese are going to invade the California coast? That's nuts."

With the help of neighboring China, as the war proponents were suggesting?

"The Vietnamese hate China."

And what of the spread of Communism throughout Southeast Asia?

"There's no threat. The Vietnamese hate China. Vice versa. So Laos is now a threat? It's a crazy war."

Reading up and learning why we were even in that war would, under different circumstances, have made of me one of the most outspoken of antiwar liberals, at least in the Lowcountry. However, if the draft board had become correspondingly enlightened as to my view of it, just as if they'd found out my true feelings about civil rights, they probably would have drafted me. Like most people in Beaufort at the time, all the board members were conservatives, if not racists or paternalistic. And even if I wasn't and they knew it, I was a native. They trusted me. I was known. It was the unknown they feared. Besides, much like Pat, I had yet to really make my views known in my hometown in a way that would threaten them. I just wasn't that sophisticated.

At the time of my appearance before the Beaufort County draft board, I was still the principal of Yemassee Elementary and Junior High School in Hampton County, but I lived in Beaufort, commuting during the week, so my draft board was Beaufort County's draft board. It was not lost on me that even though Yemassee was in Hampton County, it was Beaufort's closest neighbor, so small that its denizens shopped in Beaufort. Everyone in Yemassee was either related to or otherwise knew everyone in Beaufort and vice versa. What was good for Yemassee was good for Beaufort, which meant that what was bad for Yemassee was bad for Beaufort. And Yemassee's most prized institution, its only institution other than a few tiny churches, was Yemassee Elementary and Junior High.

I'd been a Boy Scout in Stratton Demosthenes's troop till I was fourteen years old, at which point I thought it was stupid spending half my day flailing about trying to tie a bowline and communicate with people through a sign language designed to be used on a ship when there was no ship in sight, at least not that I could see, and spend my nights fighting off insects and snakes in a sleeping bag so claustrophobic, so straitjacketed it inspired nightmares about my being carted off by the men in white coats to the insane asylum in Columbia, our state capital. Stratton was now chairman of the draft board, and all I could do was thank God I'd never told him exactly why I'd resigned my position as tenderfoot less than a decade before. Mom told him at the time that I'd wanted to spend more time studying. Ha ha ha. I knew everyone on the board. In Beaufort back then, everyone knew everyone. Unless he was military, or from a military family like Pat, a stranger in town was as odd as a UFO setting down on the banks of the Beaufort River, which to my knowledge has never happened. Plus, the inestimable Joyce Smith, so tall, so beautiful, the secretary of the board—everyone in town knew where the power lay. It lay with her because she did all the work. All the board members had their own jobs to worry about. They were businessmen. Being on the board was good for business, made them appear civic minded, respectable, which they were anyway, but being on the board institutionalized their respectability. It was like attending church, appearing in the same familiar pew every Sunday morning. It cemented the image. So to Joyce went the flowers, thrice daily I might add—morning, noon, and night—not only from yours truly but from Pat. My presentation to the board members themselves, however, had to appeal to their most basic fears and instincts, and we know what those were, patriotism be damned.

This was the segregated South. Patriotism was great but not if black people were running the country, or at least the Lowcountry.

I explained to the board in my own quiet, self-effacing way, you know how I am, that I was not really there to ask for a deferment, that in fact, with a lot of my friends either in Vietnam or heading there, I'd probably feel guilty—indeed, I told them, I knew I would—if they gave me one. The idea of my buddies over there fighting and me staying in Yemassee with the women and children—

"Women and children?"

That's what got to them.

White women and *white* children, of course.

We were at the time, I explained, surviving our first year of integration in Yemassee Elementary and Junior High. Successfully so, I could have added, instead of exploiting their fears to the max, but please, I was fighting for my life here—well, a lifestyle anyway.

My dilemma, I explained, was that, though the teachers in the school had been teaching there over twenty years, they were, not surprisingly, all women, so I was the only man in the school. Naturally, I added, anyone in my position would feel bad about abandoning them. To whom? Believe me, they knew who. Yet my friends were either in Vietnam or heading there. Clearly, I was torn. On the one hand, my buddies, my country, for God's sake. I certainly didn't want to be here, I took pains to explain, while they were over there. On the other, the women and children who clearly depended on me. Was I just going to leave them?

Again, to the board members of course, white women, white children. Alone, with blacks, unprotected?

Yemassee was almost 50 percent black, I told them, though they didn't need to be told.

So would even more black children be enrolling in the white school? The implication was clear.

At that time, the movie on at the Breeze Theatre in downtown Beaufort was *The Russians Are Coming! The Russians Are Coming!*

It flashed on the marquee right across the street from the draft board conference room. We could all see it through the window. But patriotic though they may have been, and though we were in the midst of the Cold War, only a decade or so after Sputnik, the Russians, coming or not, were at least white. No, the Russians had fled the marquee, only to be replaced in their minds and imaginations with the greatest nightmare of all: "*The Niggers Are Coming! The Niggers Are Coming!*"

"I've known Bernie Schein since he was knee high to a grasshopper," announced Stratton, as chairman of the board. Everyone there had known me since I was knee high to a grasshopper. "And if this was a 'declared' war, Bernie Schein would be the first man over there. Of that I have no doubt."

I had to admit, and not without reluctance, even hemming and hawing a bit—you know, modesty, as always in my case, prevailing—that, well, "I'd like to think so, Stratton. I would certainly hope so."

A week or so later, Ed Samuels, a board member and, like Pat, a Citadel alumnus, though of course considerably older than Pat, spotted him on the street downtown.

"That little son of a bitch," he told Pat, "not only got himself out of the draft, but every single male teacher in Beaufort County."

You'd have thought they'd throw me a party.

Naturally, Pat was elated. He hated the thought of going to Vietnam, though unlike me, he did at least have the grace to feel guilty about it.

I'd have felt guilty if I'd gone.

The draft board, as you might expect, was discreet, thank God. Maybe they didn't know any better. More likely they realized that to have exposed my professed prejudices, phony though they were, would also have exposed their own. They didn't want that fire lit. Also, hell, they doubtless believed me. And at that time, I wasn't much of a threat anyway.

Soon afterwards, only a few months later, on Mike's initiative Beaufort's first biracial council was formed, the black members of whom would eventually betray Pat worse than he would ever imagine.

In the spring of 1968, we held our first meeting.

This was the late sixties, for progressive blacks in Beaufort the *Either you for us or against us* time in our history. Their theory was that *If you white, you wrong*, and *If you black, you right*, and no one in the black community believed this more than Agnes Sherman. She was on the biracial council with, among others, me, and Pat. I thought Agnes was an asshole. If you were white—right, wrong, or even uncertain—she barely gave you the time of day. The chip on her shoulder was the size of a plantation home, but instead of weighing her down she seemed, like not a few white people back then, to have grown into it, above and aloof from the workers in the fields below. Was this a false equivalent? Yes, but I still took her attitude personally. She worked at Penn Community Center, originally a school for freed slaves, now a local retreat and conference center for both local and national civil rights activists and leaders. Dr. Martin Luther King Jr., Andrew Young, and Hosea Williams and others had planned marches and demonstrations nationwide here, including the March on Washington. Agnes's office at Penn was down the hall from Scott Graber's—Scott was Penn's lawyer at the time—and because he was white Agnes refused to even acknowledge his presence. White or black, right, wrong, or uncertain, back then we called that "stuck up." But Pat, I swear, much to my envy and admiration and surprise, won her over.

A great judge of character even then, before it became his business, he registered Agnes as a negative alert on his radar upon our first encounter with her in this, our first Beaufort biracial council meeting. Harriet Keyserling, the first female member of the state House of

Representatives and a mainstay of Beaufort's Jewish community, was in attendance, as was her son Billy who is now, almost fifty years later, our mayor. Tim Belk was there, the first friend Pat and I had who let us know he was gay, and who became the model for Trevor Poe in Pat's novel *South of Broad*. There was a fashionable local artist all lit up in bright scarves, colorful blouses, and long, dazzling gypsy-like skirts. Her name was Savannah—she never used her last name, assuming she had one—and later Pat would appropriate her name for his alter ego's twin sister in his novel *The Prince of Tides*. The only other white person I can remember there was a retired colonel's wife, originally from Connecticut who, with her husband, had made their home in Beaufort after his final tenure at Parris Island.

It was a small group of about ten people, and we knew most of them, black and white. Agnes's friend and cohort Frieda Mitchell was there, as was, if memory serves, Cory Blue, a black community activist, and the principal of Ladies Island Elementary Jeannette Fields, also black. Also present, if I remember correctly, was Juanita Washington and her husband, the lawyer Charles Washington. The year after our first biracial council meeting, Juanita would single-handedly integrate the faculty at Port Royal Elementary, where I was principal, just as her son Rowland Washington had only two years earlier single-handedly integrated Beaufort High School. We sat in a circle in an empty classroom at what was at that time the University of South Carolina in Beaufort's only building (and what was, when I was a child, my elementary school and, when my father was a child, his elementary school; where I parked my bicycle, he had parked his mule, Blackie, and his buggy).

We went around the room introducing ourselves, talking about who we were and why we were there. I talked about integrating Yemassee Elementary and Junior High School, where I was still teaching-principal. Most of the council members knew Daddy, and that provided some familiarity for me.

I spoke as a teacher. Black studies, I said, at the time a late arrival on the academic stage, at least on the white academic stage, might turn out to be an inspiration and eye-opener not only for black kids but, I was learning, also for white kids. The more they learn, especially about each other, the fewer their prejudices. Pat was teaching it at Beaufort High, and I was already seeing it work in Yemassee.

In our traditional American history textbooks, as everyone there knew, only three blacks were mentioned: George Washington Carver, Booker T. Washington, and W. E. B. DuBois. The same for South Carolina history texts. Even our local heroes like Robert Smalls, a war hero, a *senator*, went unmentioned. It was as if we were in the Soviet Union and black history had been "erased." The more I learn about it, I told them, the more I see the need for it in the curriculum everywhere.

"Been waitin' for this for a long time," said Frieda Mitchell.

Agnes looked like she was still waiting. Like white people were such slow learners they might never get there.

And we also had to look, I offered, at what was personal, at what was directly, immediately affecting these kids, at the history being made right in front of us. Why are black kids in Yemassee not allowed in the local swimming pool? How does it make them feel? They're sitting in the same classrooms now and playing on the same playground at recess and eating in the same lunchroom with white kids who up until now have only parroted the prejudices of their parents. These white kids have never even thought about how their new classmates might feel, and they've told themselves they couldn't care less.

How did I know that?

Because that's what some of them had told me outright, albeit the more I pushed them, I added, the more apoplectic they became.

"If they're apoplectic," said Juanita Washington, "that's encouraging."

It was, now that I thought about it.

I mentioned the black boy and white girl in the eighth grade in Yemassee caught fooling around at recess in the wooded area across the street from school. It was a controversy not so much that they were fooling around as that they were white and black. Since the white girl was consequently viewed as "trash," we know how she felt; but how, I wondered aloud, did that make the black boy feel? The white kids in the class had never even thought about it.

So how do we get them to think about it? To feel what a black class-mate feels?

Black kids knowing they come from black kings and queens, that their elders were and are doctors, lawyers, engineers, writers, philoso-phers, the great athletes of the Negro Baseball League . . . That can't help but inspire confidence, we know that; it encourages them to speak up, to show who they are, not just to themselves, I'm seeing, but to white kids. As for the white kids, it opens their eyes, arouses their curi-osity—they had no *idea*.

Black kids are already bringing up the swimming pool: how would white kids feel, they asked in my sixth-grade class, if their roles were reversed and they had to swim in that nasty ol' Combahee River? The white girl and her black boyfriend: I'm waiting for it to come up. And it if doesn't, I'll bring it up. They're dying to talk about it.

It's got to get personal, I emphasized. I started to tell them about how that course on the Holocaust and racial prejudice had opened my eyes for that very reason, but I was on my way to proselytizing, I real-ized, and a white guy preaching to white people is one thing, but to blacks . . . not so cool. After all, they were the ones who'd experienced the oppression. So what, at least Agnes and Corey Blue seemed to be wondering, was I doing telling *them* about black studies?

The Revolution was theirs. White people like me were just the help.

Led by Agnes and Frieda, the black members spoke factually with a mixture of fatalism and determination about the monolithic discrimination in employment and in public accommodations in downtown Beaufort. (Shopping centers had not yet appeared on the scene.) Whites owned Main Street downtown businesses and employed blacks mostly as janitors, with the exception of a few clothing stores where they employed blacks as salespeople only for black customers. Blacks and whites still drank from separate water fountains, used separate bathrooms, sat in separate waiting rooms in doctors' offices. The town was still largely segregated, the schools desegregating but with powerful resistance. A black man was still often referred to as "boy" and expected to step off the curb downtown to let a white man pass. At Penn, a cross was recently burned on the front lawn.

As we listened and spoke, it became clear a massive demonstration and boycott of downtown Beaufort businesses was in the air. A petition supporting the boycott was circulating around the room, which presented a conundrum for me. Knowing that my deferment was intact, I had, only two weeks before, signed a contract to open the upcoming school year as teaching-principal of Port Royal Elementary School in Beaufort. I knew, however, and tried to explain that if I added my name to that petition, I'd be dismissed and without a job before this school year ended and the new one even began. Plus, I'd already turned in my notice in Yemassee. Though it was early, I'd wanted to help them find a replacement who could visit the school, observe in the classrooms, and continue the program. Back then, principals were fully responsible for running their own schools. I was committed, wherever I was. Couldn't I do more to support the cause—hiring black teachers, encouraging and handling integration, working to expose and assuage white prejudice, introducing black studies into the curriculum—as a principal of a school than if I were jobless, without a platform?

Was I convincing myself or them? Let's put it this way: true or not, and it probably was, I didn't want to be out of a job, because a job, this job, as a teacher and principal, was keeping me out of the war.

So, to recap, only a few months after my appearance before the draft board, I was in my hometown's first biracial council meeting sitting next to Pat and Mike, with Agnes refusing me even a glance, though she's directly across the circle from me, my new principalship on the line, my notice at Yemassee already given, and the tension compounded in my mind by what I'm not telling them, which is that if I sign that petition and publicly support the boycott and demonstration I'll end up in boot camp instead of Beaufort.

Naturally, the council members followed Agnes's lead, greeting my reluctance with a similar indifference, with that same knowing silence.

I'm not going to Vietnam, I wanted to scream.

In my heart, if the need arose, I was ready to declare war against the military. If you can't join them, beat them.

Mike didn't fare any better than I did. He introduced himself as a teacher "over at the high school."

Agnes's eyebrows arched so high roses could have grown over them.

There were two high schools in Beaufort, which of course Mike well knew but just wasn't considering. The all-black Robert Smalls High School was located in Beaufort proper, and, though some of the kids had transferred from there to Beaufort High, it was still in operation. The schools were in the process of consolidating. Soon, Robert Smalls would become an integrated elementary school, and Beaufort High would be the only high school in Beaufort and fully integrated. Racially charged questions abounded among both the kids and their parents and the administrators and faculty as to which of the two school colors, alma mater songs, and names of sports teams would prevail. Beaufort High would remain Beaufort High in name only. Everything else was up for grabs.

Had Mike been nervous? Had he just forgotten himself? He knew immediately what Agnes's raised eyebrow suggested. Everyone in the room did.

White privilege.

And Mike and everyone in the room knew right away that Agnes was right. And Mike said so. Still, he figured he'd quit while he was behind, or so he said to me and Pat and George later.

Pat, however, won Agnes over. Instead of just stupidly screwing up like Mike or squirming and groveling like me, pleading for understanding, he did what appeared to be the exact opposite. He openly confessed to the entire group that he was a racist.

"I'm prejudiced," he told them. "That's why I'm here."

I was flabbergasted. It just wasn't true.

He regaled them with stories that just never happened, one story after another, every Southern racist adolescent cliché you've ever heard of. The most obvious, summer afternoons with his redneck friends chucking watermelons at Negroes from the back of a pickup. The truth was that as a child, a teenager, Pat didn't have any redneck friends; he was a military brat who moved, changing schools, every year. He wasn't truly a Southerner; he was migrating fowl, he lived everywhere, adopting Beaufort as his nesting place, his personal, artistic, and literary domain. Pat didn't even have a Southern accent. He talked like a Yankee. And if he did possess even a tinge of racism, it was nuked and annihilated so early by his mom he could never have even remembered it. Maybe that's why it was so easy for him to lay claim to it, I don't know. Jesus, folks, Pat had never in his life ridden in a pickup truck, except for school hayrides.

So Pat claimed he's a racist, and every black person in the room—Corey Blue, Frieda Mitchell, Jeannette Fields, the Ladies Island Elementary School principal, Juanita and Charles Washington, all of them, fall head over heels in love with him. Even Agnes Sherman, which I didn't even realize she was capable of. They were glowing, could look at no other white person in the room but Pat, who sat there looking innocent, shrugging, as if to say, "I'm a Southerner, I'm white. That's the way it is."

There I had been disclosing with characteristic modesty how I was all but the Great White Hope, how committed to The Cause I was, how steadfast and unwavering was my willingness to sacrifice myself for the good of the black community. Hell, I even told them about the Klan in Hampton County mentioning "the liberal Jewish principal from Yemassee." They didn't give a shit. This petition, I pleaded, my signature, a genuine handwringing moral quandary, wouldn't they agree? They obviously did not. Every white person in the room but Pat, who snickered, had rolled their eyes, and every black person in the room had denied me even the respect of hating me, showing only a glancing indifference, and then what happens? Pat in his wisdom lures Agnes off her throne with the simple announcement he's a racist?

This, as far as I know, was his first foray into fiction.

Yes, it was a lie, he confessed to me later—a pickup truck, watermelons? Please—but it was a lie underneath which was a greater truth.

"And what, Picasso, is that greater truth?"

"With their support, Bernie, we're in the movement, we can make things better, we're in the fight, we can change the world. Without their trust and respect, we might as well pull up stakes and fold our tents and join the Peace Corps."

I was smitten with jealousy, with envy, not because of what he'd just told me, but because I'd wanted them naturally to swoon all over me like they had him.

What school had *he* ever integrated?

Why didn't I think to say *I* was a racist? Had I anticipated the results, I'd have introduced myself like he did, only with more charm and eloquence: "Hi, everybody, my name is Bernie Schein. I'm a racist."

Pat answered that for me. "You weren't in Omaha," he told me. "I was."

"Oh, please, is that where you spent your summer afternoons hurling watermelons and throwing chicken wings at black people?"

"It was two summers ago, in the Omaha ghetto, working with the Jesuits," he said. "There's a big difference, Bernie, between a ghetto and a slum. You've never seen a ghetto, except Charleston's, and Charleston's doesn't even compare to the hell in Omaha. It was just terrible: filthy, drug-addled, lethargic, hopeless. Nobody wanted to hear about whatever good you'd tried to do in the past, elsewhere. If you were white, you had to earn their trust. Otherwise, you were just another white guy working off his guilt, as part and parcel of the institutionalized racism in this country as a white cop all too eager with his nightstick. The Jesuits were great, they prepared me for this. One of 'em said, he was funny as hell, 'In the worst they trust. And you would too, Pat, if you'd lived the lives they've lived.' So I'm white, in their eyes a racist till I prove otherwise."

Now I was caught between envy and admiration because suddenly he appeared so much wiser than me.

Pat and Cory and Agnes and Frieda became fast friends, working hard for the cause in every way they could. Pamphlets, newsletters, demonstrations, community organizing. Pat and I posted the petition, unsigned by me, that ended up protesting discriminatory hiring practices in downtown Beaufort on every telephone pole and on the doors and windows of every public space to little effect. Pat also started an underground newspaper with my assistance, exposing the shabby treatment of blacks, also to little effect except that I learned a lot. I knew pretty intimately the slums of Beaufort; never before, however, had I seen and visited a ghetto until we went to Charleston to interview the bishop, who arranged for us to visit that one and talk to people who lived there. The hopelessness and lethargy, the smell of alcohol in the streets, the threat of violence in the air, it was different, an awakening for me. We held a few antiwar demonstrations attended by the same group of liberals, no more than twelve or fifteen of us, also to little effect, since the *Beaufort Gazette* refused to cover us. Penn Center hosted a rally of several hundred welfare protestors. Encouraged by Hosea Williams and the Southern Leadership Conference, they ended up picketing the county welfare office for an increase in welfare checks to cover winter clothing needs, heating costs, and a fifty-dollar Christmas bonus for each poor child, also to little effect.

The Orangeburg Massacre occurred on February 8, 1968, in Orangeburg, South Carolina, where the local police had opened fire on student demonstrators from the local black college, later claiming that one of the demonstrators had fired at them first. It was all over the newspapers and the evening news—CBS, NBC, ABC—national and local: the white power structure against the demonstrators, the cops against the students, a symbol of what was happening all over the country. What had really happened in Orangeburg? Students were dead and injured, and cops later were reduced to the claim that before firing they'd *heard* a gunshot coming from somewhere among the demonstrators. A dubious proposition in the absence of real evidence, but even if it were true, would it have made any real difference, given the mindset of the cops at the time? And what was that mindset? It was important, agreed the council, to *Know Your Enemy*. "And it ain't," offered Frieda Mitchell, "us."

"And it ain't," I wanted to add, "*me*."

In any case, to circumvent the standard responses about the massacre, members of the Beaufort biracial council called for a debate, at Pat's suggestion: the white side, the police, against the black side, the demonstrators. Not surprisingly, when Harriet Keyserling hosted the event in her home, as with many such events in the small-town South at the time, most of the members of the council remained in theirs, which was probably a good thing in this instance since Pat and I spent most of the debate accusing each other—rightly, I might add—of saying absolutely nothing beyond what had already been said in the newspapers and on the evening news, of failing to say anything "new," of failing to go beyond what members of the biracial council had referred to as the "standard responses." Where were we to get such information back then, Pat would later ask, particularly so soon after the event itself?

"You got me," I would respond, "it was your idea."

He claimed otherwise; we argued about it forever.

In the prime of our youth, undeterred by something as silly and trivial as shameless ignorance and feckless information, we nevertheless forged ahead before our audience of two: Harriet and her husband, Herbert. While Pat took the white side, I took the side of Cleveland Sellers, the leader of the black side, whose son Bakari Sellers you now see every evening on CNN articulating so clearly and so genially what is currently the Democratic party side.

In retrospect, if it hadn't been for my dad and Pat's false confession of racism, few of the black members of the biracial council would have trusted either one of us, at least at the beginning.

By the early summer of '68, members of the biracial council had pretty much splintered off, with Agnes, Frieda, and Harriet focused on the Penn Community Center. Following Dr. King's murder in April, the commitment to his mission was intensifying. Agnes was immersed in her work for the library and museum at Penn as well as their first oral history project. Frieda in her role as codirector of the Community Development Project paid particular attention to daycare needs, with emphasis on nutrition and health, for which she would eventually gain national attention and be honored with the Marian Wright Adelman Award for Service to Children as well as the John D. Rockefeller III Public Service Award. For now, in 1968, Frieda had amassed a wealth of experience organizing voter registration, and she also organized and became the chairperson of the Beaufort County Education Committee, the central force for school desegregation. That committee's efforts led to both Frieda's and Agnes's election to the school board. They became the first African Americans elected to a school board in South Carolina.

With Mike, George, Pat, and me in schools into early June, our work too consumed our time and energy, particularly after Dr. King's death. Black kids at Beaufort High were enraged, hurt, in tears.

Pat in *The Water Is Wide*: "A contingent of black students went to the principal in a futile attempt to get him to lower the flag at half-mast. Fearing community reaction, he predictably refused and closed his office to any further discussion of the matter. Since the faculty was all white, the students walked the halls in silence, tears of frustration rolling down their cheeks and unspoken bitterness written on their faces in their inability to communicate their feelings to their white teachers."

On the breezeway at recess a few got violent, swarmed, screamed, and spit on him. One dug her nails into his flesh until "blood was drawn," he wrote. Then: "more fingernails in my arm. Someone reached up and scratched my neck. I thought I felt strong fingers close around my throat, then release it suddenly." Pat, just as he had done for his family, literally took the blows, if for no other reason than to protect those particular kids from themselves. The black kids in the school loved Pat, and even for this small contingent who distrusted any white man, including Pat, he presented himself as a safe target. "Finally," he wrote, "the entire mob convulsed with raw, demonstrative sorrow," after which, "mercifully, the bell rang."

Mike and George also listened, and an African American mother approached Mike at the year's end to thank him for his work with the kids. She knew his father, she told him. Basically, he told me, she was thanking him merely for being a moderating influence, for offering black people in the community a little hope, for simply not being a racist, i.e., for not being his father.

Because of the biracial council members all getting to know each other, our friendship and association with each other did continue, often at parties at Penn Center. The director at the time, Courtney Siceloff, was a white Quaker, and his wife Elizabeth and Harriet Keyserling were the best of friends. Friends with Harriet, we became friends with them. Courtney took me for my first ride on a sailboat. Tim Belk played the piano at parties. Pat had known them even before, through his teacher Gene Norris, who in his senior year of high school took Pat out there to meet Dr. King.

Pat loved telling the story about a group picture that was taken at Penn Center that included Dr. King and Gene Norris. In the photo, Gene is bending over to tie his shoe so that his face is obscured and he couldn't be recognized. Gene was white. He was well aware of just how hated the Siceloffs and Penn were by much of white Beaufort: they were called "nigger lovers," "outside agitators," the works. And Gene had already upset the board of education with his defiant protest of their banning the use of the *New York Times* in Beaufort schools.

Courtney was involved in training sessions for community leaders and organizers all across the South, working in health care, property ownership, and farm cooperatives, putting together a racially diverse group fighting for equality in everything from education to voting rights. However, when the *Beaufort Gazette* publicized that the United States Marine Band from Parris Island was to perform at the commencement ceremony of the Beaufort Academy, at the time an all-white segregationist academy, one of many springing up all over the South to avoid desegregation, self-effacing and soft-spoken Courtney called the Department of Defense in Washington, which immediately halted that idea in its tracks.

You can guess what the headline was in the *Beaufort Gazette* the next day. White Beaufort was not happy.

• • •

Mike, George, Pat, and I spent our summer vacation traveling through Europe, using Arthur Frommer's book *How to Travel in Europe on Five Dollars a Day* as our guide. Mike and I spent a lot of time absorbing the culture, visiting museums and ruins, which Pat also wanted to do. George, however, wanted to pick up girls, and advised Pat that it was very important for him to do too. Pat said he didn't know how, which was true, but George volunteered to teach him, and we all knew that sex—how to get it, what to do with it—was George's true subject. "This museum shit, Pat, it's boring, man. You seen one, you seen 'em all. Know what I mean? Come with me."

Pat was so much his mother's child back then, wanting to please, curious, just as he'd been in high school when you could hear him every morning on the public-address system saying the Lord's Prayer, leading us all in the Pledge of Allegiance, never missing mass. Now, with free love in the European air, he was still out to please.

George said, "Come with me, Pat," and Pat did, and for the rest of his life he'd brag that he and George had a better time in Europe than Mike and I.

I think he did. Mike agrees.

In the fall of 1968 I introduced a course on black history at Port Royal Elementary School in Beaufort, while Pat was teaching black studies at Beaufort High. I had hired Juanita Washington, the bravest woman I've ever known, as our first-grade teacher. At a school board meeting open to the public, the recently hired Dr. Walt Trammel, whom Pat would rename Dr. Henry Piedmont in *The Water Is Wide*, kept offering up excuses and hiding behind phony reasons as to why the desegregation of Beaufort County schools was progressing so slowly, so haltingly. Juanita, tall and strikingly attractive, with the most prominent cheekbones I've ever seen, raised her hand to be recognized, rose, and called for Dr. Trammel and the entire board of education (Agnes and Frieda had not yet assumed their positions) to resign.

Clearly, they were failing in their duties. If teachers in Beaufort County failed in their jobs, she explained, they were either asked to resign or were fired. The authority to fire unavailable to her, all that was left for her was to ask for their resignations.

Dr. Trammel summoned me to his office, held up a folder McCarthy-style—whether it contained real evidence I never knew—and told me that Juanita Washington was a "communist." I had no idea what he expected me to do with that information, but what I did do was absolutely nothing.

After two years teaching at Beaufort High, Pat left in the fall of 1969 to teach on Daufuskie Island, an indescribably beautiful island of black slave descendants mired in poverty, yet to catch up with the twentieth century. Located in Beaufort County, it was forty-five minutes from the mainland and accessible only by boat, an experience Pat would later recount in *The Water Is Wide*, the book that made him famous. It would take less than two years for the racist superintendent and the racist board of education to fire him.

Daufuskie's was a two-room schoolhouse. An older, African-American woman named Mrs. Brown taught right next door to him. She taught the younger kids, and Pat taught the older ones, ages ten to thirteen. It's documented how little they'd been taught. Upon his arrival, Pat was confronted with heartbreaking illiteracy and a sad absence of math skills. Here were kids in America so ignorant, so insular, so isolated they had no idea who the president of the United States was, what country they lived in.

Mrs. Brown, Pat felt, was ashamed of them. She called them "retarded" and went out of her way to confirm with great eagerness every racist trope of the white power structure. Also, at least in Pat's eyes, she was too quick to put the wood to them: old-fashioned spare-the-rod-spoil-the-child, which certainly taught them to toe the line but, as Pat discovered upon his arrival, nothing else. Also, Pat hated any kind of corporal punishment. It's all in *The Water Is Wide*, his story really, and in the subsequent movie, *Conrack*, so I won't recount it here. Pat had to inspire in them a curiosity that had been dormant. He had to make learning fun, a game.

Mrs. Brown deplored Pat's creativity, his entire attitude toward teaching, toward making learning fun and enjoyable, his taking them far beyond the shores of Daufuskie, expanding their horizons. He took them to Washington, to Emory University, to Charleston to see the Harlem Globetrotters, where the great Meadowlark Lemon patted Saul, one of Pat's kids sitting in the front row, on the head as he dribbled past him. I was sitting right by Saul, as thrilled and surprised as he was. Pat brought the kids to Port Royal for my annual Halloween parade. They stayed in the homes of white families and spent the night with their kids and the following day appeared on the floats with all the kids from Port Royal Elementary, waving and yelling at those of us watching and having the time of their lives. Black kids in white homes? In 1969? In our later years, Pat and I were absolutely stunned that we could have pulled that off. We were natives, we would conclude. Plus, as Pat wrote in *The Water Is Wide* about this very thing: "We wanted to do so much. . . . I was a cynic who needed desperately to believe in the salvation of mankind or at least in the potential of salvation. Bernie was an optimist who needed proof that his philosophy of joy and the resurrection of the spirit was not the delusion of a grinning Pollyanna. Together we were insufferable, pontifical, self-righteous. . . . We could not be wrong, because we were young, humanistic, and full of shit."

Hard, loud, critical, admonishing, Mrs. Brown in no way tried to understand what Pat was doing with the kids. It all looked chaotic to her, too much fun, which meant in her mind out of control, which probably meant out of her control. She had to have been threatened: her method hadn't worked, and the white administration had looked the other way. After all, Daufuskie was so isolated it was a problem no one knew about. That was just how it was. Negro children, in their minds, had a tougher time learning anyway, though clearly the ignorance of the children on Daufuskie went far beyond that of children in Beaufort County, black or white.

Pat hated the way she treated the kids, though he was his gregarious self with her, entirely uncritical. Did she go behind his back to undermine him in collusion with a racist administration and racist board, to defame him and get him fired? He thought so at the time. Later, however, he realized she was just a pawn, unsophisticated in the politics of Beaufort County's power structure. In a desperate request for more resources, Pat had let it be known in a board meeting open to the public that prior to his arrival the kids on the island had learned almost nothing, which had shocked him. I was at this board meeting, and Dr. Trammel looked shocked too, not at what he was hearing from Pat but that Pat was saying this in public, with the Daufuskie islanders present and in full support of him.

The county, Pat argued, had neglected the Daufuskie kids. Still, who had been their teacher but Mrs. Brown, and unfortunately for much of the black leadership in Beaufort, which included our biracial council colleagues and now members of the school board Agnes Sherman and Frieda Mitchell as well as the Penn Center board, Mrs. Brown was African American. Black incompetence was not the image leaders in the black community wanted to project. It was too dangerous in a town where whites already considered blacks ignorant by default.

In the fall of 1970, I left Beaufort for graduate school at Harvard University in Cambridge, about which more later, and the school board in Beaufort voted to fire Pat. He assumed that Agnes and Frieda had voted in his favor but had been rendered powerless with only two votes. Never once had he doubted their support, at least not then; nor did he have reason too. They were his friends, his colleagues, his comrades-in-arms. Indeed, according to Pat's biographer, Catherine Seltzer, they had voted in his favor.

His sentiment, however, would change.

In December of 1970 Pat took the case to court only to be stunned, dismayed, and horrified when he realized that the board of Penn Center, of which Corey Blue was now executive director (Courtney having left for a position in Atlanta), had turned against him, joining forces with the white administration and the board of education. As he wrote in *The Death of Santini*, Pat saw black friends sitting beside white administrators who would tell the court under oath that he was "a worthless teacher, a liar, a cheat . . . and a clear danger to the children." That Mrs. Brown was appearing with them on her own initiative or as a pawn was unsurprising. She worked for the white man. Nevertheless, the board of education as well as the board of Penn Center had to have been fully cognizant of just how terrible and tyrannical a teacher Mrs. Brown was.

Were Agnes and Frieda at the trial, colluding with members of the board of education and the board of Penn Center and a racist white administrator in their efforts to cement the firing of Pat? I can't say, I was in Cambridge at the time. Even his biographer Catherine Seltzer doesn't know for certain. What I can say is that he was so hurt by what he called their betrayal that he couldn't even tell me at the time. It would take him almost a decade, after which he told anyone who would listen, including Catherine Seltzer a few years before he died.

It was only after he revealed their betrayal that I realized in retrospect that Agnes's cold, forbidding silence in that first biracial council meeting might well have been a lie by omission. It certainly wasn't Pat who was prejudiced, as we know; he'd just confirmed hers. And according to Pat that pompous ass, along with her accomplice Frieda Mitchell, sacrificed the children of Daufuskie on the altar of her own prejudice.

Though recently married with two adopted children and a third on the way, here was a guy so devoted to doing the right thing he had gotten up at 5:00 a.m. every weekday morning, driven his yellow VW forty-five minutes to Bluffton, after which he drove what was little more than a johnboat with a motor forty-five minutes to Daufuskie. He loved those kids. They were learning! They were learning! They adored him.

I know. I was there.

III

PAT BECOMES A FAMOUS WRITER BECAUSE THERE'S NO INDOOR PLUMBING ON DAUFUSKIE ISLAND

Pat became a great writer because of his great talent, his indomitable, throw-it-all-out-there spirit, and his bang-open-the-door stubbornness, but he became a *famous* writer for quite another reason: there was no indoor plumbing on Daufuskie Island.

Initially, however, he wasn't going to Daufuskie; I was. The thought had never occurred to him. It was the summer of 1969. I was still the teaching-principal of Port Royal Elementary School at the south end of Beaufort in the tiny, unincorporated village of Port Royal, while a few blocks down the road in Beaufort proper Pat had completed his second year of teaching at Beaufort High.

Pat would later write in *The Water Is Wide* that we both wanted to save the world, but we had trouble choosing between Africa and Asia. We differed there. So we both applied for the Peace Corps, but due to a bureaucratic snafu, Pat was rejected, and I certainly wasn't going by myself. I was a small-town boy who had only been to New York once, and that was for my senior trip, until the summer of '68 when we back-packed through Europe with our buddies and colleagues Mike Jones and George Garbade. I'd hardly stepped foot out of the Carolinas. Africa, by myself? What if I got lost?

I'd heard about the poverty and problems on Daufuskie in our monthly principals' meetings with then superintendent Morgan Randal, a close friend of Pat and his family, and the assistant superintendent, Mr. McCracken. Mr. McCracken often talked about how beautiful, how isolated it was. Yet it was pretty much, as the world would later discover, as poor, neglected, isolated, and poverty-stricken as a third-world country.

What I knew at the time was that the island was all black except for a white couple who communicated with county officials by shortwave radio. In the small schoolhouse there was only the one teacher, a black woman named Mrs. Brown, who until this point had taught all the kids, all ages. Now, however, with some of the kids growing older, they needed another teacher for the next school year to teach the older ones while Mrs. Brown remained with the younger ones, according to Mr. Randal. He mentioned this almost as an afterthought, sighing hopelessly. Who, he wondered, would be crazy enough to go over there?

Someone, I thought at the time, who couldn't possibly get lost over there. The island was tiny, that much was clear.

Like Pat, Mr. Randal had been an athlete, a star quarterback at Newberry College in Newberry, South Carolina. His drinking buddy was Clyde Priester, the supervisor of buses and every kid's favorite Little League baseball coach, including mine, even though at bat I'd never gotten the ball past the infield.

Pat and I often dropped in at the superintendent's office for a drink with them after they closed at 5:00 p.m., but that afternoon after school Pat had gone to Charleston for a Citadel baseball game. I came in just as Mr. Randal pulled out of his bottom desk drawer a bottle of Old Crow.

"Schein, sit down, boy," said Clyde. Mr. Randal poured me a drink. "Here you go, Schein."

They both called me "Schein." I kind of liked that. You know, one of the guys.

"*Schein!*" Pat would yell, imitating them, though not of course when they were around. "*Schein!*"

"Schein," I told them, "wants to go to Daufuskie."

Mr. Randal looked at me as if I'd morphed into someone else, someone perhaps more like him; and Clyde, well, he just appeared dumbstruck, as if I'd shocked him somehow with a home run.

I'll confess here that I probably should have more thoroughly prepared myself for their reaction, since after the shock wore off they both just about fell out of their chairs laughing. Tears-in-their-eyes, knee-slapping laughter, the kind that seems to go on forever, feeding on itself, refueling on its own, like an animal that eats itself, pukes, then re-eats itself, starting the cycle all over again, or a new kind of car with a gas tank that, registering empty, refills itself.

Anyway, one of them, Morgan or Clyde, would stop, collect himself, glance at the other, then they'd both start up again.

"Schein, Schein, Schein . . ." This is Morgan finally, shaking his head, at the very least, dubious.

"Schein, Schein, Schein . . ." That was Clyde, shaking his head. More than dubious.

This is me, abjectly humiliated. The problem was, they knew me, and they knew there was no indoor plumbing on Daufuskie Island.

"Really?" I was stunned. "No indoor plumbing?"

Everyone who knew me knew I was painstakingly meticulous and picky about where I pooped.

A Jew in an outhouse? Disgusting.

Let me explain. Yes, black people back then were not permitted to poop in public restrooms. Yes, even on long trips they'd have to travel halfway across the state to go to the restroom or stop off in the woods. It was a problem. But it was a legal problem.

For Jews, or at least every Jew I knew, the problem was psychological. Conditions had to be clean to the point of godliness for us to poop. Pooping demanded perfection, and I'd had no idea there weren't real toilets—you know, like the ones we used at home—on Daufuskie Island.

So I told them: "Pat wants to go."

Now that made sense to then, and of course I knew it would. Pat was Irish Catholic. He could poop anywhere, no matter who had gone before him, even some poor homeless drunk who'd left half his stuff on the toilet seat.

Also, around town at the time Pat was popular because he was so gregarious and had such a great personality and had been a great athlete when ball games were the only places to go on Friday nights, so everyone knew him. Still, they made fun of him as a do-gooder and nigger lover, while he claimed in an exaggerated Southern drawl drawn out a mile that: Why, heck, he was just tryin' his best to be a good Christian.

"Pat's up in Charleston for the Citadel baseball game," I told them. "Then he's heading to Virginia to see some of his old teammates. He wanted me to stop off and be sure to tell you in time for you to get a replacement for him over at the high school. I mean, school begins again in September, right? So he was pretty insistent."

Pat was as surprised as anyone else when at the end of August in 1969 he got his contract in the mail, as he usually did, and it read: Teaching Assignment: Daufuskie Island.

It was signed by the new superintendent, Dr. Walter Trammel, who less than two years later would fire Pat from his teaching job there, inspiring the renamed Dr. Henry Piedmont in *The Water Is Wide* and the movie made from it, *Conrack*. Here was the perfect synthesis for literary success: topicality, timing, and talent. A year after the firing, by the time he was twenty-seven years old, he would be famous.

Beforehand, however, though he was still traveling by boat to Daufuskie every weekday, he'd married the widow Barbara Bolling in St. Helena Episcopal Church in Beaufort, adopting her two small children, Jessica and Melissa. Her first husband, Joe Jones, was a fighter pilot just as Pat's dad was, and had been shot down in Vietnam.

Soon after their marriage, in the summer of 1970 I met Martha Pierce Alexander while I was in Columbia consulting for the University of South Carolina Desegregation Center, running around all over the state with a bunch of their staff and consultants doing sensitivity training with teachers and administrators. A former high school English teacher, Martha was now a graduate student in early childhood education at the University of South Carolina. She was friends with some of the staff at the Desegregation Center, and I met her at one of their parties. When I asked her what she was working on, she replied with a mischievous smile: "On the theoretical level? Or the practical level?"

I had no idea, but she was beautiful, olive skinned and sensual seeming, and her smile was so clever, so expressive and radiant, so happy.

We were clearly taken with each other, so much so that when Martha visited Beaufort, Pat began warning us about our "religious differences." He was really worried. Back then in the Bible Belt, most people would have been concerned, and in many ways Pat was still very pious. A few years earlier he had been adamantly antiabortion, going on with such fervor about it one evening at Tim Belk's house that Tim, growing weary of it, told Pat that the girl he was dating at the time told him she was pregnant but that she just didn't know how to tell Pat, at which point Pat screamed hysterically, "Flush it down the goddam toilet!"

So much for that, Tim told me later.

He was much calmer with Martha and me about the fact that she was Methodist and I was Jewish. He was as patient and kind as I'd ever seen him. But he couldn't let it go; he was genuinely worried. In the living room of his home on the Point, he sat us down and talked to us separately, then together. He knew we were both thinking about marriage, which we were, but that religious differences could eventually destroy our marriage, the possibility of which clearly pained him. He didn't like saying this to us. He didn't say that, he didn't need to. Martha was taken aback by just how much he cared.

"What will the children be?" This is important, he insisted. He couldn't understand why we weren't at least bothered by the question, which just made him more insistent. I was pretty much unimpressed. It was like Mom said: If they're Jews, they'll be Jews, no matter what else they are.

"You're ignoring what could turn out to be a huge problem. Bernie, I'm telling you, this could be—"

Martha finally interrupted, probably feeling somewhat like Tim did during Pat's antiabortion rant. "Pat," she said, "you're a Catholic married to an Episcopalian."

Which was true. I'd just never thought about it.

By this time, I had given notice at Port Royal Elementary and knew I would soon be heading to Harvard for graduate school. All my buddies—Pat, George, and Mike—had gotten married. I needed to, since I was the only straight bachelor left. Tim Belk was heading for the openly gay life in San Francisco. So who was I going to hang with? Plus, I was getting bored in Beaufort. I needed to learn more. Harvard wasn't loaded with Jewish Southerners from the Bible Belt teaching black studies. Harriet Keyserling, herself a Barnard alumna, informed me, You'll be a shoo-in. Really? Why, wouldn't that be a nice surprise? Plus, this was the late sixties, and Harvard was committed to diversity. Diversity, diversity, diversity, all over their pamphlets and magazines and literature.

Well, I wrote in the essay required for admission, if you're all that diverse, prove it: take a dumbass like me.

After I got in, once I began taking classes, a professor confided in me that while my background and interviews helped get me admitted, it was my essay that got me over the top. I was surprised he'd even remembered it. As I think about it, the essay itself was over the top.

Martha and her three-year-old daughter, Lara, who already that summer I was loving and having so much fun with, went with me to Cambridge, Massachusetts. Every morning Martha would leave our apartment to drive to work at a nearby research institute, and I would walk Lara, usually on my shoulders where she could more easily use my head as a steering wheel, to the Harvard-Radcliffe preschool on the way to my classes. I was actually so fascinated with the little ones in the preschool that for three days I did nothing but observe them and take notes. Their excitement, their humor, the seriousness and intensity of their play, their openness and honesty with each other, their immediate expressiveness, made me and my friends and most of the adults I knew and worked with look, by comparison, like a bunch of clowns overcome with ourselves or a rookery of repressed duds.

At that time at the Harvard Graduate School of Education the entire campus was at your disposal. You could take any classes you wanted. You could write however and whatever you wanted. No statistics for me. As my adviser pointed out, I'd never shown in my entire academic career the slightest capacity for numbers. No footnotes even, not for me, which I had never had the patience or maybe the intelligence to get the hang of either. Oddly, neither had Pat. He was dumbstruck by numbers and had managed to graduate from the Citadel without ever having had to write a footnote.

Most of my courses, several of which were clinically oriented, centered around psychology, human growth and development, and teacher supervision, the clinically oriented ones practicums based on the work and philosophy of the psychologist Carl Rogers, whose approach to working with clients and patients was basically to shut up and listen, to offer no advice at all, to just sit there and reflect back to them whatever feelings, thoughts, assumptions—sadness, hurt, anger, confusion, frustration—they were expressing at the time. An encouraging nod, a "Yes, yes," a "You feel this way" or "You feel that way," sometimes putting words to their feelings: "afraid," "small," "hopeless," "hopeful," "desperate"; "It's all you can do not to explode"; "You're feeling a sense of urgency"; "You feel as if you're disappearing"; "You're more optimistic." If he was "reading" his clients' feelings accurately and acknowledging them as they were expressed, *without judgment*, it would encourage them and propel them forward on their own. People, he believed, were "self-governing." So that was it: no advice, no instructions, no theory for them to hang their hats on. "So what if the client needs to go to the bathroom and asks you where it is?" one of his students asked him. "Are you not going to tell him?"

"Sure, I would," said Rogers. "I just wouldn't call it therapy."

Probably to further illuminate by contrast the value of Rogers's approach, one professor showed us a film of his opposite, the psychologist Alfred Adler, who simply sat there haranguing his patients, his approach to just hang in there with them till you actually *argued* them out of their problems. Guess which of the two was Jewish? Right, Adler, the guy with the runaway tongue. Most Jews just can't shut up. Gentiles act, Jews talk. That's who they are. That's who we are. I already knew how to talk. What I learned at Harvard was not only to shut up and listen but *how* to listen. How can teachers bring students out, after all, without knowing who they are? How can we know who they are, what they most profoundly need and want, without listening to them?

Also, how can we learn without *doing*? Just because I'd learned how valuable and effective profound listening could be, did that mean I could *do* it? In the course on supervising teachers, the purpose of which was to apply Rogers's theory to the practice of supervising teachers, I had to show the professor and my classmates I could do with teachers what Carl Rogers was doing with his clients and patients, or at least some semblance of it. So, as part of the course, I supervised teachers sent out by the Harvard Graduate School of Education into public schools to do their student-teaching practicums. I'd observe their classes, taking notes, then in follow-up supervisory sessions, which I'd tape, do my best, as all the other students in my class at Harvard had to do, to listen like Carl Rogers, to mirror and reflect with exactitude these fledgling teachers' feelings and thoughts and assumptions about the class they'd just taught and that I'd just observed. Not to offer mine, but only to reflect theirs, which if done Rogers's way would result in their gradual, progressive understanding of themselves, their motivations, their strategies, their goals and ambitions, until they could get to the point where they could begin, in his words, to "govern" themselves, to do it for themselves, or at least to make it easier for others to do it with them and perhaps easier for them to do it with others.

Did I do that? Could I? Of course not, but I certainly learned how hard it was to do, how much work and training and practice it would take. Like all of us in the course, I'd then play the tape for the professor and the class at Harvard to critique. Naturally, like everyone in the class, I dreaded the prospects of the critique. Students at Harvard were critical as hell. The most promising thing they could offer about anybody's work was that it was "interesting." That's why their admissions essays had been so safe, so bland. It's why the ones I was presently reading while serving on the admissions committee, my appointment prompted by the admissions officer who had supported my own application, were so uninteresting.

Both those applying whose essays I was reading and those students presently in my classes, however, were clearly steeped in the high processes of critical thinking. They seemed to me to be great at it. Their educations had prepared them well for it. If there was a weakness, they would find it, but if there wasn't, I was beginning to realize, they'd find it anyway. This is when I began to see in my classes, particularly in the teacher supervision one I was so worried about, that my classmates were so out to impress and outdo each other that all they did was talk. No one listened to anyone else. That's why the class discussions were less than thoughtful and more like verbal crossfire in which no one had to take cover because no one was getting hit. Or if they were, they were too busy themselves firing away to notice. It was great, like kids shooting cap pistols at each other, like Jews in the synagogue who raise the chatter to a whole other level when the rabbi begins his sermon. In my classes, we were all Jews, even the Gentiles.

We were studying Carl Rogers, but we were all Alfred Adler.

So who cared? Absolutely no one! See my point? In our class on listening, no one listened. How liberating!

I wondered what Carl Rogers might have to say to that.

Pat had been fired from his work on Daufuskie. He phoned, long distance, but we couldn't talk that long because Martha and I didn't have much money and he was soon to have even less than we had. He felt anguished that he couldn't drive up for our wedding over the Thanksgiving holidays.

He'd just been fired, and he was worried about missing our wedding?

He didn't mention Agnes and Frieda.

He was also not entirely surprised that he was fired.

"That board meeting last year—"

"I was there."

"So were a lot of people."

"Right."

"I don't know if I ever admitted this to you then, but Trammel warned me not to come to that meeting. We fought like crazy about it in his office."

"No, you didn't."

"I wanted you to come. Also, I was pissed off after that meeting with him. No way I wasn't going to be there. I'm going on and on—you remember—about the county's historical neglect of Daufuskie's kids, and I swear I could see it in Trammel's eyes. He didn't like being embarrassed, and I knew I'd have to pay. Luckily, Barbara still has her job teaching at Beaufort Elementary, and that doesn't seem to be threatened."

"They love her butt over there."

"So I'm getting off my ass to look for another teaching position somewhere. Not too far from here, maybe Ridgeland or Hampton."

When I got off the phone, I couldn't help but register that Dr. Trammel had warned him not to come to that board meeting. Not only had he come, he'd brought half of Daufuskie with him to protest the conditions. Pat had a way with the wives of powerful men in Beaufort. They loved him like his mom did. They showed up too.

I also remembered Pat sending a letter inviting Dr. Trammel and his wife to dinner at his and Barbara's home, which Dr. Trammel politely refused.

I'd have never dreamed of inviting the superintendent of schools—remote, powerful, sixty years old—to dinner or anywhere else. Had Pat expected him to say yes?

I just found that request odd. Pat was always in search of surrogate fathers. Had he considered, perhaps without even realizing it, Dr. Trammel for such a role?

I also wished Pat had told me about the fight prior to the board meeting. Confronting your boss so publicly? Trammel had grown up in the mills in upper South Carolina. He was as much a street fighter as Pat was.

Never once back then did I—nor Pat to my knowledge—consider that Dr. Trammel—tough as hell, all powerful, a bully—might have been a proxy for his father and the kids on Daufuskie standing in for his family.

That invitation for Dr. Trammel to come to dinner: had Pat first sought in Dr. Trammel a surrogate father only to find, after being turned down, his real one?

Did it matter? Pat had been right fighting for those kids, no question. He adored them.

Still, in retrospect, had we considered that possibility then, it might have made his life, or at least mine, a bit easier and more peaceful as he grew older.

"You'd be a hero up here," I wrote him after we talked. It was true. Everything we'd thought or felt or said back home that had been considered so radical, particularly about civil rights or education or Vietnam, even what we'd been *afraid* to say, was merely commonplace at Harvard, a moderate take on things, far from radical. It was an exciting time: protests about everything under the sun; students taking over administration buildings; long hair, braless breasts. Young people were taking over, overrunning the place, showing America who was boss.

To LBJ about Vietnam: *"Hell no, we won't go."*

It was all over the evening news.

When Pat wrote back, he said: "Can you imagine having said that to the draft board in Beaufort?"

It naturally surprised him, as it had me, when I wrote and told him that once you left Harvard and went out into the real world to work in the field of education and you proved to be successful, many at the Harvard Graduate School of Education deemed you instead a failure. Their reasoning was that the educational system in America was so terrible, so inhumane, so racist, that to contribute to it was to prolong its inevitable demise in the same way contributing in any shape, way, or fashion to the Vietnam War was immoral, prolonging its ending.

However, I assured him, he would have been okay at Harvard. True, he'd been a success, he'd taught brilliantly, and his students had loved him. But Harvard, in their grace and magnanimity, would have forgiven him that because he'd been fired.

"Thank them for me," he wrote back. "I'm forever fucking grateful. What are they up there? A bunch of idiots?"

Ivan Illich's book, *Deschooling Society*, was the most popular book at Harvard's Graduate School of Education at the time. John Bremer's School Without Walls in Philadelphia, a system of apprenticeships where high school students went out into the real world and worked, was drawing attention nationwide. Classroom walls in public schools were under the wrecking ball. Free schools were in vogue, open classrooms up and coming.

Admittedly, the sentiment, since always I was on the lookout for educational alternatives, was exciting and appealing, if for no other reason than that promise was in the air.

I wrote up mock cases for the law school students to try in mock court. The South had risen again there, all the easier perhaps for Harvard to avoid all the muggings in Cambridge and the rage and hopelessness in Roxbury, the ghetto in Boston. I wrote up cases from a uniquely Southern perspective. Black and white schools in the South were consolidating. Conflicts abounded: for example, which school had to give up their school anthem, their school mascot, their school name, the name of their football and baseball and basketball teams? Unlike the rest of the nation, no one in the South had ever even heard of soccer back then. "'*Sock* her?'" Why would any man want to do something like that?

I looked back, as I would throughout my teaching career, at my own education in Beaufort. It had been irrelevant to me, yes. It had been impersonal, true. It had been rational. But why was there such an across-the-board absence of profound feeling, of genuine emotion, such lifelessness? Relevance mattered. Objectivity mattered. Reason certainly mattered: ultimately, things have to make sense. But without genuine feeling, some kind of personal relevance or tie-in, where's the real motivation for anyone to learn?

For my class on curriculum development, I devised and wrote up a curriculum for teachers to use with students that would bring emotion, intellect, and personal relevance into play. I selected films, stories, novel excerpts, and role-playing dilemmas I had written up, all of which were representative of conflicts the students might have experienced in their own lives, one for each lesson. In one film a girl is dumped by her best friend for the "popular group." In a role-playing dilemma, Nathan in social studies class chairs a five-person committee, which will be evaluated and receive grades as a group, doing research and reporting on the problem of narcotics in America; one member naturally sits on his ass and does zero. In a story Sally, Rosette, and Janice are shopping; Sally shoplifts a sweater, tucking it inside her coat; Rosette does the same thing. Both of them are looking at Janice, expectant. And so on, the conflicts presented to them in one form or another range from trouble at home to bullying and harassment. One of my favorites was a story about a star athlete, who is black, playing left end on his high school football team, looking to befriend the quarterback, who is white, and always looking to throw him the ball on the football field but refusing to give him the time of day off the field, leaving the black athlete wondering if the quarterback's a racist.

After each of these presentations, kids were first asked about the feelings and thoughts of the characters in these dilemmas. For example, What does the girl dumped by her best friend, just so she can run around with the "popular" kids, feel? What does her former best friend feel? What do they think? Do their thoughts and feelings match what they say? What they do? Why? Why not?

Then: Have you ever been in a similar situation? What did you feel? What did you think? Did what you say match what you truly felt and thought? Were what you felt and what you thought two different things or the same? How did you finally react, if at all?

Then: What might you feel now? Think now? Say now? How might you react now, if at all?

Finally, the kids themselves were to write up their own stories about their own dilemmas, asking and dealing with the same questions about themselves, the curriculum building on itself and continuing.

Today, can you imagine bullies, victims, sycophants, and bystanders confronting these questions? All at the same time in the same classroom? Over the years in my classrooms, they did, and you know what I found out? Every one of them was guilty. Who hasn't at one time or another in their lives snubbed, ridiculed, or at least "picked on" someone else? Who hasn't *been* rejected, ridiculed, or at least "picked on" by someone else? Hell, if a zero-tolerance antibullying policy had realistically gone into effect in our schools, all the buildings would have ended up empty.

Without fully realizing it, I was actually *creating* for the kids the education I didn't have but that I wanted and needed. It was an embryonic start, but it was a start, particularly when the kids themselves began writing up their own stories. That, of course, made them even more personal, making more personal and true too their reactions to the stories they were reading in literature classes—imagine now their take on *Lord of the Flies*—and the social dynamics taking place among themselves.

All of this expanded and developed throughout my teaching career, taking on a life of its own I could never have imagined when I first wrote up this curriculum at Harvard.

I was teaching not as I was taught, I wrote Pat, but as I was learning.

With your record in high school, he wrote back, what choice do you have?

Hard as we tried, Martha and I could find no rabbi in Cambridge, even at Hillel at Harvard, willing to marry us. Embarrassed though some of them were about it, Martha was nonetheless not Jewish.

"You've got to be kidding," wrote Pat. "Harvard? That bastion of liberalism? What a bunch of fucking hypocrites."

So, over Thanksgiving in 1970 Martha and I were married in Cambridge in Ralph Waldo Emerson's former church in Harvard Square, Lara adorably participating, my dad my best man. Pat had phoned beforehand. He'd just felt so guilty about not being able to come, it was a congratulatory call. There was little hope for a teaching job—he'd been blackballed, the word was out—his fear of running out of money becoming a depressing reality. I wished he'd called collect. He said he'd reverse the charges, but neither one us could figure out how to do it, and we talked forever.

It was in this conversation that I reminded Pat how both of us had always envied Ivy Leaguers, had entertained these fantasies of what the journalist David Halberstam had called "the best and the brightest": their intellectual status, their cultural sophistication, their inside knowledge of the ways of the world.

"Guess what?" I asked him.

He was desperate for a pick-me-up.

"We're as smart as anyone up here."

He was unabashedly thrilled. "Really? You're kidding?"

"About you I am. But not about me."

"I stop by your dad's store all the time. He tickles me. 'How's the Harvard boy, Pat? Heard from the Harvard boy lately?'" he said, mimicking him. "'Come on in and sit down, son. I'll give you a discount on a coke.'"

"That's great."

"It's wonderful."

"How's Barbara? The kids?"

"Soon to be penniless, my man. However, Conroy will rally."

He did, with *The Water Is Wide*.

I must note here too that in this period of his life Pat was still pretty much an innocent. He still attended Mass regularly. I'd only in the past few years taught him to drink, a lesson we would both pay for for the rest of our lives. All that profanity in *The Water is Wide*. Yep, before me he never even cussed. I pretty much liberated him there, and even now, in retrospect, I think it added spirit and humor to his voice as a writer. Married now, he'd only been in love once before, while a Citadel cadet, to a very pretty girl we'd both dated in high school, who'd been left pregnant and abandoned by the father of her child in Charleston. Even then, it was Pat to the rescue.

Saving the world wasn't enough for him. Just as he had tried as a child to save his mother from Don Conroy's brutality, so for the rest of his life it would be Pat to the rescue of every damsel in distress he would ever come across.

He and Barbara had their own biological child, Megan, to go with Jessica and Melissa, and after *The Water Is Wide* and *Conrack* introduced him to a world too big at the time even for him, he left Beaufort and moved with his new family to Atlanta. There, he enrolled his children in the progressive Paideia School, where I would end up teaching in my junior high classroom for more than thirty years and where Martha taught before becoming a psychologist. Lara attended Paideia, as did our daughter Maggie, born soon after Megan. Both our families were very much a part of the Paideia community in the verdant North Druid hills, which included neighborhood families from Emory University and the Centers for Disease Control as well as those from more distant Atlanta neighborhoods interested in a liberal, progressive education for their kids.

There, in Atlanta, he became obsessed with the biographies of novelists Ross Lockridge Jr., who'd written the acclaimed *Raintree County,* and Thomas Heggen, who'd written the equally renowned *Mr. Roberts.*

Both were first novels that made their authors famous all over the world, as Pat was becoming, after which they both committed suicide.

IV

WHAT PAT LEFT OUT OF
THE GREAT SANTINI

As the world would eventually learn, throughout Pat's childhood Peg Conroy, early the following mornings, before school, would obscure Pat's night visits to the emergency room with deftly, subtly applied makeup. If there was a bandage, well, he'd fallen on the sidewalk practicing his dribbling or run into a door, the usual excuses. Only, back then no one knew about child abuse. Reports of it were at most vague whispers, the statistics as closeted as the abuse itself. In the time of Norman Rockwell–type families showing up on billboards all over the country, when you were taught that if you couldn't say anything nice about anybody, you shouldn't say anything at all, when appearances were everything, when divorce was a scandal and homes for unwed mothers a vague mystery, when displays of emotion were considered unmanly in men and a form of infantile hysteria in a woman—"It's okay, baby, it's okay"—no one talked about it.

In our early twenties, when we were teaching in Beaufort, Pat hinted and hinted and hinted, but every kid grows up thinking that every family is like his own, and I just didn't get it. A psychiatrist who'd met Pat socially, back when we were teaching in Beaufort, once asked me why Pat was so angry.

Naive as I was, I didn't know what he was talking about. Angry? Pat? No, he's just joking, it's his humor, he exaggerates everything. Actually, I explained, Pat speaks in opposites. If he tells you he hates you, it means he loves you. That was actually true. Pat did speak in opposites, but that was only to people he loved.

His hatred, his anger, even when misplaced, was real. What did I know?

I'm neurotic as hell, obsessive, compulsive. Yes, the Jewish disease. But there was no fear of violence in my family. My concern, back in the forties and fifties, was that we were "abnormal" because Mom and Dad weren't as perpetually polite and well mannered, as apparently "nice," always, as Ozzie and Harriet.

I usually brought this up at dinner, when I couldn't get my way.

"Maybe," Mom offered, "if you behaved yourself and acted more like David and Ricky, then your dad and I could be more like Ozzie and Harriet." She looked at my dad. "What do you think, Morris?"

"Maybe," he said. "Anything's possible, I suppose."

While I was running my mouth, my older brother, Stanley had stolen my drumstick. "You would have been talking with your mouth full," he said, justifying it.

"Mom!"

"He's got a point," she said, amused. "That *is* impolite."

"And how many times has she told you that, Bernie?"

He was pretty clever.

As for my younger brother Aaron, all he cared about was running around the neighborhood shooting BB guns with his friends. Or to be more accurate, running around the neighborhood shooting his *friends'* BB guns. He didn't have one of his own because he was Jewish. However, he was not *too* Jewish, according to Mom, because he shot them.

"Nothing wrong with that," said Dad.

There was very little wrong with *anything*, according to Dad. Aaron was actually very much like him in that way. Stanley and I were more emotional, like Mom.

So, like with the psychiatrist, when Pat began going on and on about his father—basically just saying he was "an asshole, a shithead"—I told everyone in Beaufort he was just exaggerating. And he did exaggerate. He was known for it around town. "You know Pat," I'd tell them.

Later in Atlanta in the midseventies Pat, turning to fiction, began writing *The Great Santini*. His book was about his father, he told me, and that's how his father often referred to himself, at least within the confines of his family. His dad had seen the real Great Santini in a circus act. He was a sword-swallower and fire-eater—daring, dashing, fearless, his dad had told him, "just like I am." "Who is the greatest of them all?" his dad would ask his kids, who would answer on cue: "The Great Santini!"

His dad, Pat also told me, was in reality more a high-wire act.

When he began writing *The Great Santini*, he became more and more insistent about how brutal his father, Colonel Don Conroy, had been: his father had routinely beaten up not only him but his entire family, including his mother. Though at first fairly general in the oral telling, these stories soon became more specific: his father beating Pat with his fists, particularly when he tried to pull him off of his mother; backhanding him after he struck out in a baseball game; choking him, banging his head over and over against the wall. Who would do such a thing? *Nobody* I knew, not back then. Moreover, these *were* stories, or at least morphing into them. Pat always told stories over and over, refining them, getting them right, before he actually put pen to paper. These were going into *The Great Santini*, which was, he also emphasized, fiction. So, I wondered, was he lying? What a way to make a living! Isn't that what fiction is? Indeed, he was.

But he was also the greatest truth teller I've ever known, and he opened me, and consequently my students at Paideia, to a world of suffering, of hatred, of self-hatred, of depression and despair I had never even imagined.

It was in the early seventies in Atlanta that I began reading his first draft of *The Great Santini*. He had used the same typist Martha and I had used for our first book about teaching, *Open Classrooms in the Middle School*. Other than the typist, of course, no one else had looked at Pat's manuscript yet, not even his editor, Anne Barrett at Houghton Mifflin.

I came across a particular scene that over my objection, for good reason, I think, he left in the manuscript unchanged.

That scene was a lie, fare made palatable at the time for people like me. If you've read *The Great Santini*, you might remember it.

His father's alter ego is Colonel Bull Meecham, his mother's Lillian Meecham, Pat's is Ben Meecham.

The scene takes place in their enormous antebellum home on the Point in Beaufort, a neighborhood of old money, much of it gone, of stately antebellum homes just like Ben's, many in need of repair, and interior gardens dominated by thousand-year-old oak trees and Spanish moss. When Pat first married Barbara, they lived in one; back then in Beaufort, such homes were a bargain.

One night Ben's father, clearly drunk and out of control, brutally attacks his mother, terrifying the whole family, after which he stumbles drunkenly out of the house, down the back steps, into the neighborhood.

Afterwards, his mother tells him to go out and find his father, which he does, lying helplessly in his own vomit in the middle of the Green, a park-like quadrangle of grass and oak trees.

Ben stands over him, astride him, and he is overcome with the urge to stomp his face, to kick him in the belly, to thumb his eyes "into permanent darkness, to smash his testes." Instead, as he helps his father up, hooking his father's arm around his neck and they begin staggering toward home, he tells him he loves him.

His father looks at Ben as if he's witnessing "the birth of something wild," pulling away from him, running into the darkness, Ben chasing him all over the Green saying, "I love you, Dad, I love you. I love you, Dad. I love you." His dad just can't take it, stumbling, weaving awkwardly this way and that as if evading tacklers, tripping over himself, until finally, exhausted, he falls again, vomiting again all over himself, after which Ben hooks his father's arm around his neck again, gets him to his feet, and walks him "toward the house in silence."

Fascinating, I thought. Disturbing, yet hopeful. Love as weapon, yet no less real for it.

But I was a teacher. And a teacher is always looking for what is not said, for what is hidden, perhaps between the lines, perhaps absent from the page, and this particular scene was written in Pat's hand, above the originally typed passage, which had been crossed out.

Here's the real scene I managed to decipher with the aid of a magnifying glass, the true scene, the original typed one that been crossed out on this draft.

All is the same initially: Colonel Meecham's brutal assault on Ben's mom and their family; Colonel Meecham stumbling out of the house out into the neighborhood; Ben upon the instructions of his mother walking around the neighborhood looking for him.

As before, he finds him lying on the Green. Only, in this scene Colonel Meecham is passed out. There is no Ben chasing his father all over the Green, no "I love you, Dad, I love you."

Instead, what I manage to make out on the page with a magnifying glass shocks me forever out of my ignorance, shatters my own world, and submerges me into Ben's, into the world of over a quarter of the families in America, into a world of approximately a quarter of the kids in my classroom every year I knew I was failing, regardless of how socially polite and academically successful they might have appeared, a world, in a few words, of shame, self-loathing, and vengeful hatred, all of which Ben, through my magnifying glass, is unleashing on his father.

He doesn't fantasize doing it. He does it.

He straddles him, turns his father's face toward him, and completely unharnessing and unleashing such fury and hatred and brutality that I could never have imagined was ever inside him, he simply beats him in the face, over and over, pummels him, fist over fist over fist, one time after another, his father's face black and blue and already swollen, a bloody mess, time after time after time, until Ben Meecham exhausts himself and collapses on top him, after which he carries him home.

"Leave it in," I told Pat. "Leave it in."

"No one will believe it, Bernie. Anne Barrett won't believe it. No one will."

Perhaps he was right, I just don't know. I hadn't understood, though he'd tried to tell me over and over again. But I do now. And my students do. He came to my junior high classroom at Paideia, as he often did, sometimes to hear their stories read aloud to their classmates and to contribute to the applause, the discussions and reactions. Their stories, like his, were always personal: sibling rivalry, as old as Cain and Abel, usually a younger sibling incomprehensibly, in the older child's mind, usurping his relationship with his parents; friendship and betrayal; envy and jealousy, often of their best friend's grades, jump shot, popularity, family life, the latter particularly if their own was dysfunctional; unrequited love; first love; sex, even if only with themselves, first kiss, first sexual encounter; illness; violence; death of a loved one; ambition, usually a failure to measure up athletically, socially, academically. Like Pat's stories, they made you laugh, they made you cry. He loved them. Were you to have visited my classroom back then, you would have seen that the history of the world is in the heart and soul of every child.

Naturally, it took a lot of talk and rewriting and often difficult inside exploration and emotional excavation for them to uncover their stories, to find them, for their stories to reveal themselves to them. What was inside them that they were hiding, often from themselves, that was subtly or overtly sabotaging their souls. How do we, as teachers, bring them out so they love and create more freely and openly? Who were they really? And how could they show themselves on the printed page? It wasn't a question of what they wanted to write, but deep down inside what they felt they *needed* to write.

This was not something they could just "figure out," as they had always done before in their school years. It was something they had to discover, something inside them they were denying, something they would also realize, as Pat did, that was fucking up their relationships, their work, their lives. So the key was the heart, not the head. No way to "think" your way through this. Cut off your heads, I'd tell them. Only feel, go deeper, deeper, and the inspiration will come. From the truth of your feelings will your story, your life, begin to make sense.

So, sometimes he'd come into the classroom to just listen to them talk, to work with them, as I was, in helping them to *find* their stories.

Teaching is listening.

I brought him in to work with those kids who, like him, I had failed to see behind the false personae, underneath the deftly applied makeup, the cover-up and the excuses for cuts, welts, and bruises.

He listened to them so sensitively, so attentively, so carefully that once written it was as if their stories themselves had turned into sheets of flame. I read them aloud to the class, as I did all their stories. I'd gone through at least several rewrites with them, so by the time they were ready to be presented, I certainly knew them well enough, and I was a good reader. For whatever reason, they seemed to prefer that.

Pat was there too for the reading. He knew the entire class would be present. He knew these stories of violence and abuse had never been told in my class before, but he had faith in the kids' stories, in the kids who wrote them, and in their classmates. Because he knew kids, and because he knew the kids in my classroom, he understood that unlike the adults in the world at large, these kids in their world upon hearing them would react lovingly, which they did. Hard as it was to just get them to shut the hell up most of the time, these particular stories were met with a long, stunned silence; they were disturbed, horrified, and finally just sad beyond words for their friends and classmates who'd been brutalized in their own homes, in homes some of which had been so hospitably open to them for sleepovers, for parties, for weekend visits. The tears flowed, then one by one, a standing ovation from the entire class, including Pat. Shame, they felt, shame. Not a few wanted to go and kill the abuser, which made Pat feel great, he told them, since he'd wanted to kill his father his entire life.

For some reason, everyone burst into laughter. Pure comic relief from the master.

As I had learned from Pat, so my students learned. They knew now, as I did, of the profound suffering not way out there in the world at large but rather sitting next to them in math class, in the home where they never, in a million years, would have suspected it. Remember, the term *abuse* was yet to be a part of the common American vocabulary. The statistics at the time were not yet common knowledge. Things that went on behind closed doors remained behind closed doors. A man's home was still his castle. And it was not only these very brave young writers who were no longer alone, but also their friends and classmates. The class was more open, more intimate, more honest, therefore stronger. These kids had done to my classroom what *The Great Santini* would do to the world.

I would, of course, take the proper action with both the abusive parents and the authorities, but that is not the point here. These kids knew now, as I did, and eventually as the world would, of the battered child lost and terrified hiding behind the false and alienated personae under the makeup, hostage to their abusers, as Ben Meecham was, as Pat was. Yes, not just me, not just my students, but after *The Great Santini*, the whole world knows, and the reason is none other than my best and dearest and most loving friend, Pat Conroy.

And the scene on the Green, the original typed one under my magnifying glass? They wouldn't have believed it, he'd said. Not even his editor. So, in *The Great Santini* he gave them what they could believe, what they would believe.

The *depth* of his rage in that scene, however, which in and of itself had been so real and powerful and disturbing that it had completely blown away any doubts I'd had before, he left out. Now I wondered, what else might he have left out?

"There's always more," he told me. "In all these stories, Bernie, there's always more."

As the stories began coming out in my classroom over the years and as the world learned about the abuse happening behind closed doors in so many American homes, that would prove to be truer than I could ever have imagined.

"I hated my dad," Pat told me soon after *The Great Santini* was published, "when I was in diapers."

If that child in diapers, the child of his father, could talk, I wondered, what might *he* have to say, speaking for himself, unencumbered by the voice of the adult Pat?

In my students' stories, beneath whatever trauma they might uncover—ordinary ones like the birth of a younger sibling or more devastating ones like abuse—they usually discovered the innocent, wholeheartedly trusting child, the one reigning happily over the household before his innocence is lost or at least in doubt. And if *that* child could talk, I wondered, what might he have to say?

At the end of *The Great Santini*, Ben Meecham "fills up with love" for his father. Pat did love his father, as he often said. In fact, Pat was as "filled up" with love as anyone I've ever known. That had come from his mother, he would say. And the child in diapers, *prior* to the one who was hit, could it also have come from that love?

"I have absolutely no memory of that child. I have no memory of a time when I wasn't terrified of being hit. I don't remember a time in my childhood when I didn't hate my father."

So much hatred, but such a superabundance of love.

My daughter Maggie was born on February 21, 1975, the year before *The Great Santini* came out. Pat, decades later in his introduction to her fables, *Lost Cantos of the Ouroboros Caves*, writes that he was there at her birth.

He was, and when he'd introduce her at talks and book signings, he used to love telling the story, particularly if I were present, of how I burst out of Martha's hospital room right after Maggie was born to tell him; he was right outside the door waiting. "Bernie was absolutely out of his mind with joy and excitement, going on and on about how beautiful this baby was. Finally, when he stopped to take a breath, I asked him: "Is it a boy or a girl?"

"'Wait a second,'" he said, without missing a beat. "'I'll be right back.'"

Pat told me later he'd felt much as I had when his daughter Megan was born, particularly since he'd missed the births of Melissa and

Jessica, whom he'd adopted, much as I'd missed the birth of my step-daughter Lara, to whom Pat was very close, just as I was to his kids.

His older daughter, Jessica, responding recently to a post on Facebook about cussing, said she had absolutely no problem with that. "I was raised," she said, "by Pat and Bernie."

Both my daughters could have said the same thing.

V

THE GREATER PAT'S LITERARY FAME AND SUCCESS, THE MORE TRAGIC AND UNHAPPY HIS PERSONAL LIFE

In 1976, *The Great Santini* was in the bookstores and already on the reading list at Paideia; three years later the movie was out, premiering in Atlanta at Loew's Theatre, the same theater, much to Pat's delight, where Margaret Mitchell's *Gone with the Wind* had premiered. As he had done with the premiere of *Conrack,* he had the proceeds from the Atlanta premiere of *The Great Santini* go to Paideia.

It had been filmed at Tidalholm, a magnificent antebellum home on the Point in Beaufort overlooking the Beaufort River on the Inland Waterway. Pat had been in Beaufort, staying with his mother, Peg, in her home, for much of the filming, observing and consulting, also delighting, as his mother had, in her role as an extra. As Pat and I were sitting in the front row of the Loew's Theatre with mostly family and friends and no doubt a few local dignitaries and politicians I can't remember, he warned me, as the lights dimmed and the movie began, that they had really fixed Tidalholm up for the movie.

The house itself had always been grand and majestic. Through the enormous windows and from the fragrant verandahs, the view, especially after the morning mist had cleared, was of sunlight settling over the river in a dazzling, gleaming blue, glancing off the sailboats and cabin cruisers and, far out, even off the hulls of the shrimp boats in a bright golden hue, silhouetting the mallards and great blue herons and white snowy egrets tiptoeing about in the pluff mud, the smell of which, though less than enticing to visitors, was an aphrodisiac to us Beaufortonians, lending the sweet scent of flowers a bit of tang, of bite. It brightened up the great sweep of lawn in the front, glowing luminously in the Spanish moss heralding and garlanding the magnificent oak trees arching down the pathway to the front door, browsing among the palms, lighting up whatever flowers were in season—winter daphne, azaleas, camellias, plumbago, legustrum.

But back then, if you looked closely at the exterior of the home itself, at the molding and cornices of the verandahs, in the eaves and gables of the upper stories, you could see here and there dry tongues of paint peeling, miniature hangovers from the relentless summer humidity. Somehow, to me, it was a welcoming sign of the surrender of old money and aristocratic airs, of the growing irrelevance of an aging elite of white Episcopalians and Methodists, of slave quarters converted into apartments for rental. That decadence, a historical reminder to me of what was, was lost to me immediately in the laundered version they were showing us in the movie. It was all but airbrushed.

He leaned over to me, whispering, I could barely see him in the darkness of the theater. "Bernie, remember who we met there?"

"Are you kidding?"

It was at Tidalholm, back when Pat and I were teaching in Beaufort, long before anyone might have imagined it being featured in a movie, that we met Ernest Hemingway's first wife, Hadley Hemingway, who we'd both felt was so touchingly portrayed in *A Moveable Feast*, Hemingway's memoir about their years together as a young married couple in Paris. "If you have ever lived in Paris as a young man," he'd written as the epigraph, "then it will always be with you, for Paris is a moveable feast." So was the memoir itself for me and Pat. In an age and world of pragmatism, very much like the women of our day and very unlike the men, Pat and I were impossible romantics. To this day, it's my favorite of all Hemingway's books. Pat had it up there with *For Whom the Bell Tolls*. Back when we were in Beaufort, we had yet to meet a great writer, but we both so adored Hadley's character and the great care Hemingway took in loving her throughout the memoir that, for me at least, the anticipation of meeting her was thrilling; much more thrilling admittedly than *actually* meeting her. As Pat and I both learned through the years, that was usually the case, not only with muses and most notables of any stripe but particularly with great writers. If you want to know a writer, particularly a writer like Hemingway, know his work. That's where he is. That's where you're most likely to find him. Very simply, that's where he's looking for himself. In real life, in a social or professional encounter, that's just too much to ask of intimacy.

The owners of Tidalholm, Beaufort folks we knew at the time, had turned the mansion into a high-end B and B, and since Hadley Hemingway and her then husband, the journalist Paul Mower, were guests there, they—the owners—invited our friend Tim Belk to visit, have lunch, and play the piano for them. He brought me and Pat along for the conversation and camaraderie. Plus, he said, "Bringing two country bumpkins along will make me appear, by comparison, even more impressive than I already am." It was true that Tim was certainly more urbane and culturally sophisticated than me or Pat. Already he was introducing us to foreign films—we'd never experienced subtitles before—French literature, *Commentary*, Shostakovich, Jacque Brel, and the *Economist*. About the *Economist,* uncompromising in its professionalism, its complexity, and in its apparent eagerness to just bore the shit out of you, all Pat and I could manage was to somehow work our faces into sculptures of pensive, considered, complicated thought. I felt Pat had the look down pat, pardon the pun. Tim, however, told him he looked not like Rodin's *The Thinker* but like he was auditioning to pose for it. Tim was out of our league, no question. He was a guy, like I told Pat, who knew how to hold his fork. "The less you say," he advised us, "the better you'll look. Silence, invisibility, is your best and only option. Please, try not to be yourselves."

We weren't ourselves, not that afternoon in the parlor at Tidalholm. Neither one of us could think of anything to say. For one thing, Hadley herself, perhaps in deference to her husband as many women were in those days, was as quiet as Pat and I. Her husband, also by that time elderly, advised us that we should live out our lives revealing nothing to anyone, to always hold our cards close to our vest. Don't provide people, he added, especially those whom in your youth and naiveté you might make the mistake of trusting, with ammunition. Jesus, no wonder we couldn't think of anything to say. Later, on our way home, Tim would refer to him as "Mr. Personality."

Unlike Pat and me, of course, in the classically well-appointed parlor of Tidalholm, Tim was as cool and urbane as always, pontificating as if he were perfectly at home in these circles about movies and the latest plays in New York, airily waving his Lucky Strike, the smoke circling about his galaxy like indistinguishable satellites.

When Tim began to play, however, the melody of Rachmaninoff's Second Piano Concerto pouring so quietly, so mellifluously from his fingers, building and swirling so magnificently, so gloriously about the room, through the open windows, out over the river into the blossoming sunlight, I saw a different Hadley Hemingway, the real Hadley Hemingway, I couldn't help but think, Hadley Hemingway at work. She was mesmerized, so carefully and so seriously attentive, leaning toward the piano, toward Tim, toward the music taking over the parlor, as attentive as she had been to Hemingway himself, and as he had been to her, throughout their Paris years as a young and loving couple in *A Moveable Feast*.

I was as mesmerized by her as she was by Rachmaninoff's Second Piano Concerto.

It was during lunch that day that Pat and I both discovered that the soup in what was called the finger bowl tasted like water, well, because it was.

And now here we were at the Atlanta premiere of *The Great Santini*—think about it, only ten years later—Tidalholm all dressed up, looking perfect, celebrating the up-and-coming writer Pat Conroy. We were all excited as hell, though with Pat himself it was hard to tell. He had that stupid poker face working. I told him. He smiled. Beyond that, my reaction was to fall as much in love with Blythe Danner, playing Pat's mom, as I had his real mom, Peg. Blythe Danner actually lived on the Point during the making of the movie, only a short walk from Tidalholm. In Pat's later years, after moving back to Beaufort, on his routinely celebrated Tour of Beaufort for visiting friends he would tell them that when he was in Beaufort during the filming, he'd hold Blythe's daughter Gwyneth Paltrow on his knee and say, "Gwyneth, you're going to be a great actress when you grow up."

Who knows? Pat was probably acting himself when he told the story. But like Gwyneth Paltrow later, he could make you believe it.

Not that anyone on the planet gives a crap, but the major shortcoming of the film for me personally, knowing both Pat and Don, was that neither Michael O'Keefe playing Pat nor Robert Duvall playing Don had their charisma, their larger-than-life personalities. Plus, Don and Pat were great basketball players, and Robert Duvall and Michael O'Keefe were just horrible. Duvall played like one of those wild, flailing, out-of-control guys who, dribbling toward the basket, was so terrified of losing the ball he had to keep looking down at it—an amateurish no-no—checking to be sure he still had control of it, looking like he didn't know where he was going to end up. Watching him in the movie, I didn't either. For a minute there, in that famous one-on-one scene between father and son on the outdoor court on the Point, I wondered if he might end up somewhere in the neighborhood, maybe out on Billy Canada's dock next door, dribbling, head down, right into the Beaufort River. And O'Keefe had a decent jump shot, but he dribbled like he had a stick up his butt.

Even I was way better than both of them.

Who cares? Pat's career as a basketball player was over, but with *The Water is Wide* and *Conrack* and *The Great Santini* (the novel and the movie), his literary success was on the rise. In Atlanta he became a god, using his fame and respect for good causes, encouraging writers, getting friends either literary agents or out of jail, and, my favorite, publicly taking to task in speeches and in print Lewis Grizzard, the *Atlanta Journal-Constitution*'s mean-spirited, snarky, racist, and sexist columnist, probably their most popular one. Most of the writers in Atlanta, however—veteran novelists Annie Rivers Siddons, Paul Darcy Boles, Terry Kay, and Thomas Cook, *Newsweek*'s Joe Cummings and Vern Smith, as well as fledglings such as myself—celebrated his success with champagne at our friend Cliff Graubart's Old New York Bookshop, where we all hung out and where Pat had his own room downstairs in which to write. His fame not only as a writer but as a great public speaker was making the boy who couldn't afford a suit for the prom or dinner for his date, as he himself publicly recalled, a wealthy man.

It was about this time that Pat suggested he and I begin taping our conversations.

"For what?"

"For posterity."

"Oh, mine? Why, thank you, Pat, for caring."

I didn't know how to use one of those reel-to-reel things, which is basically all that was available at the time, and neither did he.

Sadly, however, the greater his success in the world, the greater the failure in his personal life, his family. He had left the intimacy, for better or worse, of Beaufort, he'd told me, for the anonymity of Atlanta, where he could, he said, "follow his perversions." Perversions: what a hyperbolic term for affairs. Never young babes, all mature intelligent women, never, so far as I knew, one-night stands. Whether you approve or not, hardly "perversions."

But to Pat, I think the degree of hyperbole probably reflected the intensity of his guilt, shame, and self-loathing. As much as he loved and needed women, he was Catholic, the "nice boy" his mother had taught him to be doing his damnedest to mature into the "nice young man" she had expected him to be. So I think he disgusted himself.

By this time, in the midseventies, and for most of the rest of his life—he would confess to me several years before he died—he was drinking a fifth of liquor a day.

All he wanted, he told me, was to be "a gentle, harmless man." How does "the son of Santini," as Pat often referred to himself, the son of such a violent father, become a gentle, harmless man? His father was a soldier, a warrior, a hero in wartime. He was a tyrant in peacetime, his home a house of landmines his family had to tiptoe around. Who threw himself on those landmines every time one threatened to explode but Pat? Who took his father's blows as much as humanly possible to protect his mother and his brothers and sisters but Pat? Already he'd been a child martyr. Already he'd been a warrior fighting a brutal father in his own home. His lifelong fear was turning into the man he'd fought.

Inspired by the love and the teachings of his mother, could he as a man become a warrior for good, as his mother had demanded of the child, a man who would save Jews? Befriend the lonely and the awkward? (His mother had required him to take the girl who wouldn't otherwise have been invited to the prom.) Stand up for the underdog?

He was certainly doing that. He was the bravest man I've ever known. A crusader for civil rights, women's rights, against domestic abuse, for freedom of expression. You name it, ol' Pat was at the forefront, on the right side of history, leading the charge.

His mother, Peg, never forgot that she and her sisters were children of the Depression in impoverished rural Alabama, who on the verge of starvation were fed by nearby black sharecroppers just about as poor as they were. Pat would always fight for the sharecroppers.

But how does the son of Santini, overflowing with gregariousness and joy and great humor, show anger to those he loves without letting loose unharnessed and unchecked the rage bequeathed him by Santini, without the son of Santini becoming what he most feared, Santini himself?

One thing I learned from Pat as well as my students over the years was that to tame the beast inside you, you must embrace him. The beast grows fat on denial. Opening the door wide, inviting him in, embracing him, became in my mind the key to liberation, to creativity, to intimacy, to self-respect, to love. Slamming the door on him, I saw over and over, ends up in some form of rage or fanaticism.

After the publication of *The Great Santini* in 1976, Pat literally tried his best to do that, only he was taming the beast outside him, his father, Don Conroy, the Great Santini himself, rather than the one inside, Santini's unfortunate legacy raging within, fighting for his soul. Peg divorced Don, shocking him, after which he showed up at Pat's front door in Atlanta, broken, vulnerable, a state Pat could never before have imagined, much less imagined witnessing at his front door. At last he could confront Don about his abusive behavior, which he did, then took him to Manuel's, a local watering hole, for a beer, after which Don decided to get his own apartment in Atlanta, regularly showing up at Pat's house for coffee, conversation, and the newspaper. Pat began offering up Santini's alter ego, his dad, at talks and book signings,

Santini himself proving as charismatic, witty, and endearing to the public as Pat himself.

Pat used to tell the story that at one event in Columbia, Pat introduced his father by announcing that his IQ was about "the temperature of this room." Don Conroy, the Great Santini, didn't miss a beat. His first line, stepping up to the lectern: "Damn, it's hot in here. Why, it must be 150 degrees."

It was a great start in the conversion of Santini himself into a gentle, harmless man, but what did it do for Pat other than sell books and increase his fame and show the public a hell of a good time? It was terrific for his dad, no doubt, but what was it doing for him? He was teaching Santini to be a good father, a better man, teaching him to love, yes, but he was doing so by changing *him*. What he was not doing, in failing to embrace the Santini of his childhood still simmering, waiting to explode, inside his own heart and soul, was helping *himself*.

I knew from teaching and working with writers too that to simply know and articulate your traumas and problems was not enough to liberate yourself from them, to become fully creative, fully truthful, not that that wasn't a lifelong struggle anyway. A young writer I once taught offered up in her story every detail of her father, when she was five, shooting himself in front of her. Reading it, I felt nothing, because she hadn't when she wrote it. No, like everyone else, she had to re-experience the trauma, to give up the conquest, to surrender to the feelings, the memory, to fall boldly into that black hole, the void, in order to solidly land on her feet, to come out of it whole, with both the innocence she had before losing it and the wisdom and perspective and relief and catharsis that comes from having given yourself up to it.

You just, in my experience, cannot come out of it without going through it. In that void, in that no-man's-land of tension and conflict, in that haunted house of pain is the voice of the writer, and I think this is what Flannery O'Conner meant when she said about literature that it all came from childhood. And who better, if the need was there, to tell that story than the child who had experienced it.

Pat never wrote in that child's voice. The adult was always in control. It wasn't for lack of trying, however. He said over and over not only to intimates but publicly in interviews: *"I struggle every morning at my writing desk with the little boy I once was."*

Indeed he did, and his growing awareness of that little boy produced grand writing, perhaps the most truthful, the most passionate, and the most beautiful writing of our age, certainly that I've read, but the denial of him could leave the reader, at least this one, with scenes so hyperbolic as to defy credibility, with overwritten prose his critics referred to as "purple," with melodrama, with a view of the world as black and white, Santini's view.

If only for Pat's own happiness and peace of mind, I would offer, *Let the child speak.*

Pat's whole view of art, of creativity, of liberation and wisdom, was: No pain, no gain. No pain, no joy. The question that haunted him throughout his life was this: "Why did my father beat me? I was a nice little boy." He just couldn't get beyond that question. Like most who have been abused, was he afraid, deep down, that he wasn't "nice," that he'd been in some way responsible for the abuse?

He got close, awfully close to that nice little boy, and the closest he got, while sober at least, as you'll witness in these pages, was in an interview with his biographer Catherine Seltzer at the Conroy@70 celebration, six months before he died. Publicly, it was the most beautiful I'd ever seen him. Whether in an interview, on a panel, or in a one-man show, always when he spoke publicly he was hysterically funny and also terribly moving and powerful, a one-man army rising up to decimate boredom forever in the lives of his audiences. He was always memorable, inspiring, and that's what he aimed for, giving his all. On this night, however he was different. He seemed at ease, at peace, with himself, thoughtful rather than inspired. Asked by a member of the audience what made him the man he was, so kind and generous, he rose, walked to the front of the stage, and with no attempt at humor, false modesty, or self-deprecation as would have normally been the case, he literally touched his heart and said humbly, "My mother." Tapping it, he said, "She's here. With me. Always." It was as if goodness, all he'd ever really wanted, had after all prevailed, the savage disarmed, lifeless.

But we jump ahead here. Let us to return to the post-Santini period. He divorced Barbara in 1978 and moved by himself into an apartment in Ansley Park in midtown Atlanta, where he worked on his next novel, *The Lords of Discipline.*

He also took up cooking for family and friends with a vengeance.

"Stock," he announced one afternoon at his new apartment. "Stock."

Stock? I had no idea what he was talking about. Had he learned to read the stock market page? Maybe I should too. Only he had stocks, he had a financial investor, I had no need of one. Right?

Pat looked at me like I was crazy.

"Bernie, my poor, ludicrous, ignorant friend. It must be humiliating, in this modern age of feminism, of sexual equality, of the Sensitive Man such as myself, not to know how to cook."

He went into the kitchen and returned with a large spoonful of something. I can't remember what it was, but I do remember it was something like I'd never tasted before.

We had it for dinner that night, and he began cooking at our monthly "boys' night out," for family, friends, everyone. He was happy cooking for people. He was always happy doing something for people, helping them. That was the key to a good life for both of us. It made us feel good, perhaps even important in someone's life. I learned that from my dad, yes, but also from observing Pat. Perhaps it was just one of the reasons they were so fond of each other—that, and because like all the surrogate fathers in Pat's life, my dad was unlike his.

For example, if Pat ever showed pride in *himself*, his dad would hit him. That's why, I realized, he was often so fidgety, so jumpy, especially in tense situations, his knee moving up and down a mile a minute, why he walked the earth warily, as if in perpetual fear of ambush, perhaps even why his peripheral vision, such a tremendous asset on the basketball court, was so pronounced. Back in high school, he told me, he was sitting at his desk in his bedroom and his dad caught him reading a newspaper article in the *Beaufort Gazette* celebrating his selection to the all-state basketball team. Immediately, he knew what was coming, and it did, which is why Pat could only experience joy and excitement about himself through other people, people by and large he genuinely loved and trusted.

Which is why he was so excited about my getting into Harvard and had so enjoyed Dad's excitement about it, and after I'd arrived why he was so unabashedly thrilled when I'd told him we were just as smart as anybody else there. He could never have *dreamed* of saying that about himself.

Pat could also vicariously delight in abject failure in people he loved, particularly mine. Let's return to Atlanta now, after he'd moved into his apartment and started cooking.

I had just begun taking an acting workshop over at Emory with Jeff Corey, a longtime Hollywood actor who'd been blacklisted and later became renowned as an acting coach, including, for example, Jane Fonda's. I thought it'd be fun, even though clearly I was the only man there unattired in grunge jeans and a muscle shirt exposing biceps the size of footballs. Back in the fifties, unlike Jeff himself, the actor Lee J. Cobb had "named names," as it was expressed then, of friends suspected of being communists to Congressman Joe McCarthy and the House Un-American Activities Committee, a betrayal after which, Jeff told us, this once great actor was "reduced to a series of grunts and heaves." Betray yourself, he was warning us, and you betray your craft.

"Choose material most personal to you," Jeff told us, "to present as a monologue." So I did, the next class, from Phillip Roth's *Portnoy's Complaint*, a hilarious scene about Alexander Portnoy announcing "Diarrhea! I have diarrhea!" at the dinner table, then racing off to the bathroom to masturbate in a sock.

Riveting.

Anyway, Jeff loved my performance and pronounced me a "natural actor," one who could "skip most of the ladder's rungs and vault to the top." I called Mom, I called Pat, I called everyone. This guy, I told them, coached Jane Fonda! I'm going to Hollywood! Who knows? Me and Jane might be in the same class with him. Yep. I'm going to be an actor.

No question. That was my destiny.

Yes, I'd always believed that old saying, Teachers teach because they can't do, since I couldn't do. Now, however, things would change. I was going to be famous. I was going to act. I was going to do. The whole world would now see me as my parents did, a pure and glorious joy. So what if he'd made bad grades in school. Who cared? He'd gone to Harvard. He was going to be on TV.

Before departing Atlanta for Hollywood, however, I signed up for one more of Jeff's workshops. Naturally, I walked in like a king, which people kind of thought I was because of the last workshop. Well, everyone but Jeff perhaps, though at the time I didn't realize quite why he was less than worshipful.

Here's why. For this workshop, I took a real risk. I had done what he'd asked before, to pick material close to me. Masturbation was perfect. Now, however, just to show him how incredible I could be, I ventured far beyond his instructions and selected a scene as far away from my personal experience as possible, far even from my natural personality, a scene from John Osborne's *Look Back in Anger*, the darkest, most joyless, most depressing scene I'd ever read, in which a long-married man has to tell his longtime mistress that he must end their relationship.

I was unimaginably boring, for example, playing "sad" as "sad" blatantly rather than playing against it, rather than acting out the defense mechanism, the inevitable self-protection—the blaming, the psychological sorcery, the manipulation, the scapegoating, the excuses—that might normally play out here. I didn't know any better. I hadn't yet learned to do that. In real life it came naturally, but *acting* it out was a whole other ball of wax. I was playing it all hangdog, feel-sorry-for-*me*, maudlin. I was exploiting my "mistress," the actress with whom I was doing the scene, for her pity without even knowing it. I appeared pathetic without even realizing it. The girl playing the mistress loathed me, I could tell. She was getting the shaft and was supposed to feel sorry for me?

"What do you want?" Jeff kept screaming at me. "What do you want? What's your point of view?"

What did I want? I'd never thought about that. What was my point of view? I hadn't yet been made aware of that question either.

"What do you want to happen in this scene? What do you want from it? Goddammit, what do you want?"

What he wanted was for me to sit down, to get off the stage. That was his point of view. I know this because he said, "Sit down, get off the stage."

Which I did, for the rest of my life, thank you.

I told Pat about this. Naturally, he found the episode, to say nothing of the bursting of my Hollywood balloon, hilarious.

This was during the time in Atlanta when Pat succeeded in turning his father into a warm, fun-loving, entirely decent human being. As the years drifted into the late seventies, however, the cruel tongue of the

father of Pat's childhood began slithering out of Pat's mouth with ser-
pentine venom, all that repressed anger and self-loathing. His therapist,
Marion O'Neill, or so Pat confided to me, told him that he didn't have
a passive-aggressive bone in his body, that that was one reason he was a
sucker for women, which he was, which he had been, which he always
would be.

But though he may not have been passive-aggressive with women, he
sure was with me, just as, unknowingly in his younger days, he'd been
with his father. Soon after Pat told me what Marion had told him
about this miraculous empty space in his personal armory where for
the rest of the human race passive-aggressive missiles are stored, he
remembered—one afternoon in his apartment over drinks of George
Dickel, our usual whiskey—the times when he'd be home from the
Citadel for Christmas or summer vacation and his dad would get his
report card in the mail, note his grades about which he had no problem, then spot that inevitable *F* for "Military Deportment."

Pat was the biggest slob I've ever seen, distinguishing himself as a
military man by graduating as a private. He couldn't have cared less.

"Gee, Pops, sorry about that," he'd tell him. "I'll do better next time,
you can count it on it, sir. Yes, sir. You bet, sir."

After he related this, I told him he'd sounded like an idiot, like
some Beaver Cleaver, Good-morning-Mom, Good-morning-Dad, sit-
com kind of kid, all eager to pour his Frosted Flakes, talk with his
mouth full—naturally to the amusement of Mom and Dad—and rush
out with milk all over his chin to play with the neighborhood kids.

"You bet!"

"Now that I think about it, you had to have gotten some kind of
satisfaction out of that, Pat. You could frustrate him, even exasperate
him, and it sounds like you did, but with all those good grades in your
academic courses and that phony can-do, gung-ho, get-right-on-it-sir
attitude, you could count on him not hitting you? In fact, now that I

further think about it, you must have been, on the inside of course, gleeful."

"Now that I think about it, you're right." Clearly puzzled, he added, "That's passive-aggressive, though, isn't it?"

"Guerrilla warfare at its finest. You probably drove him crazy with all that bullshit."

Pat placed his glass of George Dickel on the side table next to the sofa, which was so old and ratty it scared off roaches. I was in the recliner, our favorite chair. The whole place would have never come close to passing inspection at the Citadel. It looked like the inside of a Dempster Dumpster. I sipped my drink, surveying the wreckage. He was thinking. "I sure hope so," he said.

His weapons of social destruction, he realized, were not only available to him but readily deployable.

He fell apart as his family did. What do you do, if you yearn to be a gentle, harmless man but you're the son of Santini, and you're just really angry?

You leave.

Or with your friends you become so passive-aggressive—the tongue of Santini employed in the service of guerrilla warfare—that your friends leave you, which is what I did, and this after we went to see Marion O'Neill, the therapist, together.

The put-downs were coming so fast and stealthy and hard I felt like I was avoiding sniper fire. You never knew when they were coming, from where they were coming. I'd fire back, but I wasn't used to this kind of social and psychological warfare. My way of fighting was usually overtly aggressive—Fuck you, you scumbag piece of shit—and if I was defending myself, it usually felt good, unless I overdid it with a loved one, then I'd grovel and crawl and beg for forgiveness. Pat would *always* be passive-aggressive. It was just about the *only* available weapon in his arsenal.

One time, after I'd been published too, I told Pat he'd been a royal, raving oceanic asshole for lying to me about what a fellow writer had said about a book I'd written—I wish I could remember what it was; a real lie, I remember that much, and totally out of character for the fellow writer, a close friend—and then I felt bad about it because he looked stricken, vulnerable. He'd been drunk, and it was very difficult to tell when Pat was drunk, he was usually the same as when he was sober, only better—and I could tell he had no memory of what he'd said. I actually kind of felt bad for him, though not enough to apologize myself.

His tongue, I was learning, was as lethal as Santini's fists, particularly the more he drank. Words hurt, and he was becoming a verbal hitman the equivalent of which I'd never encountered. As he told me, he was "meaner" than me. I could certainly think murderous thoughts and feel murderous feelings and entertain murderous fantasies, which were great, but what I learned from Pat expressing them to me, to people he loved, to family members and close friends, was that if you engaged in his kind of guerilla warfare, you'd better prepare to jump in the next helicopter and get out of the rice paddies as quickly as possible. Even if you were American, as Santini himself was, Pat was the Vietcong, and you were going to lose. This was the warrior he became.

A word-sniper.

Why? To prevent the Santini inside him from exploding and reducing to rubble everyone around him. To remain in his own mind, fantastical though it was, a gentle harmless man, nonviolent, a martyr. If I'd hauled off and slugged him, which I was afraid to do anyway since I was a physical coward, he would never have hit me back. First, he loved me too much. Second, he was so miserable, so disgusted with himself at that time, he'd have probably appreciated it. Such is the way of the hair shirt, of the old Catholic ritual of self-flagellation, to which he was still hostage.

He would ridicule our friend Cliff Graubart, owner of the Old New York Bookshop, our hangout for writers, as an idiot because at the time, well, Cliff was, but Cliff was loyal and a good friend and witty and funny as hell. He just hadn't read much. Pat, in the incipient stages of the bookstore, had generously enlightened him about American and European authors from Hemingway, Wolfe, and Edgar Allan Poe to Chaucer, Tolstoy, and de Maupassant, rearranging Cliff's shelves to highlight the different genres. What had been an act of generosity, however, was now an act of exploitation. Under the cover of sarcasm, of humor, he would use Cliff's vulnerability against him, relentlessly, always with Cliff, in public. We'd all be sitting around at the bookstore, drinking and talking, and once Cliff started he could hardly finish a sentence before: "How do you know, Cliff?" Then to the rest of us: "Cliff's never read a book in his life. How do you open a bookstore, Cliff, when the most sophisticated book you've ever read is *Babar the Elephant.*"

Cliff did have that Yankee know-it-all quality, so he'd fall right into it, making some stupid pronouncement as if he knew what he was talking about. But often so did Pat. Hell, the number of times he was beating the hell out of all of us playing Trivial Pursuit, I eventually discovered, was the number of times he suddenly had to excuse himself to go to the bathroom, where he'd secreted behind the toilet *The Encyclopedia of American Facts and Dates.*

Pat's self-hatred, his contempt for the world, enraged him. He was at his worst now when drinking, and almost always after he wrote, he would begin to.

He hurt forever our friend, the novelist Terry Kay, one of the sweetest men I've ever known, who'd grown up in a poor and loving close-knit family of a million brothers and sisters in north Georgia. Terry had chronicled this in his first novel, *The Year the Lights Came On*, which Pat had generously encouraged and inspired him to write. Terry and his siblings became very successful, all well-educated. Terry had a new house built for him and his wife, Tommi, and their kids, a tasteful, lovely house just outside the city. We'd all love driving out there for a huge lunch with our families on Sunday afternoons. On our first visit, Tommi was beaming. She loved the house. It was just what she'd wanted, a house of macramé and quilts and a huge kitchen for her cooking. Her personality was all over it, as was Terry's and their kids'. As Terry began taking us through and showing us with great pride, well earned, his brand-new home, Pat—now, wealthy and prestigious—verbally backhanded him, not with his fist but with words, dropping a few disparaging comments here and there. They were subtle, no doubt coiled within the territory of Pat's humor that my wife began referring to as "harsh," before they struck, but strike they did, and they stung. "I will remain Pat's friend," Terry confided to me, "but I will never invite him to my home again." Now Pat was exploiting Terry's vulnerability as he had Cliff's, with what before he'd encouraged him to open up and write about.

I began wondering if Hadley Hemingway's husband, Paul Mower, had had a point. Pat had scoffed at the time, but now I wondered why. Had Paul Mower inadvertently touched a wound in Pat that Pat did not want opened up? Because ironically, it was from Pat I was learning that if in all innocence you expose your vulnerabilities, open yourself up to people, show them your insides for better or worse, as Pat was great at getting people to do, they can exploit that vulnerability and, lo and behold, as Paul Mower had suggested, you have—again, in all innocence—proffered the gun for them to shoot you with. Pat's sensitivity had been a beautiful thing, loving and inspiring. Now, however, I was learning that that very sensitivity, gone rogue, could be devastating.

He'd ridicule Paideia in front of his kids, who loved it there, and to me, when he was the reason I came there to teach in the first place, not that I didn't make light of it too, as did our Paideia friends, including the headmaster. But not in front of our kids. He'd tell friends who adored their parents that their parents had been "idiots." He adored my mom, but now she'd been an idiot for sending me to military school my junior year in high school, when I could have been playing basketball for Beaufort High. She'd sent me there so I could get my grades up so I could get into college after graduating. He knew that. All of us were left wondering: Was he joking? Did he mean it? We were perplexed. I had been used to the most open, inviting guy I'd ever known. Who was this? His humor was taking on such a vicious tone. He was out of control, and always, always when he was drinking.

If you didn't agree with him on some child-rearing practice, for example, he'd come after you for that, all righteous and angry, while his own kids naturally were feeling neglected by him since he'd left home. Two of our close friends, Ted and Sally Jo Orensen, were planning to take their kids to the beach over the summer, and they had yet to teach them to swim. They would—they were loving attentive parents. Pat, however, couldn't get off of it. "If something happens to those kids this summer, Ted and Sally Jo are going to hear from me. I swear."

I puffed on a joint in his new apartment in Ansley Park, which looked exactly like any other apartment.

"Well then, Pat, you should just walk right up to their front door and give them a piece of your mind. It's more than clear to me that it's time for Conroy to go into prevention mode. Stop the fire before it starts."

"Fuck you, Bernie, I'm serious."

"As am I. As am I. You just need to show them how much you care. And how little they do."

He laughed, reaching for the joint. "Ah, my piety, my sanctimony."

"No, no, no, Pat, I'm serious. I have never been more serious in my life. You just need to sit them down and calmly explain to them that they're shitty parents. Surely, they'll understand."

"What an idiot."

"No Pat, you've been sitting here fantasizing about the size of your gonads. It's time now to put up or shut up. To show them who you are. A man who profoundly, for want of a better term, cares. The only man, Pat, and I say this with all seriousness, in the entire world who cares, goddammit." I paused for emphasis. "Goddammit, Pat! Goddammit."

No one I've ever known enjoyed laughing at himself more than Pat. Everything had to be complicated for Pat, everything a crisis.

Finally: "I've got an idea," I offered.

"I can't wait, O Voice of Reason."

"If you're in the slightest concerned that Ted and Sally Jo are going to miss getting the kids swimming lessons before taking them to the beach, though why you should be I have no earthly idea, and that consequently the kids might be bored going into the water only up to their ankles and perhaps something disastrous might happen that no one wants to imagine, then perhaps you might, say, put a bug in their ear, suggest it to them; better still, ask them, 'Hi Ted, Hi Sally Jo, are the kids going to take swimming lessons?'"

Pat looked taken aback, I swear, checked himself, marveling at the simplicity of it all. "Damn," he said, as if he just couldn't get over how easy this could be. Then: "That's a good idea."

Simplicity rarely occurred to him, particularly when he was going crazy and being insincere anyway. Still, it's worth repeating that no matter how miserable he was—often because he *was* so miserable—he could laugh at himself.

Any male friends I introduced him to he judged "boring," especially if I really liked them. He was becoming not only possessive but incredibly demanding, and somewhat paranoid. People were out to exploit him, he felt, to use him. He even implied—I don't know, maybe I took it wrong; sometimes it was hard to know with Pat then—that I might, too. Meanwhile, he wanted to buy me a color television set and was hurt, really unsettled, when I refused it. It was difficult because he seemed to need to do it, but I had to hold my ground there.

What was a debtor, I asked him, to a creditor? That response, he said, was "literature."

He was so insecure, so frightened, that even that offering, I felt, was a power play, a way of avoiding intimacy, of objectifying our friendship from a superior position.

"'Literature,' Pat?"

"Literature."

Literature. That was important to both of us. But he was exploiting even that now, and no one was normally more devoted to it than he. And yes, literature is about betrayal, exploitation, but only because it is first and last about friendship and loss.

"It's not 'literature,' Pat. It's friendship."

He looked shaken, almost to the point of crying. I thought of Ben Meecham in that scene on the Green on the Point in Beaufort from *The Great Santini*, chasing his drunken father: "I love you, Dad, I love you."

I didn't know that in that post-Santini period Pat was suicidal. Again, as with child abuse, I'd been a slow learner. It was one of those things people I hardly knew did, people I'd read about. Did he hint? Of course. But even then, even after his obsession with Ross Lockridge Jr.'s and Tom Heggen's suicides after their first and only novels, I still didn't fully take in all his hints. As before with his father's abuse of him, I just had no frame of reference for it.

Ignorance, even when it's not willful, subverts the cause of empathy.

I had that problem often in my youth. The girl to whom I was "pinned" at Newberry College ultimately rejected me because I was

Jewish. She was a Christian, her family stalwart Methodists, she told me. She said, giving me back my pin, "You're Jewish."

But in the Bible Belt at that time we Jews were considered "Chosen," People of the Book, "good family people" with "good heads for business." We were so assimilated that in high school when Dick, a.k.a. "Dickless," Highgate kept asking me if "your people" believe that Jesus Christ was the Son of God, I had no hesitation whatever in informing him that we did not, that we believed instead that he was a Great Man. "After all," I explained, "he was a Jew. All Jews, Dickless, are Great Men. Consequently, I am a Great Man."

"Now if it weren't for the blacks . . ." Daddy would offer as a cautionary note.

"Should we send them a thank-you note?"

"Maybe. Something to think about, son."

Anyway, because of the absence in my mind of my girlfriend's particular frame of reference, in addition, I might add, to the fact that in this Christian college I was probably the most popular kid on campus, I honestly thought she was using my religion as an excuse, that maybe she'd just gotten tired of me, fallen in love with someone else, decided I was ugly, or something. Who knew? But not once, until I wrote a story about it several years later, did I fully register her words. "You're Jewish, Bernie, and I'm Christian." And then: "What will the children be?"

How did I know?

She wasn't anti-Semitic. She was just a Christian.

But I had lacked the frame of reference even for a respectful rejection such as hers, much less one that might have been anti-Semitic. It had been great fun growing up in Beaufort, dating, going out with girls. Religion, in my mind, had never even entered into it. Had Mom tried to warn me? Of course, but by that time I was a teenager. What did she know?

Mom on my marrying a Gentile: "What if one day she surprises you, her true colors come out, and she calls you a 'dirty Jew'?"

"I'll take a bath."

What did I know?

In 1928, her freshman year at Converse College in Spartanburg, South Carolina, where she was training to be a classical pianist, she was the only Jew, she later told me, so she had to room by herself. She'd had a frame of reference I'd no idea of.

So, Pat suicidal? I had no frame of reference for that. I had no idea, at that time too, that several years earlier on a book tour for *The Water Is Wide* he'd overdosed on sleeping pills and alcohol in Charleston, only to wake up in the room in which he was spending the night covered in his own feces.

About his body, Pat was an extremely modest man. Few have seen him naked. (That's a joke. He loved it when I'd say things like that.) But waking up as he did after a suicide attempt? That must have been so shameful, so difficult for him.

Again, my ignorance contributed to an absence of the depth of empathy Pat needed. Instead, I was all caught up in his verbal sniping at everybody, his excessive drinking, his perpetual need for distraction and entertainment, regardless at whose expense.

In almost every instance when deriding everyone else, Pat was talking about himself, of course. That was one thing I did know, perhaps because I had known him for so long. "Projection," I told him. "Pat, you're projecting all over the place." He hadn't been aware of that particular defense mechanism, which I had learned about in a psychology course at Newberry College, and to his credit he delighted in *becoming* aware of it, as always, in learning. He began spotting it himself in others and delighted in pointing it out to me. If you called him on it, it delighted him even more, that's who he was, but did it stop the madness? Of course not. It just distracted from it a bit. And Pat was always ready and eager to be distracted from himself. That's one reason he was so social, so gregarious. He needed to be entertained, to forget himself. I loved to entertain. I was funny and interesting. Pat loved that. And Pat himself loved talking, as he always would, but at that time he hated talking about himself. He hated himself. I loved myself. My parents had adored me. They were great. They both thought I was a scream even when I was lazy, shirked work, and made bad grades.

"What a friendship," I would often tell people back then, to Pat's amusement. "I love talking about myself, Pat hates talking about himself, so our entire lives are spent talking about me."

"And Bernie's eyes glaze over in milliseconds if my name even comes up."

"Right. The perfect symbiotic relationship. Though Pat probably profits from it more than me. I get exhausted. Let's face it. I'm the one who's giving here."

Actually, I was.

How could a man so filled with goodness, and he was, turn so cruel on and off for the rest of his life, though at his worst after his books came out and his families fell apart? I think it was because he couldn't bring himself to hit anybody. His was sublimated rage at its worst, out of control. Ridiculing not only Terry's brand-new home, which Terry was so proud of, but also friends' siblings, wives, friends' parents, and not least of all his own, anyone he loved, almost never in private, always in public, in social settings. It was crazy, devastating, too much for me to handle. He once told me I was the most sensitive man he'd ever known and that I'd spent my entire life trying to hide it.

He was right. I was too sensitive, but he was also wrong: his friendship was becoming good reason to hide it. Our Beaufort friend Mike Jones, now an Episcopal minister—so irreverent we called him The Irreverent Michael Jones—was often the object of his ridicule. Mike had the best defense mechanism ever. Every time, in the middle of Pat's soliloquy that was usually either dismissive or laced poisonously with humor, Mike's head just dropped, his eyes closed, and he'd fall asleep. As if on cue, every time. Amazing!

Why others stuck with Pat holds little interest for me. Let's face it, at his best, and much of the time in this terrible period of the late seventies, he was his old wonderful, charming, and winsome self, someone who welcomed and exchanged confidences. But you never knew when the tongue of Santini would strike. Having left his own family, he was hating even the *idea* of family life. "Boring" was now how he routinely referred to it. Marriage, raising kids, all that went with it: "boring." Most of the rest of us were loving it. Of course, as the older sibling, he'd been the head of his own family throughout his childhood, in some respects, taking care of his mother and his siblings, always on the alert for the eruption of violence from his father, so maybe having had to assume the role of an adult he'd never truly had a childhood. Had he also missed his adolescence? Certainly, he never drank and cussed and raised hell and lied about having sex like the rest of us did throughout ours. Maybe he was making up for it now.

He was still taking care of Barbara and the kids as a great provider; he always would. He was always great about paying the bills, supporting his children, carpooling, making sure they were doing well in school. He was protective: God forbid if he caught wind of one of them being bullied. But he had left them.

And he just hated himself for it. What had happened, he couldn't help but wonder, to that "nice little boy" so devoted to family, to never missing Mass, to being "good," to being his mother's child?

At Marion O'Neill's, where he'd convinced me to go to therapy with him, he'd say the most bizarre things to me.

"Martha drives." Martha, if you recall, my wife.

"What?"

"Martha drives you around."

"So? And?"

"Your mother drove your father around."

"So?" My father liked reading billboards. It drove me crazy. He liked me driving him around reading billboards too. "Bumpy's Tire Service . . . See that, boy, does a good business . . . Schein's Department Store, that's cousin Meyer, you know . . . Dairy Queen's got a sign up now, how about that, boy? Griffin's Esso . . . Hmmm . . . Cocklin's Kitchen . . . Yep." Jesus, this could go on and on. "Don't get to see all this every day, son." Right, Dad.

But what the hell did Martha driving instead of me and Mom driving instead of Dad have to do with anything?

Mom liked to drive, I explained to Marion. We were a one-car family. She'd drop him off at the grocery store every morning, pick him up for lunch, he'd take a nap, she'd drive him back to the store, then pick him up at 7:00 p.m., after which they'd cruise around town for a while, for all I know reading billboards together, more than likely for her to relax after being with my brothers and me all afternoon and to give Daddy a little peace and quiet, a respite from a hard day's work before coming home.

Why, I wondered, am I bothering to explain this? Did Pat miss Dad? Did he miss Mom? He thought her endearingly funny, especially when she made fun of me. I did too.

Did he now have a need for them?

"I worry, Bernie, that you'll become satisfied, content, complacent."

About what? I was about to scream.

"Your life, generally."

"Who cares? Why do you give a shit? Jesus, my entire goal in life is to work up to satisfaction, contentment, peace of mind. . . . Complacency? Sounds great to me."

"I want excitement."

"Not me. That's the last thing I want. I have so much of that going on in my head it feels like a circus, a high-wire act gone crazy."

"You want peace of mind, I want excitement."

Was this an excuse, his passive-aggressive way of trying to vacate our friendship? Is that why he'd wanted me to come and see his therapist, who because of him was also becoming mine? In retrospect, I wonder about that. Back then, I was just too flabbergasted.

"Exactly, that's right. Excitement, Pat, I couldn't care less about."

"Martha drives you around."

"Right." Then I just couldn't help it. "So I can read billboards."

His family's fallen apart, he's drinking like a madman, he's dismissive, contemptuous, incredibly judgmental, and he's just obscenely pious and sanctimonious. He's crazy, so he's driving me crazy? Am I this insecure, this unsure of myself?

Yes, I am, I realized, and not without irony he was exploiting it. This was the son of Santini himself compulsively homing in on my obsessive-compulsive disorder like a heat-seeking missile. This was not the old Pat pretending to move the pen atop my stack of writing on my desk in my study three inches over, waiting with anticipatory delight for me to jump all over him. That was gentle and funny. That made sense. He knew I knew he would carefully put it back.

This *didn't* make sense, and what is the obsessive-compulsive personality compulsive about? Resolution. The *need* for things to make sense. And crazy as Pat was, there wasn't much hope for him back then making sense. That's what craziness is. Irrationality. The inability to make sense. Crazy himself, he was making me even crazier than I normally was, and he knew it. He couldn't stop himself.

Can you imagine me coming home after these sessions, mentally going around in circles, chasing decoy after decoy, and asking Martha what the hell *she* thought Pat had meant?

Doesn't make sense to me, she'd say.

By this time, I was as relentless with her as Pat had been with me. Well, Martha, what the hell is he saying to me? What could he possibly mean? My God, was I boring her. She'd pick up a magazine, go play with the kids, make dessert, do anything to avoid, by this time, what she called my obsessive roundabouts.

I wish I could have avoided them, but I was compulsive. Ha ha.

Finally: "He's pissed off with you, Bernie, angry. He told Barbara, and Barbara told me. He's taking you to Marion's with him because otherwise he can't tell you."

"So this is his way of telling me? Talking to me about Mom driving Dad around? Talking about my need for peace of mind and his need to avoid it? That doesn't make sense."

"Of course not. That's clear. And that's all that's clear. Can't you just accept that?"

See my problem? I couldn't. Why was he angry with me? And why couldn't he tell me? *He* couldn't.

Obsessives like Pat can't let anything go either, but for different reasons. Round and round and round we go until order is temporarily restored, until another obsession takes its place, or some creative work, like writing, propels us out of it. Work, that's what makes our mental trains run on time. The obsession, hot-wired, according to Marion, itself compulsively fires up its own engine, fueling and refueling itself, running on exacerbated stress, a runaway train going nowhere, round and round and round, making us crazier and crazier and crazier until we ourselves become irrational, until we ourselves don't make sense. We become as primitive and superstitious as voodoo. Since we can't make sense of what matters to us, we start worrying about what doesn't, checking a million times whether the doors are locked at night before bedtime. I do that now. Or if we're really spinning-out crazy, ruminating endlessly about exactly how to say no if, say, a colleague we hate calls and invites us to dinner when any other time it's someone we'd more than happily say no to and delight in pissing off.

Now I was the one getting pissed off, really pissed off. I wanted to hit him where he would most hurt, to hurt him like he'd hurt me, and I did it his way, passive-aggressive as hell. His family he'd left, his friends he was leaving. The only thing he had left were his stories.

"To be perfectly honest," I told him, "I'd rather read billboards than listen to your stories. They *bore* me." Then: "So fuck you."

He was totally unfazed. He just sat back in Marion's office, palms open, welcoming whatever condemnation I could offer him.

Excessive stress does undo me, as I've said, and up until this point going to graduate school, then searching for a place in which I could teach the way I wanted, I had moved with my family four times in four years. I loved teaching at Paideia. Work and family and friends I thrived on. But the stress I had released after all that moving was returning. My best friend, according to his wife Barbara, was angry at me, above all else, for the first time in our lives, or so he'd told her.

For what?

He'd needed me, he told me, and I hadn't come through.

This was a few days after our last session with Marion on a Friday evening in late August at our "boys' night out."

"Boys' night out" was a monthly gathering of Pat, me, and all of our closest friends. Pat or Terry would cook, with Cliff's help, and a local writer and good friend, Frank Kent-Smith, would usually help me wash dishes. We'd most often meet at Pat's apartment or Cliff's house in Atlanta, since neither had family living with them. Cliff was a bachelor. Sometimes we'd spend the weekend at a mountain cabin Pat would pry loose from a rich friend. One night at Cliff's, we stayed up all night drinking and talking while Terry roasted a pig. And sometimes we'd drive down to George Garbade's family cabin on the Chechessee River about ten minutes from Beaufort, where we'd meet

George and Mike and where George's daddy would cook venison for us. Over the course of the weekend, Mike, Pat, and I would usually drive to Beaufort. Mike and I would spend a few hours with our parents, and Pat would visit his mother and his siblings still living at home.

We had all left Atlanta on a Friday morning, converging with our old friends George Garbade and Mike Jones at George's daddy's cabin on the Chechessee River. Unlike the others, I had to leave Saturday afternoon for a Paideia faculty retreat. I offered to drive my car, so everyone else could stay through Sunday, but Cliff and Frank Kent-Smith and Terry all insisted I go with them in Cliff's car. So did Pat, I hasten to add, though he left early on his own. It was Friday evening, we were all eating George's venison, which his dad had prepared for us, and drinking pretty heavily. Already Pat had unloaded on Mike, who in a parody of himself had shown up wearing his Episcopal minister's collar, touching everyone and saying "Bless you." For whatever reason, just because, I think, he presented an easy target since he was so self-deprecating, and maybe because none of us were in his wedding—his wife, devout, disapproved—Pat started in on him. It wasn't terrible, mostly sarcasm and humor, put-downs, but I know we all felt uneasy; we just didn't know how to deal with this. Mike, however, did. Entirely nonplussed, in his usual fashion, he fell asleep. Amazing, I thought at the time. Just amazing. After that, Pat started in on Cliff, who sat there confused as ever, devastated, no doubt wondering if he could possibly be as stupid as Pat was suggesting he was. I don't even remember exactly what he said to them, but I do remember their reactions. Then he turned on me.

Remember, I had no idea at the time of the depths of Pat's depression. I had no idea even of his suicidal tendencies, his first attempt, in Charleston. Again, I hadn't perceived even the significance of his obsession with Tom Heggen and Ross Lockridge Jr. Pat had yet to confide in me that he'd even contemplated suicide, much less the intensity of the hold his depression had on him. Drinking and what I would realize later was a dissociative personality obscured and deflected it. So, irrational or not, he was angry not only that I couldn't understand fully what he was going through but that I couldn't even fully see it. Not only wasn't I helpful, I didn't even realize the extent of the help he needed.

He needed the comfort of his best friend. He needed time with me, time probably over the last year or so that I probably didn't even have. He was alone all day. I was teaching and with my family. I saw him as much as I could, but in retrospect, all the time in the world at that particular moment in his life would probably not have been enough.

He listed the times he'd needed me after separating from Barbara and I hadn't been there. The problem was that even when I *was* there, instead of his telling me he was distraught, or even somehow showing me he was, he'd take to the bottle and want to have a good time telling stories or talking about anything but what *was* bothering him.

"Pat, I didn't know, you didn't tell me. I had no idea. Had I known, I would have come over and sat with you throughout the whole mess."

"I know," he said, helplessly. "I know."

But then: "You could be here now, you could skip the retreat and stay through Sunday. You could stay here tomorrow afternoon instead of visiting your parents."

Was he not going to visit his mom?

Suddenly, I couldn't help it. All the pressure of the last year. It was too much. I burst into tears.

The boys were with me, I could tell, but Pat wasn't. It was hopeless. To give Pat even only the time he needed would have been trying to fill an unfillable hole. Paideia was my job, I had to attend the retreat. I wouldn't have dreamed of being so close to Beaufort without visiting my parents.

The next morning, we went to see them, all of us. The book about teaching, that Martha and I had coauthored, had just come out. I brought them a few signed copies. They were so proud. Their son, with his wife, had written a book. Now this was something, they suggested, no question, after which Pat announced that my name was on it but that Martha had actually written the whole thing.

That's not true, I shouted, completely offended. Everyone knew it wasn't true, but why would he even suggest such a thing to two unbelievably proud parents, two proud parents he loved. Did he think he was being funny?

"I can't see you anymore, Pat," I told him when we got back to Atlanta. "I'm sorry. It's too scary, too stressful, and it's making me too crazy."

It was not what he wanted at the time, or thought he needed, but it was what I needed and wanted.

Our separation, if I can call it that, lasted for about a year, and admittedly, I was relieved. It had been too much for me.

We'd run across each other at book parties, here and there in Atlanta, and he couldn't have been more gracious and more respectful, and each time I enjoyed seeing him, no question.

I needed a respite. And he must have too. We missed each other, became a bit less competitive conversationally, more sensitive of one another. I did, and I think he did too.

We were so much alike in so many important ways, men who were in many respects more like women than men, emotionally expressive, passionate, seekers of intimacy, romantics born in the wrong century, sometimes hysterical, often anxious. We were also, however, combative men, overtly competitive, overstuffed with bluff and bravado, both of us in our youth Rebels Without a Pause, often out of control, usually wrong, lifelong learners, creative men, artistic men, literary men. We connected like we could never have with any other men. We knew that.

After a year, I was ready. So was he.

He'd reunited with his dad and was supporting Barbara through law school and seeing his kids with greater regularity; he was cooking with a vengeance now and was working assiduously on *The Lords of Discipline*, his novel about his Citadel years, which would come out a year or so later, in 1980. I was teaching my ass off, going out to breakfast with Martha, Lara, and Maggie every Saturday morning, after which Maggie and I scouted out the neighborhood yard sales for trinkets, cheap jewelry, and balloons.

After we reconciled, Pat and I would get together on Sundays to play basketball with a group of Paideia parents and faculty, some of whom had played in college or high school, some who were athletic but relatively unskilled as basketball players, and a few who just showed up for the exercise. Paul Bianchi, our friend and the headmaster, organized the games and opened up the gym for us. He usually played on the team with me and Pat. Paul had had polio as a child, so his legs hampered his mobility, but he was such a smart player, and his arms were quick and strong, and his midrange shot was as sure as Pat's passes. He was also fun to play with; not everyone out there was. The ones who'd played before and knew how to play were good sports; they had the confidence, I figured, that allowed them to be. A few weren't.

Pat believed that you could judge a man's character by the way he played the game. One guy, who was a judge in Atlanta, was a cheat. He was rough if not brutal. He'd foul like crazy and never admit to it, then whine like a baby if he got fouled. Why was he a cheat?

Because he was a judge, Pat concluded.

You could tell when Pat got pissed off with him. Pat would be sitting during a break in the action, he'd see him crashing into people and pushing them around. Pat's knee would start going crazy, jiggling, like it wanted to take off, to break into a run, to leap into the action and stop him. I think in those situations Pat saw him as like his father. Also, people like him knew to beware if Pat suddenly addressed you as "pal," just as throughout Pat's childhood when his father did it people around him knew to clear the decks and head for the hills.

That wasn't enough, however, to deter our judge from lunging and crashing into Pat when they were going up for a rebound, or, in particular, when Pat was shooting. It always ended the same way. Aware of what was about to happen, Pat would fake the shot, the judge would leap into the air, and Pat would raise his shoulder just enough to catch the judge's chin as he came crashing down on it, after which you could all but hear his teeth rattle. The game would stop. The judge, pulling himself together, would scream, "Foul! Foul!"

But where was the foul? Pat would look about innocently; the game would continue.

Pat characterized as "the bully" the highly successful corporate lawyer who in desperation would resort to stealing the ball from Paul. "He's short, he's a terrible player, and he cheats on his taxes."

In a game in which the lawyer was guarding me, Pat warned me he'd lunge and fake undercutting my legs once he saw me going up for a jump shot. "Don't worry about it," he assured me, "he'll only be faking, just enough to try to throw you off."

Why would he stop at faking it?

"He's a sneak. He cheats on his taxes. He doesn't rob banks."

Then there was a teacher at Paideia, whom we referred to as "the Pious One." He was a very good player, but he was so earnest. He played each game as if his life depended on it, but he held the rest of us, if we were his teammates, responsible. He was like your camp counselor. "Come on, guys," he'd say, banging his fist into his palm. "Let's get it together."

This just tickled the hell out of me and Pat. "Yeah, you lazy fucks, come on, man. Get it together." Then: "Hey, can't we all just *try*?"

Once Pat got on his knees and pleaded for the Lord to come down and play with us, just to help us "get it together."

Pat was driving Paul Bianchi, the headmaster, and me home after a Sunday game. I'm in the front seat, Paul in the back, since he'd be dropped off first, his house closest to Paideia, when it occurred to me that the Pious One would criticize every player on the court but Paul, who happened to be his boss. "Do you happen to know why?" I asked him, obviously a rhetorical question.

Paul was spinning the ball off his finger in the back seat, delighted with himself.

"I'll tell you why," Pat said, looking at Paul in his rearview mirror. "Because he's got his nose so far up your ass it's a miracle he can breathe."

"I know," said Paul. "Isn't it great?"

Paul was funny as hell and a great friend. He was also a great headmaster, a great leader, always the guy you could depend on to take charge, always self-deprecating about it.

As to why Paul organized all our games, Pat said: "That way he gets to play." Not that he wouldn't have gotten to play anyway, Pat pointed out. He was fun, and he was pretty good, despite being a victim of polio. "You don't get over that," he concluded.

Then: "The dark clouds of childhood, Bernie, they stay with you."

I began working about this time on "The Last of the Lowcountry Jews," a story for *Atlanta Magazine* about growing up Jewish in the Bible Belt. I had written a short story—fiction—for them a few years earlier, which the then editor, Larry Woods, prompted by Pat at the time, had asked for. Pat had bragged about it all over the place, had even sent a copy to his new editor, Jonathan Galassi, at his new publisher, Random House, just to make a point, which as a teacher I was fond of making myself, that talent was far more democratic, commonplace, and egalitarian than most writers, editors, and teachers realized.

"Hey," he'd joked, "even Bernie can do it!"

That was the Pat I just couldn't help but love. And that Pat was back.

VI

A JEW IN THE BIBLE BELT, A REBEL WITHOUT A PAUSE AT THE CITADEL

I loved Pat's writing, his wild hilarity, the spontaneous combustion of his prose; his investment in his characters, the care he took with them; his reverence for story, for twists and turns, for surprise; his heroism; his fiery, explosive anger, the latter of which I felt, as did many of his readers, he was actually expressing for me.

There was little, if any, separation between Pat, his prose, and his stories; little if any distinction between the personal and the professional, between his art and his life. He was truly at one with them. Fiction or not, he was they, they were he.

When I was commissioned to write a second story for *Atlanta Magazine*, this time a nonfiction piece that would become "The Last of the Lowcountry Jews," their new fiction editor, the writer Paul Hemphill, sent me a rejection letter in which he wrote that my article was basically a slimy, masturbatory pile of shit with not one redeeming feature.

Pat had loved the piece, was convinced that the story told the truth about what it was like to grow up Jewish in the Bible Belt, as well as the outside perspective on it. Back then to a Northerner, a Jew with a Southern accent was as anomalous as a Jewish cowboy, a Jewish sumo wrestler, a Jewish plumber. They had real difficulty reconciling a Jew with a Southern drawl that, like everything else about the South, sure seemed to them to take its time, wherever it might be heading. "Y'all?" "Come see me, you hear?" As far as "Come see me" goes, I had no idea people thought I meant it when I said it until I retired from teaching and moved back to Beaufort, by then a haven for Northern retirees, and they showed up at my door.

When I was growing up, they didn't even know we Jews lived down here in the Bible Belt. Northerners back then, on familiar terms with the gentlemen's agreement in their part of the world, assumed that if we were down here then we must have been catching anti-Semitic hell. In these small towns, we weren't. We were different, yes, but not only were we People of the Book like everybody else in town, we were "Chosen." Plus, we were too few and too assimilated to be threatening. We attended synagogue, but if we didn't open our stores on Saturday we'd go broke. Gentile friends, if they were spending the night anyway, attended synagogue with us on Friday evenings, and we often attended church on Sundays with them, especially since without them there'd be nothing to do on Sunday mornings.

Daddy told me that the only time he ever experienced any anti-Semitism at all in Beaufort was a salesman's joke. Harmless, he noted. And though Mom would never forget the social nightmare of having to room alone in college, she was fully aware that, though her college was distinguished for developing musical talent, it was also considered socially elite; in other words, she'd say, it was "snobby," like a "finishing school." Sorority charters excluded Jews from sororities, and while Jews might appeal for a charter of their own, it certainly took more than one, and she was the only one there. She'd grown up in a town even smaller than Beaufort, Williston, South Carolina, which offered up to her only one story involving anti-Semitism. Her mom, my grand-mother Esther, was working the cash register in their downtown department store and this woman, a long-time customer, began appearing in the store dressed entirely in black, warning Esther that if she did not accept Jesus Christ as her Lord and Savior she would burn in hell forever.

After a few weeks of this, my grandmother Esther, according to Mom, reached into a desk drawer behind the counter and pulled out a list of customers who had yet to pay their bills, eyeing one in particular. "You're going to burn in hell with me, honey, if you don't pay me for four pairs of stockings and the slip you bought three years ago."

The story for *Atlanta Magazine* was eventually published in the *Atlanta Journal-Constitution Sunday Magazine*. However, they wouldn't have even known about it had Pat, furious over Hemphill's rejection, not delivered it himself, without my even knowing it at the time, to the editor, our old friend Lee Walburn.

It was controversial. Small town Southern Jews loved it, identified with it, particularly with what I wrote about the condescension toward us from city Jews and northern Jews who'd grown up among their own, steeped in Jewish culture, who could throw about classically Old World Yiddish idioms with greater ease and facility. Even their humor sometimes seemed foreign to us, leaving us baffled and them wondering why. To them, and this is what really pissed me off, we seemed less than *real* Jews.

However, many Atlanta Jews, city Jews, particularly Establishment Jews, loathed it. Spokesmen for the Anti-Defamation League and the Southeastern Division of the American Jewish Committee attacked me personally, one accusing me in a letter to the *Atlanta Journal-Constitution* of anti-Semitism, the other accusing me of giving him "indigestion." Still another, this one from New Jersey: "Try Judaism, Bernie Schein, you'll like it."

So not only was I an anti-Semite, a notion I'd never in my life even come close to entertaining, but also, according to that ignoramus from New Jersey, not even a *real* Jew, a notion I had encountered particularly at Camp Blue Star where Mom sent me every summer for the Jewish experience and where they all spoke in northern accents and were as curious about me as they would have been about a Jewish Tom Sawyer. There, however, it was all friendly and in good humor: I might have been an object of curiosity but certainly not one of hostility.

I was hurt, I was furious. So I wrote my own letter to the editor in response. The one common thread running through all these critics' letters was the accusation that I had "aired dirty linen in public."

Dirty?

I hadn't considered it dirty in the slightest. Who cares if we're oblivious to what's under the hood of a car, if we're finicky about peeling shrimp since it's against the rules for us to eat shellfish, if at the time at least, few of us were going out for middle linebacker on the football team?

On the other hand, as I had suggested in the article itself, was there a cultural tradeoff with assimilation? Of course there was, and that notion also bothered the Establishment Jews. When I was growing up, Jewish doctors, like all doctors in town, had no choice but to have segregated waiting rooms; to do otherwise would have been illegal. For Dad's first cousin to have hired a black manager in his upscale downtown department store would have signaled all the whites to stay away. Restaurants, run by Jews or anyone else, were by law segregated. By and large, we Jews were more moderate, particularly regarding civil rights, than the Gentile community. We weren't amalgamated, we were assimilated. We couldn't afford not to be. Did that mean we were soon going to take up hunting, fishing, and NASCAR? Spend our family vacations at the Grand Ole Opry?

Did a photograph in the *Beaufort Gazette*, which I had described in the article, of a Jew who happened to be a local politician standing in his boat holding up a record catch suggest a close proximity, on his part, to racist views? What would it take to drink a little beer, play a little poker, take up hunting and fishing, join the country club? What would it take, I'd asked in the article, just to be "one of the boys?" The question, particularly for small-town Jews, was a real one. But so was the one I'd asked following it: "*Just* one of the boys?"

Like it or not, for better or worse, I insisted, there was a tradeoff. As the former president of the American Jewish Committee, Morris Abrams, from Fitzgerald, Georgia, once noted in an interview, "There was very little, if any, anti-Semitism in Fitzgerald, Georgia. Of course, we were assimilated. On the other hand, if a Hasidic Jew, dressed like he'd just gotten off the bus after a long ride from Crown Heights, was seen strolling down Main Street . . ."

That was my point, I wrote in my letter to the editor.

Admittedly, I couldn't help in my letter also pointing out that "indigestion," to say nothing of irritable bowel syndrome and every other gastrointestinal disease, was the Jewish Condition, and that for the chairman of the southeastern division of the American Jewish Committee to imply otherwise by blaming me for *his* was a denial of his own Jewishness, itself an act of anti-Semitism. I also confess to going after the spokesman for the Anti-Defamation League: Since when, I asked, is "Jewish linen" considered "dirty linen?" He too, I wrote, was an anti-Semite.

"'Try Judaism, you'll like it?'" *Real* Judaism, I wrote, or hers?

I signed it: Bernie Schein, Jew.

P.S. Go fuck yourselves.

It was on my desk waiting for a stamp one day; then the next day, after a visit from Pat, it wasn't. He stole it, he confessed later, and on his way out threw it in the trash can. He thought it was hilarious, he said, particularly the signature—"Bernie Schein, Jew"—but it was hilarious in the sense that like anyone who would have read it, he found himself laughing at me, not with me.

"If Hemphill had characterized that stupid-ass *letter* as 'a masturbatory load of shit,'" he said, "I would have agreed with him. 'Bernie Schein, *Jew?*' This is ridiculous. 'Go *fuck* yourself?!' How welcoming. You've already said your piece, Bernie. You've got the Temple Board holding meetings about how to deal with this. Letters are pouring in to the *Southern Israelite*. This letter makes you look like a fucking joke. No, let me correct myself: this letter simply reveals to all of Atlanta what those of us who already know you know: You *are* a joke. Can't you just keep that to yourself?"

Then he added, all but falling all over himself, so pleased was he at my apparent ridiculousness: "Just that one little piece of 'dirty linen'?"

He saved my butt. The letter was carried off by the garbage truck.

Pat was a Catholic who still wanted to be a Jew. We were both outsiders, and it showed up in our work and our lives. Our conversations, as he would tell me on his deathbed, were "great."

They were. That article in the *Atlanta Journal-Constitution Sunday Magazine* had grown out of our discussions. As Pat later said, "I contributed to that piece only when I disagreed with you." He was right.

"You had to explain it to me before you could convince the reader." He was right. "You did," he said.

"Thanks, Bubba."

"Fuck you."

The Lords of Discipline reflected another commonality we shared. He had gone to the Citadel, and I had gone to Broward Military School my junior year in high school. It was there I learned to cheat really well, honing my skills, which prepared me solidly for my senior year at Beaufort High.

It was there also that I learned to loathe the military. I saw it at its worst. Poteete, the cadet in *The Lords of Discipline* so victimized by the relentless hazing at the Citadel that he kills himself, is based on a cadet I told Pat about at Broward who was beaten so badly he was either pushed or jumped out of a third-story window of the barracks, and the last I saw of him was a sheet-covered body on a stretcher carried off in an ambulance.

The plebe system at the Citadel and the first year of Broward, where you were a "rat" instead of a plebe, were unspeakably cruel. For Pat at the Citadel, it was the specter of Santini all over again, and for the rest of us whether we were at the Citadel or Broward some diabolical variation on him. For all of us rats, the iconic Santini was everywhere—in the library, on the quad, in the showers—coming at you relentlessly, often out of nowhere, in the form of upperclassmen—PFC's, corporals, sergeants, lieutenants, majors, colonels, on up the ranks, senior privates even—screaming in your ear one after another, working you over when you were showering, terrifying you every minute of the day and night because you never knew when he was coming, you couldn't escape him, you couldn't even close your door, everywhere, everywhere, everywhere, all the time, reminding you minute by minute how little and small and cowardly you were, how big and strong and invulnerable he was.

His purpose was to completely break you down, every defense ripped away, reducing you to a puddle of vulnerability and nakedness. It was torture. Not only were we paddled regularly and beaten by upperclassmen, we also regularly bent over for the same treatment by faculty members.

At Broward at least, we were brainwashed. Every evening at dinner in the mess hall The Old Man, the school's founder and head, Colonel B., would harangue us over the microphone: *"Men stick it out. You're not a man if you can't stick it out. Men stick it out."*

Every night: *"Men stick it out. You're not a man if you can't stick it out."*

We were boys. High school boys. We believed him. We weren't allowed to call our parents unless an upperclassman was standing right there at the phone with us. Letters were opened and censored.

This was in the earliest of the early sixties, still culturally the fifties at least where we were. Adults were to be respected, authority to be honored. Colonel B. was the father of Broward, and he was the only father we had there, and that was where we lived, our new home, and while we were rats, our only home.

I never even thought about running away, sneaking uptown to a pay phone, begging some local for a quarter, to call my parents. I was too frightened. Was I not a man if I couldn't stick it out? If not, who was I? What was I? A baby?

I didn't want to be a baby, I wanted to be a man. So, like Pat, like most of us at the Citadel and at Broward, I stuck it out.

Broward's greatest casualty became the Citadel's: Poteete.

I hated both places. So did Pat, at the time. When you tear a boy down to build him up, to make him a man, what and whose man is he? Certainly not his own.

We wanted to be our own men. Pat wanted to be his own man. As a teacher, I wanted my students to be their own men and women. Pat wanted the world that way.

By the time Pat began working on *The Lords of Discipline*, minimalism and irony were making thin gruel of just about the entire literary scene, so many writers falling in line with each other like the good soldiers they were, ladling out prose lemming-like with all the spit and bite of prison food, nothing to really savor, too little meat on the bones. Pat's voice, however, was nothing but his own, anything but understated, anything but reserved. He was his own man. Always Pat would rather add than cut, expand rather than contract, overstate rather than understate. Thank God, as he himself would say, for great editors. And that editor, at this stage of his career, was Jonathan Galassi, curious, delightful, perceptive, with the uncanny ability to prune Pat's prose flowering here and there beyond the realm of credibility, to show it at its best. *The Great Santini* had been an episodic novel, held together by time and theme more than by a conventional plot. Jonathan was showing Pat through his work on *The Lords of Discipline* something new for him, how to plot.

Pat's prose in *The Great Santini* had been written under the influence of the poet James Dickey, whose poetry class Pat had taken after *The Water Is Wide* came out. Dickey, whose novel *Deliverance* had been published in 1970, hadn't even known who Pat was. That was Pat: all he was in there for was to learn, to feel and bear the full heft and weight of Dickey's knowledge and insight. "Originality of phrase," that concept was key. Language, according to Dickey, must be new for the poem to be anything other than derivative. Pat took this to heart in writing *The Great Santini*. Poetry, in other words, Pat's own, was what he felt would elevate his prose. He wanted his language, as was Dickey's, to be original, new, expressed in a way that had never been expressed before. He did that, but I also wondered if in *The Great Santini* he'd been so keen on elevating the literary quality of his prose that he'd straitjacketed some of the natural spontaneity in his voice I so loved in *The Water Is Wide*.

Now, however, with *The Lords of Discipline*, he was once again coming out swinging, much like he'd done in *The Water Is Wide*, only now he was flat out swinging for the fences with every sentence, his antiauthoritarianism defying not only classic military tradition, upending it for the world to see, but the literary style and fashion of the times.

Essentially, he was saying to the whole world, "Fuck you." Fuck you if you think the Citadel is a nice place to send kids. Fuck you if you want to look the other way in the face of unspeakable cruelty and violence. Fuck you if you want me to shut up. And fuck you, critics, if you think storytelling is beneath you, if passion is beneath you, if a

Southern drawl makes you feel about us Southerners the way you imagine we feel about blacks.

What, he was asking, gives *you* the right to decide for history what literature is? *You*, he was saying, are the provincials. I am a man of the world. Fuck you, Iowa School of Writing. Fuck you, burgeoning MFA programs. Fuck you, English professors and literary critics. I am Old School, of the European and American classics. Give me George Elliot, Hemingway, Dante, and Wolfe. Give me the passion of Cheever, even of Mailer. Do not give me the minimalists, do not give me what is posing as fiction now in the *New Yorker*, *Esquire*, and the literary magazines.

Pat took everything personally. That was his curse, that's what made him true in the moment, it's what made him interesting, it's what made him passionate, it's what, in short, made him care. It was his gift.

VII

PAT MARRIES LENORE

Pat was unprepared for beautiful women swarming about him, particularly, as always, damsels in distress. *The Great Santini* certainly, to his astonishment, had brought pretty women to his door, contributing to the breakup of his marriage to Barbara. With the publication of *The Lords of Discipline* in 1980, the numbers banging away to get at him increased exponentially as his fame and fortune did too.

Most, however, he kept at bay. Pat was not one for one-night stands or even younger women, had no interest in hot babes. He needed love, maturity, and did not seek sex without it.

Pat's mother, throughout his childhood, had been his damsel in distress. He was her knight in shining armor, her golden boy, always on the lookout for her husband's blows, secreting her and his siblings away from them, absorbing them to protect her and his siblings from them, his body throughout his childhood on the line.

Now his damsel in distress was Lenore Fleischer, who as his mother had done, was warding off what Pat felt was the evil husband—in Lenore's case, the evil ex-husband—and he fell in love with her. As Pat would remind me, it was I who not only introduced them, but beforehand informed Pat that he would end up marrying her.

In the beginning, she was magical. A parent on the Paideia campus, the atmosphere of which (reflecting the Reaganesque times) was becoming more and more corporate and conventional, she was all vivid, wild-eyed, flirtatious, a dark Jewish beauty enchanting, seductive, and charming as hell.

You felt upon first knowing her that the apparent delight she took in your presence was visceral. Or at least I did. Her brown eyes lit up whenever she saw me. She seemed *excited* to see me. Did they light up around everyone? Now I doubt it. At the time, however, I knew they'd light up around Pat.

In retrospect, I wonder: was that why they lit up for me? Was I, his trustworthy best friend, merely obligatory, part of a scheme to get him to the altar? *Had* she schemed?

Whenever I'd run into Lenore around Paideia, she presented herself with such charm, humor, and immediate intimacy—that was either her gift or her gimmick—and such admiration and affection for me, I had no idea that she too might have been out to exploit Yours Truly in order to get to the rich and famous Conroy. Nor did I realize at the time that, like Pat's mom and every other woman in his life, Lenore indeed was a damsel in distress, her seductive charm a cry for help.

With Lenore, Pat could embark once again on what would turn out to be another grand crusade in which he would arm himself for battle, fleeing the helplessness and emptiness in his heart and lose himself, only to find himself, once again at war.

On Pat and Lenore's first date, Martha and I double-dated with them. Pat picks us up, we arrive at the Lion's Gate apartment complex, which happens to be across the street from Paideia, and Pat parks in front of Lenore's apartment, where she lives with her two children, Emily and Gregory. Martha remembers an arrangement where, instead of going inside to get Lenore, Pat waits in the car with Martha and me for Lenore to come out, which she does, a few minutes late.

Pat's in the driver's seat, Lenore slips into the front seat beside him, and Martha and I are in the back. After enthusiastic greetings, she apologizes for being late and begins explaining why. She tells us that, as she was getting herself ready, she was looking at herself in the mirror and she hadn't been able to tell who she was looking at, which evidently set her back a bit. The impression I got was that that wasn't at all unusual for her.

Pat and I found this fascinating. Martha, upon arriving home that night, most definitely did not. She was then a teacher at Paideia, knew Lenore from around campus, and liked her. She was also on her way to becoming a psychologist. For whatever reason, what Lenore said that evening suggested to her that Lenore was an "emotional mess." In retrospect, I believe what Martha registered was an alarming degree of dissociation. She also told me I needed to warn Pat. She was really worried.

Like Pat, I found the stories circulating in the Paideia community about Lenore interesting as hell, to say nothing of dramatic. Pat told me, surprised I hadn't heard it since it was "all over Paideia," that when she was still married to her husband, the neurosurgeon Alan Fleischer, he was returning home late one evening from a liaison with an also-married Paideia parent only to find Lenore waiting for him at the bottom of the staircase in their home, standing naked, with an upraised knife in her hand.

Tell me that's not a classic noir image, right out of an old forties movie. A few years later, Lenore and I were having a drink on their deck waiting for Pat to get dressed. We were going to meet up with Martha to go to a Peachtree Publisher's party and then to dinner. The deck was about four or so feet off the ground, and there was no railing. My lower back had been giving me all sorts of problems. My chair slipped backwards, and I fell off the deck, landing on my back. Not only was it shocking, it was painful. The laughter that spiraled out of Lenore's mouth was insane, orgiastic, out of control, or so it seemed to me. No offer of help at all, no calling out for Pat to come help, just sadistic laughter that sounded like Barbara Stanwyck. It was so horrifying, it carried my pain off with it.

Only later, during the fifteen-year hiatus in the friendship between Pat and me, would I relate it to the story of her naked at the bottom of the stairs, a knife in her hand, waiting for her husband. Had Martha been right? Was she crazy?

What idiots we were, Pat and I.

Well before her meeting Pat, Alan and Lenore were seeing a therapist. After a session, she got in her car (they had driven in separate cars) and was beginning to drive off. Alan put his body in her way, taunting her, daring her to run over him. What did she do? She drove her car right into him. He was on crutches for weeks, had to urinate through a catheter. That too was all over Paideia.

That's passion, Pat and I told each other upon hearing the story. Old school, a woman scorned, Alan had betrayed her. Vengeance was hers. That's real passion, old school.

I tried to piss Martha off so she'd run over me. "That would take real passion," she said, "real passion, old school," and so declined.

After their first date, Pat and Lenore began seeing each other regularly, evolving into a couple. They went to hear Cleo Laine sing in Chastain Park. He was still living in his condo in Ansley Park, but he spent a lot of time with Lenore and her two kids in her apartment at Lion's Gate.

Her relationship with Alan became increasingly volatile. One day he showed up at her apartment to pick up the kids and take them out to spend time with them. Pat was there. To avoid the possibility of Alan and Lenore fighting, he showed up at the door to manage the kids' departure.

Alan had a drink in his hands. He threw the drink in Pat's face. Pat picked him up and threw him into the nearby shrubbery. Lara, my stepdaughter, who was there babysitting Lenore's kids, witnessed the entire incident. Alan charged Pat with assault and battery. Having witnessed it all, Lara was infuriated, asked to be subpoenaed, and was fervent about testifying on Pat's behalf. Pat never forgot things like that.

Pat won that legal battle and countersued, which did nothing but prolong the drama.

The custody battle for Lenore's two children, Emily and Gregory, was the most vicious I'd ever heard about or seen. It wasn't so much about the children as it was about Lenore and Alan. They seemed to feed off their loathing for each other. And Pat, the defender of Lenore and therefore the children, was frankly no match at the time for Alan.

Alan seemed to invite violence, to get off on it. Pat told me Alan baited him by "keying" Pat's car. "Keying" is dragging the sharp point of your key around the body of a car and scraping a thin line all the way around it. That bait Pat had no problem whatever avoiding; he couldn't have cared less. But every time Pat in his own way fought back—for example, when he countersued Alan over Alan's assault and battery charge—he realized, he told me, that Alan was like the Tar Baby: the more you punched back, the more you got stuck to him.

But in 1981 he married Lenore, and he championed his new family. Jim Landon, an old friend whom Pat would visit every Sunday for brunch and a lazy reading of the Sunday *New York Times*, hosted the wedding together with his sister Jane in his condominium on Peachtree Street, which was in close proximity where Jim did his pro bono work for the Atlanta Symphony.

"The boys" and our families were all present. Cliff Graubart, all decked out in yarmulke and tallis, officiated, referring to himself as Rabbi Cliff throughout the evening, saying to each person, "Bless you, my son." It was clear Cliff was not at his most serious. Why would he be, he would say later. It wasn't *his* wedding.

I was Pat's best man. I stood next to Cliff through most of the ceremony in a small semicircle that included all the guests. As he murmured his way through the necessary prayers on the way to pronouncing Pat and Lenore man and wife, I felt a hand on my butt, tickling it. Cliff, keeping a straight face, was trying his damnedest to make me laugh, and it was all I could do not to. The more he tried, however, the more he started trying *his* damnedest not to. You know what happens then, every time. We made the mistake of looking at each other, after which we lost it. We couldn't help it. And once we started, while not a single soul there who had any idea what we were laughing about, neither one of us could stop. We just had to let it run its course, after which, teary-eyed, with everyone wondering what the hell was going on, we pulled ourselves together, making every effort to appear more solemn and dignified than we ever had been in our lives, and Cliff resumed the ceremony.

Lenore, so far as I know, never forgave us.

As Cliff later said so magnanimously: "Can you blame her?"

"No," I told him, "But I can blame you."

"Excuse me. Now who's the unforgiving one?"

The custody battle raged on, until one night in the home into which they had moved in Ansley Park, nine-year-old Emily confessed to Pat that Alan had regularly sexually abused her, holding a pillow over her face so she couldn't scream. I won't go into details she provided; suffice it to say that she said he had raped her. Already disgusted with Alan, Pat was shocked nonetheless, and to ensure objectivity he wrote down, word for word, everything she told him.

After hearing Emily tell her story—for the first time, so far as he knew—and writing down everything she said, to avoid her having any contact with Alan, Pat began making plans to move his family to Rome, Italy, where my stepdaughter Lara would spend the first summer with them.

I must confess that by this time, for whatever reason, if it was just Lenore and me, say, in her kitchen chatting, I found myself becoming vaguely restless, vaguely bored, without knowing why. Had we run out of anything of substance to talk about? Other than Emily, and of course Pat prior to their marriage, and the drama and chaos around the custody battle, had we ever had anything of substance to talk about? I didn't seem to have much to offer her, and she didn't appear to have much to offer me. Cliff felt that, although she was certainly polite, she didn't seem sincerely welcoming to him either. Maybe she was unforgiving about our behavior at the wedding.

Though she'd been a red-diaper baby raised by parents who'd been communists, she loved spending Pat's money so much, according to Cliff, that he began referring to her as a "Neiman-Marxist," a play on the name of the high-end department store, Neiman-Marcus, in Atlanta. Was she more style than substance?

I asked Martha what she thought.

"That's the least of your worries."

VIII

PAT WRITES, PAT TEACHES

Before Pat actually put pen to paper on all of his books, he first told all the stories that were to be in them to family, friends, in speeches, to just about anyone interested in hearing them. His literary idol, Thomas Wolfe, did the same thing. So like Wolfe, by the time he actually did put them on paper, he'd been through a great number of oral drafts. This was a good thing, because the more Pat wrote, the more his once beautiful, feminine handwriting miniaturized and cramped into an almost indecipherable script. Thank God for typists.

One of the stories he told Cliff over coffee in the Old New York Bookshop that would later be included in *The Prince of Tides* was about the caged tiger on display in the parking lot of a famous Esso service station in Columbia, South Carolina. The sign above it so big no one could miss it was "Put a Tiger in your Tank!" which was the Esso logo familiar to just about everyone nationwide at the time. Naturally, the presence of a real tiger garnered all sorts of attention. People brought their kids when they stopped for gas so they could throw chunks of red meat into the cage.

Pat's idea, as he described it to Cliff, was to relocate that tiger to the Lowcountry island on which were living his alter ego, Tom Wingo, and his mother, father, brothers, and sisters in *The Prince of Tides*, people of the rivers and woods, intimate with nature and the animals, conservationists and preservationists (as critics would note) before their time, the last holdouts on an island vacated of residents for an oncoming nuclear facility. (The island is based on New Ellenton, South Carolina, where even the corpses in cemeteries were dug up and relocated with the residents for a nuclear facility, the Savannah River Plant, presently under controversy for their storage of plutonium.)

In *The Prince of Tides*, the family cares for the tiger in his cage in their yard. They're safe among the snakes and predators, but not from the evil giant Callanwolde, a murderer and rapist who steals onto the island into their home one night when their father is away and attacks the family. Tom stealthily opens the cage, and who does our tiger have for dinner? Right, a big meal.

Pat, as he usually did after telling a story, sits back and awaits Cliff's reaction like a man who's just enjoyed a full meal himself. But Cliff's not reacting.

"What?" Pat challenges him. Silence always drives Pat crazy anyway. It makes him tense, wary of a stray fist, verbal or physical, coming out of nowhere, which is one of the reasons he *tells* stories.

"I have a question."

Pat motions him to hurry up with it.

"How does the tiger know who to eat?"

In the winter of 1984, Pat brought over to my house in Atlanta the first three hundred pages of *The Prince of Tides*. Here I entered a new world, so magical, so illuminating, so wondrous that in losing myself in it I forgot my own. I read it all in the same evening. When I couldn't bring myself to stop for dinner, Martha got mad at me, until, that is, I started handing her the pages. The spirit, she concluded, was hungrier for sustenance than the body. This was before his new editor, the estimable Nan Talese at Doubleday, worked on it, so it was more epi-sodic (as in *The Great Santini*) than fluid (as in *The Lords of Discipline*) but so magical and captivating we didn't care.

A few months later, he brought me another six hundred pages. For me, they just lacked the drama, the momentum, the interest of his first three hundred.

"Why do they feel so different?" I asked him.

"The first three hundred pages were inspired," he answered, entirely unsurprised. "After those, I lost my inspiration."

He went back to it, confident he could make it all work, and I'm sure he did, because this time he sent it straight to Nan.

The work Nan did on *The Prince of Tides* both Pat and I thought was nothing short of majestic, magical, editorial wizardry the likes of which we'd never seen. Pat's first typed draft, the one Martha and I had read, had been close to a thousand pages. The chapters had been long, interesting but overly episodic, somewhat chock-a-block, one chapter in the present, the next in the past, the following one in the present, again the next one in the past, and so on. Still, the language was so beautiful and powerful and the scenes so dramatic I stayed pretty much glued to it, though I knew, as of course Pat did, that the manuscript would have to be cut.

Nan simply made major cuts that neither Pat nor I missed in the slightest, and she made a chart for Pat with arrows pointing forward and backward, right and left, for every scene—not for each chapter but for each scene—alternating those reflecting the past and those reflect-ing the present, including and interweaving past and present *within* each chapter, integrating them all into the whole of the novel, making it read more fluidly, making it flow.

Pat needed Nan as much as Thomas Wolfe had needed his editor, Maxwell Perkins. And Nan loved Pat more than any editor and pub-lisher ever loved a writer, so much so that even with her natural grace and New England reserve, she found herself, following Pat's funeral, unable to leave his gravesite.

With *The Prince of Tides* pretty much under his belt, as he put it, he volunteered to teach a creative writing course to high school kids, who would enroll in it by choice. It was a course I'd taught annually but no longer had time for. Naturally, I was delighted when Pat offered, and I was able to take his place on those few occasions when he couldn't be there. We worked together beautifully: When I assigned them letters to write to their parents, letters they were not required to show their parents, Pat's subsequent assignment was for the kids, *as* their parents, to write themselves back.

Mikey McMahon wrote a story so powerful that Pat wanted it included in the Paideia High School literary magazine. In her story, Mikey attempts suicide because of her father's failure to give her the attention she needs, which he had done and so much enjoyed when she was younger. Now, in her story, he's just absent or inattentive a lot of the time. Like most adolescents, she doesn't tell him; instead, she seriously attempts to kill herself.

"It's a love story," Pat announced to the class, after reading it aloud.

Had she not loved her father, he explained, she wouldn't have cared. There would have been nothing for her to write about. The class loved and admired the story, particularly her honesty and bravery in telling it.

Not every faculty member in the high school did, though, including the woman who ran the computer center and the high school administrator. Pat had to fight like hell to get it in the magazine. They challenged him all the way. Pat, as far as I know, never, ever drank in the mornings. However, fortified with the courage of George Dickel for a morning meeting in Paul's office, he finally confronted them and got his way.

They had made it very difficult for Pat, who loathed censorship of any kind, a loathing grounded in the cover-up of abuse during his childhood. Why would they go to such lengths to block Pat on this? Well, the high school administrator, the Pious One, was the guy who played basketball with us on Sunday mornings. He didn't like losing, and if Pat was on the other team, he did lose. That's when he would get all self-righteous and tell his teammates to "get it together," even when they had it together. He was pretty passive-aggressive.

As for the computer woman, she apparently felt that Pat hadn't known who she was before this and left the meeting satisfied. How do I know? Because I saw her coming out of the meeting, walking across campus, and asked her how it had gone.

"I'll tell you one thing," she said to me, "he knows me now."

And if he hadn't been famous? If he hadn't been such a winner on the basketball court, would he have had to go through all that?

In a world of censorship, was there no "safe space" for Pat? And more importantly, for Mikey McMahon?

Pat in the Old New York Bookshop in Atlanta, late seventies.
Courtesy of Ellis Hughes

Best friends: (from left) Pat Conroy, George Garbade, and Bernie Schein
on the Chechessee River in Beaufort in the late sixties.
Courtesy of Michael Jones

Bernie

The bright crystal cruets of your smiling
give refreshment in a land of desert people
   And the world sings   a bird - heavy world
all cymbals and chime   and children clap
to tambourines hysterically mastered by circus chimps
   And the symphony begins here:
a maestro with a silver laugh
who sings an aria of gladness —
a face of the singing morning.
   And the ballerinas dancing only for the love of the dance...
and the world.

Pat's handwritten poem "Bernie"
written in late sixties.

Bernie

The bright chrystal cruets of your smiling
give refreshment in a land of desert people
   And the world sings , a bird-heavy world
all cymbals and chime, and children clap
to tambourines hysterically mastered by circus chimps.
   And the symphony begins here:
a maestro with a silver laugh
who sings an aria of gladness-
a face of the singing morning.
   And the ballerina dancing only for the love of the dance...
and the world.

Pat Conroy

Pat's poem "Bernie"
typed and signed by Pat.

Bernie and wife, Martha, in Atlanta, 1975.
Courtesy of Charles Rafshoon

At the Old New York Bookshop, circa late 1970s. From left to right:
Frank Kent-Smith, Bernie, Cliff Graubart, and Craig Matthews.
Courtesy of Ellis Hughes

Bernie's and Pat's coffee mugs, which hung
near the front door of the Old New York
Bookshop. *Courtesy of Ellis Hughes*

Bernie and Pat with Bernie's daughter,
Maggie, in Bernie and Martha's home
in Atlanta in late 1970s.

"The boys" (left to right); Terry Kay, Frank Kent-Smith, Pat,
Paul Darcy Boles, Cliff Graubart, and Bernie at Pat and Lenore's
wedding ceremony in Jim Landon's apartment, Atlanta, 1981.

Our monthly "boys' night out" at Cliff's house in Atlanta, circa early 1980s:
(front row, left to right) Daniel Sklar, Terry Kay; (back row, left to right)
Cliff Graubart, Pat, Frank Kent-Smith, and Bernie.

Fans line up to have Conroy sign their copies of *The Prince of Tides* in 1987 at the Old New York Bookshop in Atlanta.
Courtesy of Ellis Hughes

Bernie with students from his Paideia classroom, 1980s.

Bernie's class at Paideia School, circa 1990s.

Bernie with colleague Bonnie Sparling and students in
Paideia classroom, circa early 2000s.

Bernie and Pat, with Bernie's daughter, Maggie,
in Bernie's home in Beaufort, circa 2009.

October 2010, Pat and Bernie signing Bernie's *If Holden Caulfield Were
in My Classroom* and Pat's *South of Broad* at Pulpwood Queens and
Timber Guys book club in Jefferson, Texas.

Pat and Bernie on Bernie's front porch, circa 2010.

Pat and Bernie at the Great Santini's gravesite, National Cemetery, Beaufort, circa 2010.

Pat, Bernie, Scott Graber, and guest at our weekly lunch group, Griffin Market, Beaufort, circa 2011.

Bernie, Pat, and two of Pat's fans at the weekly Griffin Market lunch, circa 2015.

Left to right: Sandra Conroy, Pat, Martha Schein, Maggie Schein, Jonathan Hannah, and Bernie at Maggie and Jonathan's wedding in Sandra and Pat's home, Beaufort, November 2013.

Left to right: Pat, Martha Schein, Maggie Schein, Jonathan Hannah, Sandra Conroy, and Bernie at Maggie and Jonathan's wedding.

Bernie and Pat at book launch and signing for Bernie's
Famous All Over Town at the Arsenal, Beaufort, 2014.

Maggie and Bernie at book launch for *Famous All Over Town*.

Left to right: Pat, Bernie, John Warley, Scott Graber, Margaret Evans, and friends at the Anchorage Inn, Beaufort, circa 2015.

Maggie displaying her book, *Lost Cantos of the Ouroboros Caves*, together with Pat, who wrote the introduction, 2015.

Pat and Bernie at Conroy@70 Literary Festival, the Arsenal, Beaufort. 2015.

Bernie and Pat in Pat and Sandra's living room, Beaufort, circa 2015.

Pat and Bernie in Mina Truong's gym, Beaufort, 2015.

Pat, his personal trainer, Mina Truong, and Bernie in the Mina & Conroy Fitness Studio, Beaufort, 2015.

Bernie, following Jewish tradition, places a rock on Pat's tombstone at
Brick Baptist Church Cemetery, Beaufort, in 2016.

Pat's writing desk.
Courtesy of Jonathan Hannah

IX

FAME FRIGHTENS PAT

Pat had no fear of greatness. He was ambitious. He wanted it. He worked for it.

He was terrified, however, of fame, he'd confessed at boys' night out in the sitting room of a rustic mountain cabin in Sapphire, North Carolina. The lordly roaring of the fire and the crashing of the waterfall outside our windows made his voice seem small, himself vulnerable. This was in 1985, right before he moved to Rome. Fame like he'd never imagined was coming, he told us, with the imminent publication of *The Prince of Tides*, so once again the specter of Santini haunted him.

To Pat fame was an overwhelming tsunami of praise, the dangers of which were everywhere. Pat was generous in his praise to others, but Santini, the angry father he had internalized, had beaten out any joy he himself might have gotten out of it. It terrified him, yet no one needed it more. He trusted it from me. I don't know why. He looked at me when I offered it as if he'd never before really seen or experienced it himself, exactly the way I felt when he first told me how beautiful Beaufort was. Coming from me, it delighted him, just as he could laugh at himself over any criticism of his work I might make. His editor for *The Lords of Discipline*, Jonathan Galassi, would write "too too" in the margin of any of Pat's overblown scenes. Jonathan was always right, and Pat trusted him, but for reassurance Pat would check his notes and the scenes with me. In an early draft of *The Lords of Discipline*, Pat had imagined this absurdly gargoyle-like sea creature, some deviant, diabolical sperm whale offshoot, if I'm remembering correctly. Naturally, it was hideous, nightmarish, so it was something I spent a lot of time and energy repressing. What I definitely remember was that it was so far beyond the realm of credibility that I just ended up, as he had so often done to me, laughing—at him, as I hastened to point out, not with him.

Pat's response to Jonathan, so he told me: "If Bernie thinks it's too much, it has to be, because Bernie is."

After which, as *he* hastened to point out, he and Jonathan laughed at me, not with me.

But he couldn't truly accept praise from almost anyone else, much less the entire world. Nor criticism, unless it was from editors of his work like Anne Barrett or Jonathan or Nan. He knew they made him better, that they could teach him what he didn't know, that they could repair and improve whatever he did wrong, that he could learn from them.

And remember, Pat was always learning. As a teenager, like many writers, he'd gone through his Holden Caulfield stage, sounding much like Holden and nothing like himself. Back in Beaufort in our early twenties, he wrote a play about our small group of friends, Tim Belk, Mike, George, and me. It was funny as hell, but as Tim pointed out, everyone else in the play sounded exactly like me or Pat.

"I realize," I offered with my usual magnanimity, "what's wrong with everybody sounding like Pat, but what's wrong with everyone sounding like me?"

It would have made the play a masterpiece.

Pat aspired to greatness, but he was terrified of praise—what a paradox. Look how much he learned from one work to another, from *The Boo*, a vanity press publication, to *The Water Is Wide*; from *The Water*

Is Wide to *The Great Santini*; from *The Great Santini* to *The Lords of Discipline*; and from *The Lords of Discipline* to *The Prince of Tides* to *Beach Music, My Losing Season, South of Broad, My Reading Life*, and *The Death of Santini*.

Critics have said that he wrote the same thing over and over. Presumably, what that means is what they dismissively see as his "fucked up family—same thing, over and over." But that observation is simply not true. The topics themselves are all different from each other, and so are his styles, his voices. *The Boo* is a tribute to Pat's surrogate father at the Citadel, the assistant commandant, whose decency and charitableness led to his downfall. *The Water Is Wide*, about his heroic efforts to teach impoverished kids on Daufuskie Island. *The Great Santini*, a story about his father, a man at war with the enemy in wartime and at war with his family in peacetime, a story about the military family, about child abuse, which illuminated for the world the crimes committed against more than 25 percent of the kids in America. *The Lords of Discipline*, excavating and placing above ground for all to see the cruelty and horrors of hazing, the sadism that inevitably follows in its wake. In *The Prince of Tides*, he did as his mother had asked, he made her beautiful, a lovely and compassionate Southern lady, which is all she wanted to be; he showed us the honey, but he also showed it dripping with vinegar; he showed us for all time that one person's success is another person's failure, in this case a wounded brother and his damaged sister; he illuminated the contrast between the modern South and the modern North, and the infringement on and destruction of nature; he showed us insanity, his way, and consequently, the way of much of the world's. In *My Losing Season*, we see that failure is a better teacher than success, losing a greater teacher than winning. *Beach Music*, among other things, defies the doctrine among literati that only Jews can write about Jews, that only blacks can write about blacks, minorities about minorities, and so on; suffering, he suggests, over the long haul of history, is human. *South of Broad*: sexual abuse in the Catholic Church, violence in the Holy City of Charleston, orphans out of the mountains of north Georgia, the AIDS epidemic in San Francisco, Charleston's aristocracy, Charleston's lowlifes, the magic of friendship, the integration of the high school football team, the joy of the ideal father-son relationship, perhaps even overly idealized but nevertheless a total contrast with the abusive father-son relationship that his critics had charged him with over mining. In *My Reading Life*, he shows us that a great critic must be a great reader, and he was the best reader, the most curious, the most prolific, and the most perceptive I've ever known. And *The Death of Santini*, a memoir, shows us a son redeeming his father, teaching him to love by loving him, becoming himself his father's hero, Santini's hero.

Redemption was a theme that ran through Pat's life as it ran through his stories: his relationship with his father; his relationship with the Citadel; his relationship with his adoptive home town; his relationship with the Holy City of Charleston; his relationship with his friends, certainly his relationship with me. For fifteen years, from 1990 until 2005, as you'll see, we didn't speak to each other. The atom splits, the explosion is devastating, the atom fuses. Chaos, but also creation, governed his thoughts, his feelings, his imagination, his relationships, his life.

I'm a character in several of his books: *The Water Is Wide*; *The Great Santini*, for which I actually named Sammy Wertzberger, the character based on me; and more recently, *The Death of Santini*. In all of these, Pat's love for me is there for all to see. But also clear, at least from my point of view and no doubt from that of those who know me best, is Pat's idealization of me: my activism and sense of humor and youthful daring in *The Water Is Wide*; my outrageousness, to say nothing of the breadth of my vocabulary at the time in *The Great Santini* (though he does realistically capture my cowardice there); my role as muse, loyal best friend, and court jester in *The Death of Santini*. Was I funny, radical, loyal, inspiring? Yes, but (with the exception of my cowardice in *The Great Santini*) flawless? Where was my obsessiveness, my hysteria, my self-centeredness, my self-protectiveness, i.e., my defensiveness, my instinct to go on the attack when threatened and to act like a baby when my defeat looked like a sure thing? Where was my hypocrisy, my vast open-mindedness in the face of global and national crises, on the great issues of the day—unless they affected me, my family, friends personally, unless, as Herbert Keyserling had said, the bumblebee stings me on my nose? I was a traitor to all I believed in, or professed to believe in: where was that?

If Pat had written about me in the course of our fifteen-year rift, a rift he wrongly, I must add, blamed entirely on me at the time, what might have he said then? I can tell you. He would have exaggerated my failings. He would have blamed me for 9/11.

See how it works?

To create, one needs material—in Pat's case, stories—to work with, and the source of Pat's material was anything and everything. Nothing was off limits. Not only would he beg, borrow, and steal, *especially* if what you were telling him was personal, he would let you know he was doing it. At least that's what he did with me.

For so many people, he was such a good listener and they were so inspired and appreciative, they ended up all but offering him the keys to the safe. I witnessed this a thousand times. And why not? The retelling of a story you've told, whatever else it might be, is a compliment, an act of praise.

Less than a decade ago, probably around the fall of 2010, Pat and I were heading to St. Augustine, Florida, to meet the novelist Janis Owens to join her in readings and presentations. Pat loved and admired Janis and her work. Her bailiwick, which she so irreverently referred to as Cracker culture, she illuminated with such loving care I began thinking of myself as a Jewish Cracker. That's who I am, I realized through her novels and cookbook, *The Cracker Kitchen*. I regularly informed her that I loved and admired her and her work much more than Pat did—my way of getting the upper hand—and we both fell head over heels in love with her whole family, her mom and dad, her kids, and grandkids; her husband, Wendell, who frequently offered to beat up anyone we didn't like, poured us great bourbon, and handed out fantastic cigars.

Janis had gotten us the speaking gigs in St. Augustine, about an hour or so drive from her house in Newberry, Florida, and while she went shopping for her Xanax and Pat for my Woodford—she bought only the best kind, and so did he—Wendell drove me to a small nearby town called Pixie, Florida, where he pulled up and parked across the street from a very nice house in a very nice neighborhood, where we had a view of it. It was just after 5:00 p.m.

He opened the windows and produced two cigars. He pulled out a flask and poured us both a drink.

We're sitting there smoking and drinking, and Wendell, pleased with himself, is luxuriating in his cigar. It's a Saint Rey; they're fantastic, so satisfying, the best thing short of breast feeding.

"Wendell, what the fuck are we doing here?"

He pointed across the street. "See that house, Bernie?"

"Yep."

"See that house next to it, on the right."

"Great house."

"The lady who lived there until a few years ago was apparently the Lord Bitch of Pixie. Everybody in town knew her, and everybody in town hated her. Especially the mayor, city council members, civic organization people, hell, even the guys at the service station where she got her gas, even her fucking hairdresser. She just spread poison everywhere she went. She was like Midas, except everything she touched turned to shit. Her family apparently loathed her. They were all over Florida. They had a code, a signal worked out. If anyone of them got wind she was on her way for a visit, they left town, only to call and check with each other as to where she might be headed next."

"Damn."

"Her neighbors . . . need I say more?"

"I can imagine."

"Well, as I think about it, you're good at that, you, Janis, Pat, all of you."

"Yeah, but I'm better at it than Pat."

"Aw hell, Bernie, no question, everybody knows that."

"It's why I'm a wealthy man, destined for greatness, while he remains on his hands and knees crawling around through the literary rubble."

"That house directly across the street, the one next to hers? The city planner's. So he was getting it from her at every town council meeting, where she'd just drive everybody nuts but really go off on him since he was the one doing everything and getting paid for it, and then she'd wait for him to pull up into his driveway and from her front yard give it to him again."

"She was *that* bad?"

"One night after a late town council meeting, he pulls in his driveway, gets out of his car, and there she is, screaming at him from the front lawn; she knew better than to trespass on his. He calmly, without so much as a word, walks over to his tool shed—see it right there, off to the side, toward the back?"

"Yep."

"Walks out with an axe, strolls over to her front yard, and chops off her head. He knew what he was doing, knew what to do with an axe, I'll tell you what. Chopped her head clean off. Saw the pictures myself. Hell, probably go online in a few years and get 'em if you're interested. Want me to check for you? Here, have another drink."

After a few minutes, I turned and looked at Wendell. Right when I was about to ask him what we were still doing sitting there, a Lexus pulled into the driveway of the same city planner's house.

A middle-aged man with graying hair and an incipient paunch got out of the car carrying a briefcase and some loose papers, waved our way in case, it seemed, he might have been expected to know us—Southern politeness reigned in Pixie—and turned toward his front door.

"That was him," said Wendell, driving off.

"That was him?"

"Yep. Recognize him from the photos. I've been here before, obviously. Pixie's only tourist attraction, far as I can tell."

"He's not in jail, on death row, serving time?"

"Not a minute, not an hour, not one day. Hell, Bernie, everyone in town knew the woman: judges, lawyers, all the public officials. Even if her lawyers had tried cherry-picking jurors favorable to her—which they didn't, since they disliked her as much as anyone else did—you couldn't have found one anywhere around here who'd indict, much less convict, the guy."

"What's he do now?"

"Oh," said Wendell, "he's still the city planner, too young to retire."

"An axe murderer got off scot-free because the whole town hated her?"

"Yep, and the mayor, the town council, just about the whole town all but sent him a thank-you note."

"This is unbelievable."

"Yeah, that last line is, I agree, even Conroy would have left that one out."

Conroy loved that story. So naturally he retold it himself a million times. But you know, for the life of me, what I can't remember is whether he used Wendell's last line about the thank-you note.

Retelling a story *is* high praise, that's how it lives on through the years. It's Pat in praise of Wendell's story. Pat could do that because it wasn't in praise of Pat, though he was always grateful, and expressed it, for a good story.

Criticism, however, he was always on the lookout for, as if for the approach of an advancing army, and always in his mind it was the approach of Santini. He walked the world warily. I mentioned that I wondered if his acute peripheral vision on the basketball court, all those deft and polished no-look passes, was the offspring of his wariness. I found myself wondering too if his ball handling and sure and ready passing, his "setting up" of teammates to score, was *not* because he wasn't a good shooter, as he claimed, but because the applause and slaps on the back go primarily to the man who scores. Vicariously, Pat, I know, could enjoy that like no one else.

On the other hand, Pat *was* a good scorer. He could drive to the basket and make the layup or the short hook shot with the best of them. And he did. In the clutch, he wanted the ball, he *wanted* to take the shot with the game on the line. When I asked him about this, his answer: "I wanted to be the hero."

Scared of applause, of accolades, a young man yearns for heroism. Is that why he wrote? To work out that tension? His protagonists all become heroic.

Cliff used to tell Pat, facetiously, that he was "a simple, uncomplicated man." Was he complicated, as Cliff in his facetiousness was actually suggesting? Or did he only appear that way, as I suggested to him, because he was so fucking defensive? I shortchanged him there, as you can see. He was defensive, no question—Santini raised him—but boy, was he complicated.

He once told my wife Martha, before she became a psychologist, that there were five faces in front of his own, layers of faces, one in front of the other, behind which was his actual face. I'm not a psychologist, and neither was Martha then, but even a layperson can grasp the degree of self-protection, of dissociation here.

Who was he protecting himself from, dissociating from?

• • •

From St. Augustine, after our presentations, Pat and I drove to Newberry to meet Janis, who would be waiting for us, and with whom we'd spend a few days. Wendell was already on a flight somewhere to play golf. Pat always drove. Slow. Like Mr. Magoo. So slowly, I'd complain, that it felt like we were going in reverse. Then, naturally, he'd drive even slower. You could never tell Pat what to do.

Once we arrived in Newberry, we were to call Janis via cell phone so she could give us directions to her house, so upon arriving Pat phoned her, and I could hear her trying to give Pat directions. Unbeknownst to us, her house was evidently right around the corner. Janis and my wife Martha give the most confusing and circuitous directions I've ever heard in my entire life. As I listened to Janis over speakerphone, I wondered, Are Pat and I about to embark on a trip around the world? Should he refill his tank? Should we have bought winter coats? Iceland's cold. Newberry was a small town. We were there, just off Main Street. Could her house have been so far away as to warrant fifteen minutes' worth of directions?

As he was listening, Pat pulled off to the side of the road, his face tired, a pathetic picture of consternation, confusion, exasperation. It was a nice spring afternoon, the windows were down, and he began waving his hands frantically as if slapping away at unseen flies or mosquitoes.

He couldn't seem to get away from them, whatever they were. He was flailing, but at what? There was nothing there. He looked frightened, confused, even as he hung up. Then he just sat there, immobile, in his own world.

"What the fuck was that about? You looked like an idiot. Are you going nuts? Jesus, let me out of here."

"It was Santini," he realized, surprising himself.

"What brought *him* up?"

"Not knowing where I was going, the confusion."

"Well, her directions were confusing as hell."

"I was warding off his backhand. The blows kept coming. I never knew when."

It never occurred to me to wonder whether he was referring to Santini, his nickname for his alter ego's father in *The Great Santini*, or his real father, Don Conroy, because for Pat they were one and the same. "Remember, when we'd move every year, changing schools, and we'd always leave at nighttime, drive all night. Dad drove, and I had the map in the back seat: I was the navigator?"

I did; you may too. The scene is in *The Great Santini*. Pat's alter ego in that scene and throughout the entire novel is Ben Meecham, who, like Pat, is the oldest of all his siblings, and just as Pat's dad had done with Pat, Ben's dad has appointed Ben navigator; whenever Ben made a mistake—which was inevitable, they were driving all night—his dad hit him, just as Pat's dad had hit Pat when he was navigator.

My god, I thought, he's still warding off those blows. It takes almost nothing to set him off.

No child could have tried harder than Pat; he had to.

It took us two hours to get to Janis's, so Pat would swear later. I wasn't paying much attention, though I do remember passing and repassing Dunphy's Hardware and the courthouse downtown and the YOU ARE LEAVING NEWBERRY and WELCOME TO NEWBERRY signs. It was while we were on our way that I remembered, more than twenty-five years earlier, the smallness of Pat's voice amid the sounds of the great fire in the fireplace and the roaring waterfalls outside our windows and the ice-rattling glasses in the living room with "the boys," in the twilight shadow of the Blue Ridge Mountains in Sapphire.

It was the voice of the Navigator.

And it turned out he'd had good reason to be frightened of the fame that would come with the publication of *The Prince of Tides*.

X

ROME

In 1985, Pat, Lenore, Emily, and Gregory moved to Rome, where Susannah was born. Both he and Lenore adored her, doted on her. She was beautiful, as I would discover several years later when they returned to Atlanta.

In Rome, Pat continued fighting Alan for custody and sought to expose him as a sexual predator and the molester of his own child. Publicity, he figured, was his best offense. As always, Pat wanted a public light on the problem.

Why the need for publicity, I was never quite sure. Emily would tell me later, as a student in my class, that it was her story, that she didn't want it in the newspaper. Pat felt, of course, from his father's abuse of him and his family, that the great sin is always the cover-up. Thus, his lifelong fight against any kind of censorship.

Pat said if he could make Alan a public figure by exposing him in the newspaper, then he himself would be free to write or speak publicly about him without Alan being able to sue him for libel or slander, and the sustained exposure would be so damning that Alan would be prevented from seeing and having custody of Emily.

By now, Alan had married the Paideia parent with whom he had been conducting the affair. They moved to Phoenix, Arizona, where he continued his work as a brain surgeon. Did Pat think that publicizing Alan's abuse of Emily would lead to his indictment? Dekalb County's grand jury in Atlanta did indict him in August 1986 on one felony count of sexual molestation of Emily; the incident, according to the Dekalb County assistant district attorney, allegedly occurring between December 1, 1982, and January 1, 1983. Any return to Atlanta would result in his arrest.

The problem was that when the doctors checked Emily out, they could find no evidence she'd been sexually abused. That's why the Dekalb County prosecutor in Atlanta didn't go for a conviction. He believed Emily but was afraid that without the physical or medical evidence, with Emily's history of lying, they'd lose. And fully aware of just how vengeful, given the opportunity, Alan could be, Pat wanted to make him as uncomfortable as possible, to cost him his job, to break him, to render him powerless, to destroy him. Would publicity do that? I think he felt it would.

There were articles by reporters in the *Atlanta Journal Constitution*, where he had long-time contacts, and probably most importantly of all, in the *Arizona Star* in June of 1987, where Alan's indictment for molesting Emily was plainly stated for all of Arizona to read and in which, Alan admitted, caused "panic" in the hospital in which he was practicing surgery, with some looking at him now not as a doctor but as a child molester. Still, Pat remained desperate, worried that the Georgia indictment and publicity were insufficient to fully stop Alan from seeing her.

Before moving to Rome, Pat had taken Emily to a family therapist in Atlanta. Pat had wanted her to know Emily's story so she might testify for her and against Alan in court. Had Pat asked her to do that prior to Alan's indictment? I don't know. I never thought to ask him then. Now, however, he was phoning from Rome, and he wanted me to talk to her about it, so I can only suppose that he'd already tried. I knew the therapist—she was highly respected in the Paideia community—so I met with her and gave it my best shot. The only testimony she could offer, however, which may well be what she'd already told Pat, was that Emily had *told* her about the abuse.

That wasn't enough. Pat was furious. Now even from Rome, he was rallying an army, from the newspapers to the Paideia community, since Emily had attended Paideia since kindergarten.

He mailed me a letter that he wanted distributed throughout the entire Paideia community. From Rome, he phoned, insistent, letting me know how important this was.

Without going into the details, the letter was an embarrassment; it would have been entirely counterproductive. He was assuming too much to expect a bunch of academics and artists and intellectuals, from parents to teachers, to jump on the bandwagon with him without physical evidence, without proof of Alan's abuse of Emily. And faculty had been made aware of the doctors' report.

Also, Emily had the reputation of being a chronic liar among the teachers who had had her as a student at Paideia. Her fabrications were convincing, presumably because for her own psychological survival she'd learned to lie to herself—she'd had to, having been a victim of abuse. Given all this, it was too much to expect them to actively and aggressively support such a nakedly emotional plea from Pat. Plus, the Paideia community had learned over the years that Pat's insistence and his self-righteousness were integral to his makeup. They loved Pat, and they didn't doubt him; they just weren't ready for a loyalty oath, in my view. The pressure I was feeling from Pat was tantamount to being asked to sign one.

Who knows? Pat might have been drunk when he wrote the letter. But there can be no doubt, he wanted it out there. Martha thought worse of it than I did, and what I thought was bad enough. I threw it away.

Pat never mentioned it, even upon his and his family's return to Atlanta from Rome in 1987, which catapulted Emily into my junior high class at Paideia, an event that would change our lives forever.

XI

THE SLINGS AND ARROWS OF FAME

The Prince of Tides was out. It was everywhere. And Pat, as he had feared, far from having gotten himself together, was not ready for the slings and arrows—envy, jealousy, hostility—coming his way, especially from family, friends, and fellow writers.

Pat's beloved sister, the poet Carol Ann, so lovingly and cleverly portrayed as Mary Anne in *The Great Santini* and by far, more than any of us, Pat's most intimate friend, severed her relationship with him. Her alter ego in *The Prince of Tides* was a portrait of insanity, her insanity. A writer herself, and a very gifted one, she felt herself and her story exploited.

To me, Carol was always very pretty, though I don't think she knew it. To Martha and to me, of all the Conroys she seemed the most reasonable, the most sane and clear minded and fair. I never quite believed Pat's view of her as intermittently psychotic—until a few years before they went to Rome, when Pat, one evening in the kitchen of his new home in Ansley Park, showed me a note he'd gotten from her that day. She was living in New York at the time. Pat presents this entire scene in *The Death of Santini*, so I'll just share with you here that his depiction of the note was exactly as I'd remembered it. To paraphrase, her message was basically that, for $5,000, she would refrain from killing herself. So she was either in dire need of money or manipulative as hell.

As he also wrote in *The Death of Santini*, my advice to him was not to give in to her extortion, not to send the money. It seemed she was holding him hostage psychologically. I can guarantee you he did, though. Had I been in his shoes, I'm sure I would have too.

For Pat, when she cut her ties with him after *The Prince of Tides*, it was as if his twin had died. No matter how he tried to reach out to her, she refused to see him. His helplessness was palpable; he couldn't stop talking about it, thinking about it, figuring what he could do about it. He would refer to it with finality, acknowledging that the relationship was over but would say so again and again, as though he couldn't quite believe it. For her, in his view, he was guilty not only for his literary and commercial success as a writer but for having been the apple of his mother's eye, the "golden boy" of the family. He had thought that by making her character a highly respected poet it might offset in her mind his writing about her psychosis. She would have none of it. Pat wrote in *The Death of Santini* that Carol Ann said to him: "I have only one mortal enemy in my life. . . . Pat, that enemy is you."

As far as she was concerned, Pat told me, he had exploited her, had exploited the most precious relationship in either of their lives, and had stolen her identity. He couldn't help but wonder: did she see his success as her failure? That's what he believed, from what I gathered. What she actually thought, I have no idea.

She was in fact a well-respected poet in New York, where she worked with the Teachers and Writer's Collaborative to foster creative writing programs in schools and in the community. Her book of poetry, *The Beauty Wars*, would be published by Norton in 1991. All her literary friends in New York, she informed Pat, didn't see him as a serious writer but dismissed him as someone who wrote "trash for the mob," as he recounts in *The Death of Santini*. His response is to tell her he doesn't give a shit. He didn't. But he did care about her, that was certain.

An Atlanta journalist Pat and I both knew as an obsessively bitter, envious man did a huge piece in *Atlanta Magazine* featuring Don Conroy, debunking Pat's portrait of him as a wife- and child-beater in *The Great Santini*. Pat's brothers and sisters knew better, his mother had known better, Pat had known better, but journalism in this case did nothing but perpetuate the abuser's denial.

At a writers' conference in Atlanta, a bestselling, critically acclaimed novelist was standing against the wall all by himself looking painfully morose. When I asked him what was wrong, he glanced over at Pat, who was being mobbed by admirers. To his credit, he admitted he was jealous. Pat told me later that he'd gotten "bad vibes" from him, which is why, he also told me, he stayed away from most writers, whom he characterized as "piranhas."

One fellow novelist who disappointed him was a close friend. He had had a moderately successful career most writers would envy, but after Pat's success with *The Prince of Tides*, he began routinely at dinner parties and in social gatherings accusing Pat of selling out, of writing for money.

Even at Paideia, as happy as people were to see him around campus, he was more aware than ever of subtle putdowns coming his way. One math teacher, referring to his dialogue in a particular scene, couldn't wait to see him, she told him, just to let him know that "Pat, no one, no one talks that way! No one!"

While on tour in Chicago for *The Prince of Tides*, he visited and had dinner with his grandmother and his aunts and uncles on his father's side. His aunts and uncles cheered as his grandmother, who had Alzheimer's, flicked pasta and meatballs, one piece after another, in his face—encouraging her, laughing at his humiliation. His aunt Mary announced that Pat had gotten "the big head." When they found out

Pat was staying at the Roosevelt Hotel, his Uncle Willie said, "Oh, he's too good to stay here, he's got to put his shoes under a bed at the Roosevelt Hotel." Pat told me they felt that, with his heightened fame and success, he'd gotten too big for his britches.

Too big for his britches. "The world doesn't forgive that easily," he told me. "Fame sucks, I told you it would, but I can handle it. My father prepared me well for it. Besides, the backhands are verbal. At least I'm not getting hit."

As for me, Pat's fame, initially a source of great enthusiasm, became a pain in the ass. I'd never been invited to so many dinner parties in my life, only to hear: "By the way, do you happen to know how I can get in touch with Pat?" "By the way, I don't." Ha ha ha.

After which I'd give them the wrong number.

I had to change the message on my answering machine. "This is the home of Bernie and Martha Schein, obviously unavailable at the moment, the reasons too intricate, too complex, and too weighted with profound implications to go into now. However, if you're looking for Pat, I will go into them. I should let you know that it will take you no less than three full working days to locate him. He is in a remote mountain cabin high up in the Rocky Mountains. He is completely isolated, without a phone or any means of communication with the outside world, except for nearby animals, which he strangles with his bare hands for food. Incognito, he's grown a beard, which I wish he would trim. I should warn you, he stinks. He needs to clean up a bit, but that's just my opinion, which last time I visited him he didn't seem remotely interested in. So you know what I say to that? Fuck him. Right? Right. Whatever. In any case, no vehicles can even approach getting up that mountain. Plus, there are no motels or rental cabins there. Too dangerous. So with the trek to the cabin taking at least three days, bring camping equipment. To avoid becoming food for bears, bring a shotgun. If you need firing lessons beforehand, call Kill at Will. Mention my name. They'll take care of you. As for myself, I could certainly use a holiday. But you know, babysitters are so expensive, and boarding dogs now, wow. After that, no money left for vacation! Ha ha ha. But hey, Thank you for calling. Thank you. Thank you for being you. Thank you for being a Jew, if you are one. If you're not, let's just leave it at: Thank you. Thank you."

"Your message, Bernie, it's so funny!"

It was Diana Epps, a real beauty, the former Miss Beaufort, Butch Epps's wife. Butch, also from Beaufort, was an old classmate and friend, just a fabulous guy, now a lawyer. As Pat so often said, South Carolina is so small, everyone and everything seems to connect with everyone and everything else. Butch had been influenced by Gene Norris, the same teacher who had so influenced Pat. He rented an old Victorian house in Edgefield, South Carolina, smack dab in the middle of the impoverished Corridor of Shame, moved a bunch of lawyers into it, and took the state of South Carolina to court for failing to provide even a "minimally adequate" education to the children in the schools. He was relentless in his own quiet way, worked his ass off, sacrificed monetarily, and as far as Pat and I were concerned, became a hero.

His wife, Diana: "Bernie, Butch is chairman of the South Carolina Defense Lawyers Association, I'm not sure whether you know this or not. Anyway, they're having their annual meeting on a yacht!"

"Really?"

"It's huge, right? It would have to be. That's a lot of lawyers. Anyway, they're really going all out for this, and naturally they're looking for a speaker."

I couldn't help it: "I'd love to, Diana. What an honor. Thank you. Please tell Butch. Wait, let me get my calendar, mark down the date. . . . You can count on me, Diana."

After that, I again changed my message.

"Hello. So nice to hear from you, whoever you may be. If you're looking for Bernie or Martha, please leave a message if you think it might be interesting, somehow useful, perhaps worthwhile. If not, don't. That's my take on it. If you're looking for Pat, we don't know him. We hate him. He's dead. Kill yourself."

By this time, I was truly hating Pat's fame as much as he was. I was writing Pat's blurbs for other writers' forthcoming books, which up until now, I'd really gotten a charge out of doing. A friend would call, ask if I could get his advance reading copy to Pat for a blurb, since Pat never answered his phone. I'd say sure, no problem, the friend would drop it off at my house or mail it to me, I'd write up the blurb myself, and sign Pat's name, often without him even knowing it. When he'd see these writers at festivals or parties swarming him with appreciation and gratitude, at first it took him by surprise, but I must say, over the long haul he adjusted well.

I loved writing them. To blurb a book, you don't really need to read it. I remember Terry Kay phoning James Dickey to ask him for a blurb for one of his novels. "What's it about?" asked Dickey with absolutely no hesitation. "I'll get you the advance reading copy," said Terry. "Don't worry about that, Kay. Just read me what's on the back cover."

See how it works?

Writing a blurb was an exercise in writing short fiction or akin to haiku. What I liked about it was you got to exaggerate all you wanted, heaping praise on people you liked, giving them a fighting chance, and making them happy. Everything about it made me happy, including Pat's frustration at being caught by surprise.

"Bernie," he once asked, "Have you ever written a *sincere* blurb in my name?"

"Have you?"

He hadn't. And he'd been right. Blurbs aren't literature. They're advertisements, like some famous model hawking Clairol. They're like job recommendations. Why write them unless you're helping someone find a job.

To be so free to write so utterly irresponsibly, what freedom! What joy it was!

But that was because it took so little of my time then. Now Pat himself was getting so many requests he all but disconnected his phone. It got so bad he actually *wanted* me to write his blurbs for him, which I no longer wanted to do since there were so many.

"I'm getting too many requests myself," I told him.

"Bernie, in all sincerity, I cannot tell you how odd that sounds."

"Too many for one person to handle. I'm getting out of this business."

Which I did, mostly.

Every once in a while, I would feel the inspiration coming on. Not to brag, I told Pat, offering my back to him so he could pat it, but I managed through sheer strength and determination, those old standbys, to fight it.

XII

A MOMENT OF CLARITY

The headmaster Paul Bianchi asked me a question over drinks at Manuel's Tavern, a local watering hole. It was a prescient question, though at the time I had no idea of that. It barely registered. An elderly group of women at a nearby table were oohing and aahing over the yellow leaves that all seemed to be falling at once from the gingko tree outside the windows.

He'd put all three of his kids in my class, and he had a pretty good idea of why Pat had wanted Emily there. He knew me.

"If it comes down to a choice, either totally going all out for Emily or supporting Pat, which way would you go?"

"Emily, of course."

After which I gave no thought about it at all, but I should have.

In retrospect, I'm not even sure why Paul asked the question, unless he was remembering the conflict over Mikey McMahon's story being published in the high school literary magazine. Paul was familiar with Pat's fury. He'd been in the middle of that fight, which had been bruising not only to him but to Pat as well. In fact, though Pat, with Paul's support, ultimately won the battle, Paul may have supported him as much out of fear of him as conviction.

Paul was pretty eclectic and pragmatic. If he was thinking about the Mikey McMahon controversy at the time, it was probably on my behalf as much as his. He was a good friend but also professionally very protective of me and my classroom. Paul knew what could happen if you crossed Pat.

I didn't, not really. I just saw him as a fighter for good causes.

Pat had wanted Emily in my class badly. He had reminded me of it nonstop over the summer when he got back from Rome. He was a fervent advocate of our creative writing program, which was controversial in the Paideia community because it was so personal, with kids' stories coming from conflicts in their family lives and social relationships, conflicts usually from a much earlier time in their childhood. Almost all had to do to one degree or another with a loss of innocence: loss, perhaps rejection, perhaps failure, perhaps abuse. At bottom, as Pat had said about Mikey McMahon's, all were love stories or no one would have cared.

He wanted Emily loved. And by that time, he had learned, as I would, that not only would it not come from her biological father, it would not come from her mother. Lenore loved without reservation Susannah and Gregory, Pat told me. Always they were uppermost in her mind. But as much as he loved Lenore, she just couldn't give Emily the love and attention she needed. It would have to come from him, as indeed it was, and he needed my help.

From the beginning, unsurprisingly, Emily had problems in my classroom, as she'd always had in school. In my class, telling the truth was paramount, whether you were telling a story or writing one. There was a premium even on telling the truth about lying; that could really get you a round of applause. But Emily lied chronically, and her lies were so time consuming and frustrating to unravel—lies about her work, her family, her classmates, her social life. Add to this that she tried to fit in socially by undermining others, gossiping, dividing and conquering. All of her lying and manipulation inevitably boomeranged on her, as you might expect.

She confided to me that she was pregnant, and the responsible party was a boy at Camp Blue Star, in North Carolina, the camp she had attended on their return from Rome before her school year began. Not true. According to Lenore when I phoned her about it, Emily's Tampax was in the trash can.

Over the years, with my help and guidance, the kids in the class had written their own class constitution which they regularly revised and amended. It included laws and rights and provided for an elected congress and a court system with lawyers, judges, court officers, the works. Emily abused the class court system by vengefully charging a classmate, who'd gone out of her way to befriend her, with petty stuff, anything she could find: leaving her lunch bag on the table where kids worked, failing to return a borrowed pencil, disturbing the peace by whispering during work time, misdemeanors no one ever charged anyone for unless they got really out of hand. Then when this same classmate retaliated by charging Emily with vengeful prosecution, Emily lied about it.

Her lies, in almost every situation, metastasized to the point where she drove not only her classroom lawyers but the entire class crazy. And amid the chaos, there stood Emily, sheepish but nevertheless the center of attention.

I must note here that I think everyone in the class loved Emily. She was certainly interesting, intriguing, and a character. She had a great sense of humor. She wasn't just needy, she was also empathetic and loving. Yes, she could be envious and jealous and passive-aggressive and the worst sort of rumormonger if it served her social advantage, but she could also show a keen interest, a curiosity in her classmates and their work, and in the works of the great writers we read. You can imagine her fascination with Holden Caulfield. She was searching, no question, but to find what she was searching for she had to work, and her lying about whether or not she had done her work drove me nuts. She was just too psychologically scattered to actually do it.

I wondered at the time if Lenore's unresponsiveness to Emily, her seeming inability to give her attention, might somehow be her way of dissociating from the sexual abuse Emily had suffered at the hands of Alan. However, wouldn't therapy have helped Lenore with that?

Moreover, faculty at Paideia told me she had been that way with Emily from the beginning, from the baby carriage. Pretty like her mother, they said, Emily nevertheless had looked a bit slumped and awkward in the baby carriage, with something of a wandering eye, as if she had something less than full muscle strength, though looking at her as she grew older one could never have surmised that. One faculty member told me that when Lenore would pick up Emily and carry her into preschool, she seemed to be holding her at arm's length.

Whatever the reason, Emily had a teacher who loved her and a stepfather who not only loved her but had saved her. He was her lifeline. But he couldn't replace her natural father or her mother.

I think the only thing Pat *knew* then was that he wanted her story out. He had heard and read the kids' stories in previous years, from the most disturbing and the most tender to the lighter, more amusing ones. He wanted Emily freed as much as possible from shame and self-loathing, wanted her understood and celebrated publicly in my classroom, among intimates, if for nothing else than for her honesty, her art, her survival. He imagined, I'm sure, that not only would her story be read aloud to the class, as the best were, but it would be featured in *Hidden Places* too.

It turned out that her story was the one thing she could focus on. She'd turn in a draft, then after talking more about it with me and her classmates she'd remember something she'd left out, or when I'd read parts of it aloud to her she'd immediately grab it back and go to work on it. The story focused her, I realized, rather than the other way around. Also, she'd already told it to Pat.

Emily wrote her story with the door to her shame wide open: the repeated rape, the asphyxiation so she couldn't scream, the cover-up. I read it aloud to the class, which was the highest accolade a student could get in my classroom. Afterwards, the class gave her a standing ovation. They applauded her courage. It was a great story, dramatic, disturbing, horrifying, and brutally honest. It was entirely clear and coherent. Naturally, in their responses the kids expressed their own fears, their own personal reactions, and her answers were thoughtful, clear, wise. She understood their fears, their questions, had had them herself. Several of the kids brought up their own instances of having been abused and the resulting feelings of shame, of guilt, and of bearing responsibility. Had they encouraged it somehow, without realizing it at the time? Emily's story suggested otherwise, giving them greater permission to tell their own. The class, above all, wanted intimacy, to be able to trust each other, and Emily had helped create, ironically, a safe zone for that, for genuine friendship—for strength, not power—to flourish and grow.

For all her craziness, this was her moment of clarity, and it had made her in the eyes of her tearful classmates, now smothering her with hugs, embraces, admiration, a champion.

But, indeed, it was a *moment* of clarity.

Intelligent and well-intended though she was, much of her other work she was just unable to complete. Her neediness, which manifested itself in her hunger for attention, interfered. Which is why I encouraged her to write about her relationship with her mother. That, however, was a wound too painful for her to touch.

She could talk about it and did so happily, but it was because talking distanced her from the feelings that writing about it would have brought out in her; also, it was a clever way of getting my attention.

I begged Lenore to try and give Emily the attention she craved. She said that she would make time for her and Emily to go "running" together every Wednesday afternoon. I hoped that would be a beginning, but it wasn't happening. When I phoned Lenore to ask why, she told me her leg hurt.

"Lenore, do you know *why* it hurt?"

She did, but, I was beginning to realize, there was nothing she could do about it. Therapy? Didn't seem to help. Finally, I did the only thing left for me to do. Emily would be going into high school the next year. The high school teachers paid serious attention to every student's cumulative record folder. I told Lenore that if she couldn't somehow work to give Emily the attention she needed—since in my classroom it was clear she wasn't doing so—I would have to write that in Emily's folder so the high school teachers would know what to expect.

That didn't work either. Nothing did; the child was falling apart in my classroom, and if there was something I could have done about it, I did not know what it was.

For his part, Pat raved about her story. But, as involved and supportive as he was, it just wasn't enough. Her wounds were too damaging, too deep. She'd been neglected, abused, and abandoned. She needed her mother.

Much to Pat's displeasure, I decided against publishing her story in the school magazine, *Hidden Places*. Martha felt it would leave Emily vulnerable to high school boys on the make. Also, the majority of our readers, other than junior high kids themselves and their parents, were elementary school kids and their parents, and the contents of the story were not for young children.

Soon after hearing it read aloud to the class, Alana Goldberg told me that Emily had told her the same story back in second grade. Alana's own father was as sensitive and kind as a kid could have, but Emily's story had so frightened her that until the day she told us about it she had lived in fear, every night, that her father would enter her room and violate her in the same way. She had never before told anyone this fear, and he never knew. When she matured enough for a bra, the idea that her dad might somehow be aware of it and perhaps might go with her to buy one horrified her.

As a second grader, she had been too young, too innocent, to hear Emily's story. Emily told her because she assumed all fathers did that to their children, that it was normal. And there was no teacher, no class, no discussion, to tell her or Emily herself otherwise. Emily hadn't yet encountered Pat.

Several kids in my class said that, even though, hearing the story, they weren't worried about their own fathers abusing them, nevertheless they would have left the classroom feeling disturbed and vaguely fearful had it not been for the class discussion that followed the reading.

When I was considering including her story in *Hidden Places*, I talked with Emily privately about the possibility. I knew she hadn't wanted Pat to publicize her abuse in the newspapers. It was her story, no one else's, she had said. What did she want now? Did she want her story in the literary magazine? What I heard coming out of her mouth was chilling. It was not the voice of a child. She sounded like someone who'd been brainwashed.

"Twenty-five percent of children in America have been sexually abused. I definitely want it in the magazine. Not to include it would be censorship of the worst kind. The abuse must be stopped. The only way to do that is to make it public."

The voice was Pat's, not hers. She wanted so badly to please him. He had saved her. He was still fighting for her. He desperately wanted the story published. It was so important, in his mind, that the community know.

What I heard in her voice was Pat fighting for her, but not in any way, shape, or form did I hear Emily fighting for herself.

"Emily, you've written a great story. It's an incredible contribution to the entire class. They love you for it. So do I. I love you even without it. And that's why I'm not going to publish it." I reminded her of what had happened with Alana, how the sheer power of it, particularly without the context of discussion, could leave young ones scared. I told her what Martha had feared. Would it leave her vulnerable once she entered high school? Some boys weren't nice. "It's not your decision," I told her. "I know you want it in there worse than hell. I wish I could do it for you and for everyone who needs to read it, but I can't, and I'm not. I know you're angry. You have every right to be. Go back and just tell Pat that Bernie's an asshole, a hypocrite, and as much as Bernie knows you want it in there, as mad and upset as he knows you are, that it won't be, he's decided against it."

"If you have to choose," Paul had asked, "who will it be? Emily or Pat?" I had chosen Emily. But so had Pat. We were both fighting for her.

So that was it. When I did that, he began avoiding me. The few times we were together he seemed unengaged, preoccupied.

At the time, I couldn't be sure why. I thought I knew, but I couldn't get him to talk about it. I knew Emily would tell him I was a jerk—I wanted her to, to let herself off the hook—but did I expect him to truly believe it? He felt, I'm sure, that I'd betrayed him. Had it been *his* magazine, I asked him, would he have allowed someone else to make this kind of decision for him? I explained to him why I had made it. He was dismissive. Alana? He dismissed that as an issue too.

I asked him if my refusal to publish her story was why he was angry with me. In my family, yelling and screaming was normal, par for the course, often the only way to walk off with the argument in your pocket. Volume counted. But, with us, there was no threat of violence in the air. It was safe, fun. With Pat, of course, I knew otherwise, so I assured him that if he told me why he was upset with me I would not yell, scream, act like a Jew, or sound like Santini but would be so respectful and kind and understanding that he would be glad he told me.

"You're upset, Pat, I know that. You've been avoiding me."

"Nah, I've just been busy."

He couldn't do it. And so he ended the friendship.

And I ended up hating his guts for it.

XIII

THE RIFT

For fifteen years, we didn't speak to each other.

We talked *about* each other all the time, Pat publicly, in his speeches all over the country, telling the same stories he'd always told, usually funny ones: how my noble, lifelong crusade against the use in American education of the IQ test was based upon my horrific discovery of my own IQ, sixty-seven, which he'd so generously offered up to me after combing through my old cumulative record folder back in the sixties when he was teaching in Beaufort High School. "My God," he quoted me saying, "I'm stupid! I'm an idiot! *Sixty-seven*?"—a score, he would then confide to his audience, he'd made up. His excitement so great upon receiving an invitation to the Oval Office from then President Jimmy Carter that he immediately phoned his buddies at the newspapers with the scoop, only to discover to his utter embarrassment and humiliation when he phoned the White House, as requested, to confirm, that *I'd* made the whole thing up, even the printed invitation, which I'd gotten a kid in my class to do, after which I asked the art teacher to give her an A. Barbara Streisand phoning him out of the blue about a film she wanted to make based on *The Prince of Tides*, surprising him so much he was convinced that whoever was calling, Bernie had put her up to it, and told her if she really was Barbara Streisand, which he knew she wasn't, to sing "People," her standard, which she did. I won't repeat all the stories here. He'd told them forever, to the point that, once we reunited, I suggested he come up with new material.

Privately, apparently without realizing it at the time until friends informed me, I talked about him all the time too.

But all this was after Pat had left town, moving to San Francisco with his family in 1991. In the brief interval before he left, he turned on me viciously, telling our writer friends and my colleagues at Paideia that I'd been "mean to Emily." In his mind, I was now the mean guy and Emily my victim, or so Paul, the headmaster, told me. For a time, it was confusing. I wondered, what exactly had I done? Was this solely because of the omission of Emily's story in *Hidden Places*?

After he'd left for San Francisco with Lenore and his family, I did find it initially disconcerting and later insulting that he was celebrating our friendship in the stories he was telling all over the country as if nothing had ever come between us. Because of it, people, most of whom I'd never met before, would introduce themselves, offer their hand, even embrace me, with stars in their eyes.

It seemed crazy to me. Unreal. Because it was. How could he compartmentalize to that extent?

Shortly after he'd left, he returned to Atlanta for a talk at Emory, just a few blocks from where we lived. Without telling me, Martha went to hear him, slipping inconspicuously in the back row. She missed him. Like me, I don't think she understood what had happened. Mostly, he talked about me, his "best friend Bernie," telling the stories he'd always told. Inconspicuous in the back row, Martha found herself weeping.

Part of my job at Paideia was to supervise and work with other teachers. It was just like working with writers, which some of them were. As with students in my classroom, my rule with fellow teachers or writers was: Open hearts create open minds. Cut off your head; it's in the way, a bumbling clerical functionary. Don't think. Be true to your feelings, true feelings, not only to what you need and want and aspire to be and do but to your feelings about whoever or whatever might be undermining that—a friend, a partner, a colleague, a sibling—and you will discover what undermines your teaching, your work. Truth, hard as hell to get to—what one teacher I worked with called the "organizing emotion"—sires logic, reason, coherent thought. Who are you? What do you feel, deep down? From true emotion, your thoughts will come naturally. So, whatever it is you're not fully aware of that's mucking about in your heart and soul usually comes out in almost every aspect of your life that's important to you, not just your teaching but your art, your writing, parenting, your relationships with your partner, your parents, your friends, your colleagues, the parents of the kids in your classroom, the community, in your relationships with the kids themselves. It can affect your pickup basketball games, your approach to photography if that's your interest, the advice you give kids playing soccer, conversations with parents, with colleagues, with friends, with each other.

The group of teachers with whom I worked, dubbed "The Teachers' Group," met in my classroom every Wednesday afternoon after school. In these sessions, where you began is far from where you'd end up. A teacher complaining about the kids continually "acting out" and disrupting her classes realizes she's resisting the need to discipline them because she in no way wants to be like her older sister, who intimidated and bullied her. Afraid of becoming the bully, she shows up in her classroom as the target.

Attendance was purely voluntary, but that didn't prevent one faculty member from perpetually complaining about "spending all this time on feelings," dismissing the process as "touchy-feely" only to discover she was denying her own. She realized too that when she'd go on and on about being "tired of all this mess," she truly was exhausted. She'd been the "whitewasher," the "good" kid, in a family of alcoholic parents and a raging rebellious brother. To be the one, she told us, always putting on a happy face, keeping up a good front, putting on a great show while doing her best to hide the flaws of her family, was awfully tiring. How did this directly affect her teaching? Open to her own story, her own childhood, she could be more empathetic and more open with the kids. She could listen. Also, she could drop the act. Denial is exhausting.

One time, we had a real moralist in the group, sage-like, gently pious, sanctimonious, nudging everyone in his own aw-shucks, avuncular fashion, as if he were merely wondering aloud, no offense intended naturally, if we all might find it in ourselves to somehow approach kids with just "a bit more sensitivity," perhaps "a bit more maturity." He encouraged us all to be "open minded." Why, thank you, said one teacher, but wasn't that why we were all here? Why the condescension? Was he talking about us, asked one teacher, or himself, because as she told him, flawed though she may be, she was a hell of a lot more open minded than his judgmental ass, pardon the "insensitivity," the lack of "maturity."

Why the need to be such an asshole? we asked him. Surely, he knew better. Is it "open minded" and "sensitive" to judge us from on high instead of just telling us how he feels? Who among us was he really talking about? Anyone in particular? Are people here not sensitive enough to you? we asked. Have you been insensitive in some way with the kids? Perhaps condescending, like you were with us? He'd been ignored, he said eventually, neglected, and consequently unbearably lonely as a child, basically almost entirely unattended to. An only child, he had been brought up in a very wealthy family in an enormously spacious home in upscale Tuxedo Park in upstate New York, where not only was a child not heard, he was not seen. Even now, he added, walking into a Buckhead mansion or any large, expansive house was a brutal reminder of his childhood, which is why his own home in Cabbagetown in Atlanta was little more than a bungalow. He offered up a pained smile, after which he graciously and sincerely thanked us, then informed us sadly that we, our help, had arrived too late. We had no idea what he was talking about until we read about it in the papers after he was fired. He was a Peeping Tom.

Not only was he a Peeping Tom in his neighborhood, a member of the Paideia community reported that he had taken lewd photos of high school students. "Sensitivity?" "Maturity?" In his self-righteous judgment offloaded like baggage onto our shoulders, there was denial, we were learning. We also learned that for our own sakes it was important, if not to question it, to fight it.

I was saddened that our moralist felt it was "too late" for him, though obviously in retrospect I could understand why he felt that way. Clearly, to fully reenter the spacious mansion of his childhood had always been too much for him. What saddened me more was there had been no signs of struggle, no fight inside him, only blame and despair. It was as if he was the opposite of Pat. Whatever else he might have been, Pat was a warrior: *"I struggle every day . . . with the little boy I once was."*

That struggle made all the difference in the world not only for Pat but for those who in his revelations gained insight into themselves.

As for me, a teacher with whom I worked in my own classroom, Bonnie Sparling, once brought up Pat. "He's an asshole," I said. The whole group looked so taken aback I just moved on. We had bigger issues to deal with. Romero Vardan and his assistant teacher, SaraBeth Haverford, were driving each other crazy. She was overstepping her authority by presenting herself to parents as the lead teacher in the classroom, while Romero undermined *her* role as his assistant in the same way that, as a child, he'd undermined his mother. How? He made himself late for school and his mother late for work by taking forever, on purpose, he now realized, to tie his shoes. Why? *He'd* wanted to run the show, even though it wasn't his to run, just as SaraBeth now wanted to do in his classroom, which wasn't hers to run. And now that the show *was* his to run, his mother was still in the way because he was still taking too long to "tie his shoes": to get SaraBeth the materials she needed or to notify her of schedule changes, or, not surprisingly, of parent-teacher conferences, which frustrated SaraBeth, making her even more controlling.

Romero was so passive-aggressive that he stopped attending our sessions, then resumed, blaming his absence on his hurt feelings because I hadn't sought him out to ask *why* he had stopped attending.

"It's not a fucking cocktail party, Romero. You didn't want to come, so you're blaming me."

"This is what he does to me!" cries SaraBeth. "It drives me crazy!"

But she was driving him crazy too. Her ambition, her need to run the show, she admitted, was real. She wanted the classroom to be hers, not his. In her heart, she wanted their roles reversed. Did she realize the likelihood of that happening was nil? Of course. But Romero exacerbated her need with his subtle undermining of her just as she did his need by undermining him.

Teachers' Group was a place I didn't have to deal with Pat. Like the other teachers with their issues, I wasn't fully aware of my feelings about him at the time. Besides, though I did some of my own work in these sessions, it was more to set an example. The sessions were about them. Sure, the subject of Pat came up over the years, most often brought up by me, as I would later realize, but I too compartmentalized. As time passed, I didn't want to have anything to do with him. I just dismissed him as an asshole, ignoring the peculiar looks I got from people.

That changed, the result of a phone call in 1995, which is about the time Pat separated from Lenore and returned to Beaufort, living on Fripp Island only a few blocks from the ocean.

John Berendt, the author of *Midnight in the Garden of Good and Evil*, whom I'd never met, phoned me one evening from the Surrey Hotel in New York. He was interviewing Pat for an article he was writing about him for *Vanity Fair*. Pat had suggested he talk to me.

"You've got to be kidding."

"Actually, no, I'm not. He asked me to call you. In fact, he and I are in the same hotel. I could get you guys together on the phone if you'd like. You could talk to each other."

This, to me, was fucking crazy, to say nothing of infuriating.

"Write this down, John. I want to make sure I'm painstakingly clear. Put this in your piece."

He was ready.

"Pat Conroy is a traitor. He's shit for a friend. He's a complete fucking asshole."

"He's moved back to Beaufort now, you know, living on Fripp Island."

I hadn't known that. "I pray his plane crashes on the way home."

"Sure you don't want me to get you two together? He's right down the hall."

I vented about this in the next session of the Teachers' Group. Bonnie Sparling said, "Bernie, you talk about him all the time!"

She was right. I did. Constantly. Pat this, Pat that. Here's what Pat would say, here's what Dickey told him, how much Pat loved rewriting, and this, folks, on top of his telling all his stories to family and friends long before he began writing them. I'd tell my students about his penchant for rewriting. Writing, I'd emphasize, is rewriting. You know what Dickey told Pat? A poem is not a poem unless it's been rewritten at least fifty times. How many times has this been rewritten, I'd say, holding up their poem or story or essay. As Pat would say, I'd tell kids and adults, whoever I was working with, Go deeper. Go deeper. Let it come, let it come. Try it. And if you're uncomfortable in the slightest afterwards, there's usually a reason. It means you should be. Trust that feeling, that discomfort, rewrite. Don't get stuck on what you've written. If it's good, save it, you can use it somewhere else, in a different story. Be open to the reality that what you're writing may not *be* your story. What's the most interesting part? *That* might be your story. Rewrite with that in mind. Your real story might be buried somewhere in the one you're writing, particularly if that kernel, no matter how small, makes you uncomfortable. You write, Pat says, to find out *why*. That's what he meant by Go deeper, Let it come.

And the stories, they were never ending. One of my favorites that I loved telling the Teachers' Group was how crazy made us crazy, especially me. Pat and I were going to visit our old friend Lukie Brown in the insane asylum in Columbia. On the drive down, I told Pat, "He'll come after me, watch."

Pat was curious, surprised. "Why?"

"Crazy people, insane people, nut cases, especially paranoids, they spot weakness, vulnerability, the soul of a sissy, a heart made of mush in, pardon the pun, a heartbeat. An instinctively open one, like mine, brings out their worst. They won't come after you. Your heart, wisely, is closed, slammed shut, as impenetrable as Fort Knox, primed, instinctively armed and ready for battle, for the surgical preemptive strike. You are a warrior. I, I am a Jew. Smarter, more intelligent than you, yes. You are a dumb Irishman, but dumb Irishmen survive. You have character. Strength. Me, I'm easy game, doe eyed, standing there in the middle of the clearing, right in their line of sight without even realizing it. In short, you are a strong man. I am a weak one. Thank you for listening."

Pat looked at me like I was nuts.

"Wait, you'll see. He'll come at me like a sadist. Let's stop for a drink so I can fortify myself."

He was always ready to do that.

So we arrive at the insane asylum, walk upstairs to Lukie's room, the door's open, and there he is, right across from us, sitting on the lower bunk, his bunk, buck naked. We're the only ones in the room. We sit on a couple of folding chairs in front of him, his dick blatantly announcing itself as he drones on for over two hours, offering a detailed diagnosis of every single person in the hospital who has worked with him: psychiatrists, psychologists, pharmacologists, social workers, social psychologists, medical doctors, psychiatric nurses, head nurses, regular nurses, orderlies, security personnel, hell, even the custodians. He spoke in this dreadfully soporific monotone, with no pause whatever for a Jew like me, screaming inside with boredom, to wiggle into. No. On and on and on. I could see Pat had spaced out with that fake look of attentiveness he'd mastered by the time Lukie had gotten to the psychiatric nurses.

And of course, there's Lukie's dick now resting comfortably against his leg, his right one, like a lapdog sleeping with one eye open; periodically, with Lukie's slight movements, rearranging itself.

So Lukie finishes his monologue, waiting for our acknowledgment and approval. Pat tunes in, then spends all his energy trying to avoid looking at Lukie's dick all cozied up right there with Lukie, right there in front of us, and I just couldn't help it. All those people who were supposed to be helping him, the ones he'd just consigned to the loony bin? "Lukie," I asked him, "are they all naked too?"

Lukie didn't skip a beat. In the same flat monotone he cited my low SAT scores, my poor grades in high school, my academic probation my freshman year at Newberry College, the rejection by my girlfriend there and a reference to who she'd "fucked" instead of me at the time, my failure to get into law school because of my low score on the law exam (my first attempt to dodge the draft), all the teaching jobs I didn't get after graduating from college and having to end up with the one in Yemassee because they couldn't find anyone else who'd want to live there, my ending up marrying a divorcee since all the single women had rejected me, my having gotten into Harvard because I knew somebody, my professed commitment to education for all dubiously reflected in my teaching at an "elite" private school . . . and on and on and on.

On the way back, Pat began laughing: "Gosh, Bernie, he knows you so well."

After getting over himself, he said, "It wasn't because you were weak that he went nuts on you, Bernie. It's because you're a wiseass."

If I did speak about Pat all the time, I still didn't want to see him, be with him, talk *to* him—he was an asshole. But he'd been a huge influence on my life, on my thoughts, my feelings, and I did go on about him like he did about me.

He'd been so hateful. He used to see me as such a good person, I knew that, someone with a good heart, and naturally I had supported this opinion with great enthusiasm. And he'd always felt inside that he himself was incapable of truly loving. But if that were the case, I told the Teachers' Group, how had I felt so much love from him?

In that moment, I wanted to tell him that. But then I'd remember just how much hate I'd felt from him.

It took another ten years for me to get over it. Maybe realistically it took the same amount of time for him, I don't know. Maybe he'd been drunk when he'd asked John Berendt to phone me.

In the early fall of 2005, he called on my birthday, singing, "Happy Birthday" in that horrid singing voice he had.

He was married by then to his new and last wife, Cassandra King Conroy, the bestselling writer and novelist, and was still living on Fripp Island. He invited Martha and me down for the weekend.

For the rest of my life, I will never understand this, but as soon as I walked into his home on Fripp Island and saw him, all the negative feelings, too many to count, were no longer anywhere in sight. All I felt was the old love.

"I don't understand," I told him. "I wanted you dead, I hated your guts—and now, suddenly, nothing but love and good feelings?"

"I knew this would happen," he said.

He did. He did.

Isn't that something? Wasn't he something?

XIV

RAPPROCHEMENT AND RETIREMENT

After our visit with Pat and Sandra, Pat would phone several nights a week and we'd end up talking for well over an hour each time. He had me back, he said, and he didn't want to lose me again. So why had he lost me for fifteen years?

Lenore was conniving and manipulative, Pat said. She separated him not only from me but also from his dad, with whom he'd become very close, as well as Jim Landon and Cliff Graubart, both among his oldest friends. She'd lied about me being "mean to Emily," though he couldn't seem to remember what she'd actually said to him, and to get rid of Jim she'd told a terrible lie about his lawyering for them, one so outrageous I'm not going to give any credence to it by repeating it here. Now, sadly, she had turned their daughter Susannah against him.

He spoke of Lenore's "Iago-like" mode of dividing and conquering, a strategy Emily had apparently learned from her, he said. Lenore was a social climber, indifferent to suffering, including his own when he was bedridden with severe back pain and, more importantly, that of Emily, who had become more and more depressed and suicidal in San Francisco. Lenore in his mind had transformed into the evil one, this former red-diaper baby of Jewish card-carrying communists now obsessed with money and status, his money, his status, which she may well have been.

Was he talking about her now as he had talked about me, and perhaps Jim, right before he left Atlanta for San Francisco? Blaming her as he had blamed me? I know how head over heels in love he had been with Lenore back then, in Atlanta and Rome, but how could he have believed all that crap? He'd never in his life done anything he didn't want to do.

Emily's story, the omission from *Hidden Places* . . . If he'd been mad about that, couldn't he have told me? In fact, if he'd been mad with me about anything, couldn't he have just told me? And why didn't he tell me how he felt when I'd asked him directly? If you're mad at your best friend and can't tell him why, what can you do but leave?

When he left, he couldn't tell me why. Why should I believe he could do so fifteen years later?

Still, Pat was genuinely surprised when I brought up all my entreaties to Lenore to get her to give Emily the attention she needed. I'd tried for almost a year, and he hadn't known about that? She hadn't told him? Was it possible that the pressure I put on her made her resentful, causing her to turn on me? Pat had shut me off around that same time I'd been forthright with Lenore. Of course, this was also when I'd told Emily I wasn't publishing her story.

I didn't know the answer then, and I don't know now. But indelible in my mind is how genuinely surprised he was about my entreaties to Lenore on Emily's behalf. And had Lenore indeed turned Susannah against him—"the most painful heartbreak" of his life, as he told me? Had she ruined his life, as he'd claimed? That was surely an exaggeration. His father had done that. Still . . .

I retired from Paideia the following year. I truly loved the place, Paul, my fellow teachers, certainly the kids in my classroom and their parents, but I was sixty-two, at heart a small-town boy, and I was ready to come home. Like so many independent schools at the time, Paideia had begun in 1971 as a radical argument against traditional education. My agreement with Paul when I came was that I could teach any way I wanted. "Why not?" he'd said at the time. "Nobody knows what to do with junior high kids anyway." Which was true.

The school had not only survived, it had prospered, but as the times grew less radical and more conservative, so did the school in general, while the longer I taught, the more I learned from my students, the more progressive I became. For example, the better my students' writing became, the more flak I'd get from the more conservative quarters of the community. Political correctness was a literary assassin, and to avoid the school, the kids, and, needless to say, myself getting hit— much to Paul's relief, I'm sure—I stopped publishing *Hidden Places*.

One of Pat's favorite kids during my first year at Paideia was David Biederman—terrifically bright, excitable about anything and everything, hyper, funny as hell, and, as his parents Sandy and Jolayne, who adored him and found him amusing, took pains to explain to me, "full of shit," which was their theory as to why he could talk a great game but couldn't put pen to paper.

He was skinny and Jewish and nerdy and wore glasses, entirely unathletic running around all over the playground or gym accomplishing absolutely nothing, much like he did in class, putting out weird theories of alligator farms in Florida and stories about how he was working out a deal with "their people" to bring at least one to Paideia. One morning after Pat dropped his kids off at the elementary school and stopped by my classroom just to say hello and to see if anything interesting was happening, David brought up the alligator farm to Pat, no doubt hoping for an investment, which Pat found hysterical.

"Where are you going to put them, David, in the bathtub?"

There was still one in the bathroom at the time.

David was always entwining and twitching his fingers, his eyes lighting up, looking like a mad scientist: "Good idea, Pat! In fact, now that I think about it, an *excellent* idea. I'll get to work on that! Right!"

So, naturally, thirty-three years later, Paul arranged for David to speak at my retirement party at Manuel's Tavern. Pat couldn't come. He joked he was worried about his fame and celebrity status taking attention away from me. I think his diabetes was acting up. The idea of David speaking, however, almost got him there.

David was now a highly respected author and professor of international law at Emory, and he told the story of how I finally got him to write.

Bernie's classroom, he began, on the first floor of an old Georgian mansion, included a living room converted into a classroom, a kitchen converted into a conference room, and study area, bathroom, and wardrobe closet turned into a study area with a small table and bench surrounding it that could accommodate two or three kids. It was a pretty small space.

It was in this wardrobe closet, he said, that he learned to write. Bernie was going crazy, his parents were going crazy. He simply couldn't bring himself to put words on paper. He talked a great game, he explained, and he talked incessantly, but writing? It just didn't come. Had he wanted to do it? Yes. Had he needed to do it? Yes. But in the end, all he could do was talk about it.

Martha was also a teacher of his. Her idea, since he got so excited talking, was to have him talk while she wrote down his words, like they did with kids in the preschool, until he was able to take over the writing himself. The problem there was that he liked that *too* much; he loved telling stories, he just couldn't write them.

Bernie and his parents agreed, David went on, that they had no idea why he couldn't write, and trying to figure out why was an exercise in frustration and futility.

The wardrobe closet was Bernie's last resort. His parents agreed. During school hours, while other kids were in classes, David would be in the closet. After school hours, he would remain in the closet. He could leave it only to go to the bathroom. He could come out only when he'd written ten pages or a complete story. There was no escape. At night Bernie and his parents would bring him food, and they would take shifts in turns, at which time he could not talk with them and they would not talk with him. Once he'd completed the writing assignment, he was to slip it under the door and wait for Bernie to read it.

Pleas of "I've got it, I've got it," "Open the door," fell on deaf ears. They would only respond to writing slipped under the door.

It took an entire school day, that night, and most of the following day to do it, but he got it done. He'd never been so excited in his life. Bernie thought it was terrific; naturally, so did he, and Bernie read it to the class.

The problem for Bernie, he said, was that he couldn't stop writing after that, including a seventy-page story about the mayhem created all over the world when the Earth tilted too far off its axis, which Bernie had to read. Bernie hated science fiction, especially seventy pages of it from a thirteen-year-old kid. However, he had it easier than David's parents. They had to listen to him read it aloud, all seventy pages.

He had no more trouble writing after his experience in the wardrobe closet. After graduating from law school, he had penned seven respectable books published by Oxford University Press and Harvard University Press.

He did find, he concluded, that he did most of his writing on planes, in close quarters, with passengers on either side of him. The more crowded, the better.

Why not? He had learned to write in a closet.

Now, in the year 2006, could I have gotten away with that unorthodox approach? Not a chance. If I couldn't truly take risks, I was ready to retire. Avoiding risks, I'd learned, at least in many cases, meant perpetuating problems. If there's a risk, Pat used to tell my classes, take it.

I couldn't wait to get back to Beaufort, to get back home. At sixty-two, I could begin collecting social security. I could do some teaching there, write, do a few workshops. Martha could begin a practice in Beaufort, which she did. Pat was there. Sandra was to become a dear, dear friend. Mom was there. My brother Aaron and his wife, Nancy, had retired there. I could see my older brother Stanley and his wife Isabelle, both of whom worked in Washington, when they came down to visit Mom. Old friends who'd gotten me through high school like Billy Canaday were ready to throw me a party. Billy Keyserling, then in real estate, could get Martha and me a house.

Juanita Washington was there. I wanted to drop by and visit with her like in the old days.

"She's got Alzheimer's," Pat told me upon my return. "She won't even know who you are."

Together we attended her funeral.

XV

BEAUFORT, ONCE AGAIN

The Beaufort years were great, they were fabulous, just lovely and beautiful and fun. Ten years, ten years. A treasure, I can safely say, for both of us. And on those few occasions when they weren't, not only did the Jew compulsively speak up and talk about it, but something had happened to the dissociated Irish Catholic: he could talk about it too. And not only could he talk about it, it came naturally, instinctively, and easily to him.

He was now diabetic, physically soft, did not exercise at all, and walked as slowly as he drove. Well, almost as slowly. Walking, he at least moved forward. I could get impatient. It took him forever to get anywhere; I was always having to pull up and wait for him.

We'd park downtown, then walk over to Blackstone's or Wren's for lunch. I'd be starving. But not only was he slow, he'd have to stop and talk to every single tourist, all the locals, pet their dogs, kiss their babies, ask about people they both might have known. He'd even ask about their businesses, how things were going, understanding absolutely nothing of what they said and having absolutely no interest in the subject. "Fascinating," I'd note afterwards, "just fascinating." That was space-out time for both of us, after which we'd talk about what we'd been privately daydreaming about. "Where'd you go?" I'd ask him. "Where'd you go?" he'd ask me. Then we'd stand there on the sidewalk arguing about who went where first.

Pat was so indiscriminately hospitable he'd stop the horse and carriage tours and welcome all the passengers with open arms, even if they didn't know who the hell he was.

Afterwards: "The horses are crying, Pat. You neglected to kiss them. They feel left out."

"Oh darn, you're right. Wait, I'll go back."

Or: "The restaurant's closing, Pat. Can you hurry the fuck up?"

At which time he'd start walking backwards on purpose.

Beaufort was now a resort town, a tourist town. Where once you couldn't find a stranger when you went downtown, now they were everywhere. It was like a miniature Charleston. With so much development overwhelming the natural beauty of the Southeastern coast, *Travel and Leisure* and *Condé Nast* and *Southern Living* were hailing Beaufort as one of "the best small towns in America" and the "most romantic," "The Last Paradise." Beaufort had fought overdevelopment and was still fighting it, with Pat now taking the lead. For developers and most of the local politicians, green meant pro-money, not pro-environment, and they were as bloodsucking as mosquitos. Check their back pockets, my mom told Pat and me, if you were looking for the motives of the local politicians, many of them our friends, When the pro-development alliance proposed sixteen thousand new homes, which would increase Beaufort traffic by at least twenty thousand more cars, we met with conservationists, retirees, and Beaufort natives and locals, rallied five hundred people for a public protest, and, with Pat's celebrity bringing in the television cameras from all over the Lowcountry, halted that development in its tracks, "changing politics in Beaufort forever," according to city councilman Mike Sutton.

Like my brother Aaron said, it had been fun, a great way to spend our time. Of course, he was retired. And it was only right, he pointed out, that Pat should lead the charge. After all, with Pat's books and the movies made from them, he had put Beaufort on the map, all but issuing the developers an invitation. Great to be on the map, he said, but on our terms. It's our town, not the developers' and politicians'—or as Pat put it, not for sale. Barbara Streisand and Nick Nolte, Tom Hanks and Robin Wright, Robert Duvall and Blythe Danner and Michael O'Keefe, Kevin Kline and Glenn Close had all starred in movies made at Tidalholm. Producers had plantation homes here. Tom Berenger lived here. It was now a haven for retirees. Where once the *New York Times* had been banned, there was now one in every fourth or fifth driveway. Lincoln Center's Charles Wadsworth annually presented his chamber music ensemble here.

The sad truth was, it was because Pat had drunk himself into a physical wreck that he was slow as hell. At lunch, there were times when I could tell he could hardly digest the food or taste it. He'd nibble cautiously, then box it all up for Sandra to eat later.

Pat had been an absolute aficionado of food. His taste was impeccable. One day at a downtown restaurant I will not name we were both having boiled shrimp. We were looking forward to it because it was shrimp season in the Lowcountry. Pat took a few tiny bites of one and said, "Bernie, these are good."

They most certainly were not good. Not only were they not local, they weren't even fresh. They were frozen. Any Lowcountry resident would have known that at once, and not so long before, Pat would have been the first among them.

He'd gained too much weight. That was a worry too. Sandra fed him wisely and carefully, but because he got no exercise we joined the Y and went to the gym. He wanted to see if I still had my jump shot. So, like when we were young, he'd talk about getting the oven heated up, which meant he wanted to rebound the ball and pass it to me until I got hot.

I was surprised. It was so sad. He tried his best, but any movement toward the ball on his part was dangerous, so prone was he to falling. The greatest ball-handler the Citadel had ever seen could no longer even dribble standing still. So that's what we worked on, and he lied, standing there, only dribbling, up, down, up, down, "It's coming back," he said.

"It is, isn't it? I think it is, Pat."

"I can feel it."

He broke my heart that day.

Sandra and I were both frustrated. He'd go the Y and exercise, but he still wasn't taking care of himself and, as always, was drinking too much.

Evidently, I wasn't entirely taking care of myself either. I took thyroid medication daily and had run out. Still in Atlanta closing out her practice, Martha had prepared me for this eventuality, giving me the phone number to call and reorder, but I'd forgotten about it. After a few weeks I began losing weight. I felt I was jumping out of my skin I was so anxious. I couldn't eat. I had no idea what was happening. I could barely leave my bedroom, much less the house. I could barely get out of bed. Talking on the phone was like trying to find your way at night through a dark strange house in which the electricity is off. I had acid reflux, which I'd never had before, and it was getting progressively worse. I was in bed so much my back, which had given me problems forever, was spasming. The emotional pain I was feeling was so agonizing, so unbearably chaotic, and terrifying, however, I yearned for the back pain to continue, for the reality of it to somehow ground me.

Finally, I began hallucinating, which I'd never done before. A spaceship appeared in my bedroom like a high-rise condominium to take me off to another planet, to who knows where. It was frightening, because I was too weak to get out of bed to do anything about it. Was I to get in the spaceship? Who, what, was at the controls? I had no control over myself, my mind, or my body. A knife appeared in my hand. Was it to kill me? I fought against it. Was I supposed to go into the bathroom and kill myself? The spaceship, the knife, appearing, recurring, over and over.

Pat was calling every afternoon from Highlands, North Carolina, where he and Sandra were vacationing, the only time I could bring myself to talk at all. I can't tell you how empathetic, how sweet, how wonderful he was. He knew just what to say. Did the depression lift? Of course not. But his attentiveness was reassuring.

He and Sandra returned to Fripp. He phoned, telling me they wanted to drive into Beaufort and take me to lunch. He asked me what Martha had said when I'd last talked with her on the phone.

"I told her I was depressed, but she said she didn't want to talk about it, that it was too boring, that she talked to depressed people all day."

Which was true. Since I'd never been depressed, she probably assumed I just missed her or wanted a little attention. Besides, she was coming to Beaufort that weekend anyway, she'd see me then.

The next day was Thursday, Martha had decided to come down a day early, and when she saw me she looked terrified, stunned. For one thing, I'd lost so much weight. She arrived just in time to meet Pat and Sandra for lunch.

At Barbara Jean's seafood restaurant, I tried to put on a cheerful face, for some reason, probably because Pat and Martha and Sandra were looking at me like they'd never seen me before. I tried to eat but ended up just pushing the food around on my plate. I tried to laugh, to show my appreciation, if Pat said something funny, but all I could offer really was a painfully weak smile.

By the time Martha and I got back home, there was a phone message from Pat. "I know this is a sensitive thing to talk about, but Bernie, I just don't want to lose you, not again. Sandra and I are both sufferers, as you know, from depression. Yours is worse than anything we've been through. We've talked about it. I think your depression is somehow physical. It's different from ours."

How had he known? He was right, of course, but I had had no idea at the time. I hadn't paid much attention to the message, but Martha even before hearing it was packing up a suitcase to take me to the hospital.

In the hospital, I can't stop crying. They have me in a wheelchair wheeling me to my room, and along the way people ask me what's wrong, and all I can say is, "I'm depressed, I'm depressed," bawling my eyes out.

Martha's sitting at my bedside. Some kind of doctor comes in with a clipboard asking me questions that mostly Martha answers, the usual ones they ask everyone once they're in the hospital. Then: "What medications, if any, are you taking?"

"Levothyroxine . . . But now that I think about it, I haven't taken it in five or six weeks."

Martha's jaw dropped. This apparently was her second shock of the day. I thought she might faint. "You haven't been taking your thyroid meds?"

"They never sent them."

That's when it hit her. I saw it on her face. "You haven't taken your meds in five or six weeks, Bernie?"

"I told you. They never sent them."

"You just stopped them all at once?" asked the doctor. "Cold turkey? Just suddenly stopping thyroid medication, by itself, can cause depression. You stopped taking it all at once? That's one hell of a shock to the system."

That was enough for Martha. She took me home, called the insurance company, which overnighted the meds. I was feeling better just knowing the cause and the problem.

The thyroid, Martha and the doctor told me, regulates mood, and therefore can have everything to do with depression. Pat had been right. The cause had been physical. And the doctor had been right: just suddenly going off the thyroid medication can result in a "thyroid storm," a downpour of depression.

I had had no idea that the thyroid had anything to do with mood and depression. Neither had Pat. I called him when I got home from the hospital. You know what he said?

"You know what's going to happen now, Bernie? The "thyroid" causing depression is all you're going to hear about now. It'll come up all over the place. Just watch."

The next morning, I get up, and walk outside on my front porch, first time in five or six weeks. It's bright and sunny. My next-door neighbor, Andy Woichicheski, is washing his car in his driveway.

"Hey, Bernie? Where you been? Haven't seen you."

"Depressed."

He looked up, curious.

"Oh," he said. Then: "Thyroid?"

Back in the house I switched on the television, PBS: a documentary about an elderly artist who'd spent decades in the insane asylum before the doctors discovered it had been caused by his thyroid, after which they adjusted his medication and released him, free of depression for the rest of his life.

Boy, was he pissed off. All that time in the looney bin, and it was his thyroid?

For the first time in over a month, I go out with Pat and Aaron for lunch at Steamers. Pat's hearing aids weren't working too well that day, but I saw my brother Aaron's ears perk up. Naturally, he knew all about my depression, the meds, the thyroid, Pat's sentience, the whole business. Anyway, he was overhearing something interesting at the table next to us. By the time I tuned in, I could pretty much pick up what they were talking about, particularly when once again the words "thyroid" and "depression" were used in the same sentence.

"Should we tell Pat," Aaron asked, "Or will he get too cocky?"

"Synchronicity," he explained. "I adjusted my hearing aids when I saw Aaron's ears about to pull up a chair at our neighboring table."

'Synchronicity?' What the hell was that? I asked him.

Aaron didn't give a shit. His food had arrived.

"Literature," Pat said. "Jesus, Bernie, do I need to spell it out for you? Literature? Coincidence? Synchronicity is about coincidences somehow connecting, relating. The world picks up on these things. Everything's circular. One thing can't help but connect and relate to another, once you learn what that one thing is, which you just did, and it becomes part of the collective consciousness, then the world of coincidence opens up to you. Jesus, what a genius I am."

"The experience sure opened my eyes."

"I rest my case, thank you, thank you, all around."

"What goes around comes around."

"Jesus, Aaron, can you believe this? Bernie's an idiot!"

"Oh sure, I can believe that," Aaron said, his mouth full of pasta.

Craig Washington, a local musician Pat had taught in high school, and I were chatting at the church reception following his mother's funeral. His mother was our old friend, Juanita Washington. We were talking about old times, commenting on who was there at the reception, when he spotted Pat in the fried chicken and collard greens buffet line.

"Ol' Pat," he said chuckling, "ol' Pat, that boy been eatin' a lot of 'poke' lately."

I thought this was funny as hell: "Ol' Pat been eatin' a lot of 'poke' lately."

So, sitting down next to Pat and his fried chicken, I couldn't wait to tell him. I honestly thought he'd think it was funny too. Pat enjoyed laughing at himself more than anyone I knew. Craig was over there off to the side in the crowd milling about, still chuckling.

Pat did look like he'd been puttin' down a lot of poke recently, but I can't use that as an excuse. Facts didn't mean anything. Humor did, almost always. Intimacy did. And Craig couldn't have said that to just anybody. Right?

I'll tell you this: he sure couldn't have said it to Pat, because when *I* did Pat went apeshit, in front of our entire table, most of them elderly black women except for the preacher's wife.

"See, this is what you do, Bernie. Jesus, who would say that to somebody? I can't believe it. Nobody, nobody. Why would you do this? It's not funny. It's not funny."

It wasn't? I thought it was. I thought it would be to him. Frankly, I was embarrassed. About his physical appearance Pat was as vain, I realized more and more, as he was modest. In that way, and only in that way as far as I could tell, Pat was like everyone else. Until then, I saw him as entirely unique.

But what really struck me, beyond all expectation, was his honesty, his directness. Pat was pissed off, and *in the moment* he'd told me.

Did this mean we had a future together? I believed it did. Did it mean also that he was so physically decrepit now that his fear of his father's rage exploding inside him, napalming everyone close to him, had subsided? That he had come to realize that guerilla warfare—his passive-aggressive behavior, his taking his bat and ball and going home when he couldn't tell his intimates he was mad at them—had been self-defeating?

Had he learned something else about himself over the last fifteen years? The failure of our friendship, also of his friendship with Jim Landon, with whom he'd breakfasted every Sunday morning in Atlanta; the failure, though to a smaller degree, of his friendship with Cliff—and with who knows who else. His loneliness afterwards was for one reason and one reason only, and it must have been extremely painful for him: he couldn't trust himself to tell us *why* he'd been upset with us, why, in short, he'd been angry, even that he *had* been angry. At least he'd been unable to tell me.

I could never be close friends with someone I couldn't truly talk to. Had Pat learned that he couldn't either? That in an intimate, lifelong relationship, it's inevitable that at some point you're going to profoundly piss each other off?

If in his close relationships his father's rage had been kept on the back burner, as it had been with me, had he subsequently learned that getting mad and expressing it was not as scary as he might have imagined? That if he didn't, the only thing left to do was to leave, creating even greater loneliness, greater suffering, in the wake of departure?

Time would prove that he had indeed learned to say openly to me what he felt, hopefully also to Jim Landon, Cliff, and perhaps other friends. I can't speak for them.

With us, the recurrent theme of his life, estrangement and reconciliation, had played out, as with his father and the Citadel.

What of his estrangement from Susannah, whom he adored, and Lenore, whom he had once adored? From Pat, there was blame, scapegoating, and righteous indignation, as there had been with his father, the Citadel, his friends, but unlike with us, there came no reconciliation. And as much as he wanted it with Susannah, his rage against Lenore had gotten in his way. About Lenore, his tongue was lethal, as it had been about us. Did Lenore deserve it, as his father had? Susannah was a child when he left; she certainly didn't.

One of the first things Pat told me when we reconciled was that Susannah had visited him and Sandra on Fripp Island back in 1998 and again in 1999. Why had Lenore allowed the visits if she was turning Susannah against him, as he also said? Susannah was still living with her. Pat's answer: she had come as a "spy," an "informer" for Lenore, with whom Pat was warring over alimony and child support.

Sandra confided to me that during her second visit in 1999 Pat had said hurtful things to Susannah about her writing, to which at the time she was devoted. Susannah clearly adored and admired Pat, but when he offered to mentor her, it was clear she preferred the tutelage of a particular creative writing teacher in San Francisco, which hurt Pat's feelings. Remember too, Sandra said, he was drunk as hell the whole time. What exactly had he said? Sandra couldn't quite recall—she did vaguely remember words like "overblown"—but whatever the words, most hurtful was his tone, which had a "Santini-lash" quality to it.

That was the last time, Sandra said, he had seen or heard from her.

Shouldn't we remind Pat of this? I asked her. Time has passed. He's dying to get her back.

Oh, as soon as he sobered up and realized what he'd done, he was horrified. He wrote her the sweetest letter in the world just apologizing profusely, wanting to do anything and everything to make up for it, but by that time so much shit had hit the fan with him and Lenore, it was too late, Bernie. Too late.

You know what else is so sad to me, Bernie? If you brought it up to him now, he would have no idea what you were talking about. He was just too drunk then. And not just depressed—he'd been suicidal. It'd just confuse him. And for what? Right now, there's not a damn thing he can do about it.

When Emily visited Beaufort and went out to dinner with Martha and me, Maggie, her husband Jonathan, and Pat, I asked her to please let me know if I'd done anything to hurt her when she was in my class. If I had screwed up in any way at all, would she please let me know so I could somehow make up for it? Pat was so uneasy, so clearly uncomfortable, particularly when I brought up Emily's story, that he could never go back to that restaurant again.

She couldn't remember my reading her story to the class, their standing ovation, the great love and support, the admiration not only for her story but for her courage, the empathy and understanding. None of it, which even now I find curious. Maybe it was a threat, a reminder, if she had remembered it, of what she hadn't gotten.

Her only response: "Why didn't you publish it?"

I was delighted to hear her ask and answered exactly as I had back when she was in my class. Pat just looked so disturbed, so uncomfortable, almost pained, hurt, or at least threatened by it, I couldn't stand it. Was he uncomfortable because he could remember, or because he couldn't? Because he couldn't, or because he wouldn't allow himself to?

Or was it just coincidental that he was so disturbed while we were talking about Emily's story going unpublished? Turned out it probably was. Emily was staying at their house on Fripp Island. When she wasn't spending time "projectile vomiting," as she referred to it, probably due to anxiety, Pat felt, she would complain there was no food in the refrigerator, which there was, according to Sandra, food Sandra had bought just for her.

While she was there, Pat told me, he received a phone call from his accountant in Atlanta. Pat gave Emily a $500 monthly allowance, and Ed, his accountant, would unfailingly send her the check at the same time every month. Maybe Emily had needed the money earlier this month, but for whatever reason she had phoned Ed loudly, angrily, haughtily demanding her check at once, reminding him as if he were a mere peon that she was a Conroy: "Do you know who I am?"

Pat was furious. She was using his last name as her own and pulling rank in a way that just embarrassed the hell out of him.

Pat wasn't the man he'd been. Tired, fat, sick of fighting, diabetic, weak, at this point in his life he was looking for a little peace and contentment, a respite from all the chaos in his past, of which Emily, through no fault of her own, had been such a recent part. He had rescued her from her father, had tried to save her from herself, from her suicidal urges. Now he just wanted to write, sit on his porch and smoke cigars, read, drink liquor and hide the empty bottles from Sandra, watch the news on television (he was a self-described "news junkie"), and talk the time away either on the phone, on my front porch, or his.

And that very afternoon, no doubt unaware of Ed's phone call to Pat, Emily had asked him if he would be her father.

He was her stepfather, he finally told her. He was not her father. She was close to forty years old. He wondered: had she always wanted him to adopt her? Much as he loved her, much as he'd cared not only about her but for her, charming, amusing, and personable as she was, this damsel in distress he could not save.

By the time he'd gotten to the restaurant, he told me on the phone later that evening, he was shaken to the core. His discomfort came from trying so hard to hide it. As to taking care of her, he just felt he had given all he could.

If she ever treated Ed that way again, he also told me, he was taking away her allowance.

Right.

And as for her story, its nonpublication, why he'd abandoned our friendship, that he'd abandoned it at all: after that evening, it just didn't seem so important anymore. It remained what it was, a minor chapter in the greater, heartbreaking tragedy of Emily.

As to the friendship between Pat and me, I was learning. Now that Pat seemed to be able to express himself intimately and honestly to me and with me, we were probably closer in these last ten years than we'd ever been.

When I wrote something he didn't much like, he didn't avoid stating what he felt. I'd written a very personal piece about the Jewish cemetery in Beaufort and the Jews who were buried there for an anthology entitled *State of the Heart*, which would be published by University of South Carolina Press. It comprised essays by South Carolina writers about places in South Carolina that in some important way were memorable for them. I loved mine. To this day, looking at it again, I still love it. Pat didn't, referring to it as "Bernie-lite," probably meaning sentimental; I'm not sure.

"I'm sorry, Bernie; I wish I could give you more on this."

"Don't worry about it, Pat. You're giving me everything."

He was.

A bestselling novelist had ridiculed him for spending so much time signing books and talking with readers. Why do it, he'd asked Pat, if you don't need to?

"Do you know why, Bernie? I'm afraid," he said helplessly, "that they'll stop coming."

His daughter Susannah, now around twenty-five years old and living with Lenore, was still refusing to see him. "My greatest hurt," he told me then. "What can I do? I write her letters, but I think Lenore gets to them first and hides them. When I'm in Atlanta, I leave notes on the door, but with Lenore there, I doubt she even sees them. A couple of times I've knocked on the door and waited, calling out her name. Once, through a window I think I saw her hiding. Lenore's gotten to her. Neither one of them will even open the door for Cliff, bless his heart for trying."

Someone who had been close to both Pat and Lenore had told Pat that after he left San Francisco Lenore found a stack of letters to women with whom he'd had affairs and read them to Susannah. Several years later, this same person told me that if Susannah had expressed any tendency to repair the relationship with Pat, Lenore would have begun "working" on her.

He was vulnerable, and he showed it, whether he was drinking or not. Most of his bluff and bravado had all but disappeared.

Had mine? I asked him, puffing away on his back porch.

"Nah, you're just as fucked up as ever."

The problem to which I keep returning was that he was still drinking way too much. The anxiety would usually hit him around 5:00 p.m. after he'd finished writing for the day, and sometimes he'd drink so late into the night he'd be fairly high the next morning. This was in 2007. He was working on *South of Broad*, and he was working hard, but he knew when not to, when it would just be a waste of time and energy, when the story seemed elusive and inaccessible to him. He knew when writing could get him to the story, and he knew when to wait for it to come to him. I marveled at his confidence, but he'd been at it a long time.

Often, he'd show up at my house around lunch, and we'd drive all over the Lowcountry looking for interesting spots. They were everywhere: tiny lovely prayer houses out on the islands; a nest of ospreys atop a telephone pole; avenues of oaks heralding the old plantations; cemeteries; blackwater swamps; backwater rivers; glorious sunsets and ocean vistas, brilliant fruit and vegetable stands; the Old Sheldon Church ruins on the road to Yemassee, which, with sunlight filtering through a canopy of leaves, was, Pat felt, "the most beautiful road in South Carolina," which is why it appeared in his novels; my favorite, the nearby Yoruba African Village on the road to Pocotaligo, welcoming tourists with a sign suggesting an authentic African village "As Seen on Prime Time" national television. My least favorite jaunt: his back-road route that he assured me would keep us off the crowded highways during a hurricane evacuation, which seemed a lot more important to him than to me.

Sometimes we'd stop by Scott Graber's law office in Beaufort, where John Warley was also working at the time, both old Citadel buddies of Pat's. Scott had spent a lot of time in Africa, was even writing a novel about it: *Ten Days in Brazzaville*. Ten days? Only ten days? Pat would tease. "In my real life, Pat, just to clarify, significantly more than that."

On one of these occasions I asked Scott about that Yoruba African Village just off the highway on the road to Pocotaligo.

Turns out Scott had paid a visit to the village while he was representing a nearby landowner who'd complained that the villagers were wringing the necks of chickens, sacrificing them while performing ancient rituals.

"The villagers are actually from Detroit, Bernie. And I did go out there and indeed met with the chief. Needless to say, gentlemen, Detroit is not in Africa, but the chief did look resplendent, I might add, in African robes. He also had an African name, which despite my time in Africa, I frankly cannot come close to pronouncing. Present at the meeting are the chief himself, his interpreter and translator, and I, the inimitable Scott Graber, attorney at law, right here in our lovely town of Beaufort, South Carolina.

"The interpreter explains to me the proper protocol for addressing the chief: I am neither to look directly at him nor speak directly to him. I must present myself humbly, head lowered, when the chief speaks.

"When the chief speaks, he will speak into the ear of the interpreter. The interpreter will then speak into my ear, translating the chief's Africanese into English, after which I may speak into the ear of the interpreter, who will then speak into the ear of the chief, translating my English into Africanese.

"So, what, no doubt you're wondering, happened?"

"We are," said John, "to state the obvious."

"Nothing," said Scott. "Nothing. You want to know, as did my client, what was discussed, decided, negotiated. A perfectly reasonable expectation, I must add. Indeed. Were they slaughtering chickens in ancient rituals? Did they have an acceptable explanation? Could we reach an agreement, some sort of compromise that might satisfy my client as well our African villagers from Detroit? The chief and his interpreter were speaking in a dubious facsimile of Africanese in each other's ear, which I couldn't possibly understand, and which I began wondering whether they could either, particularly once the interpreter began translating what the chief said into my right ear. There were in the verbal atrocities committed against my right ear a few vague Old Testament references to Abraham and Isaac, who it may surprise you to hear, in the considered judgment of the chief, were black. No doubt, in their minds, about that. No doubt, in their minds, about anything. No doubt, in their minds, about the incomprehensibility and the absurdity of this entire triage. Who was I talking to? Who was talking to me? I was to arrange a compromise with African villagers from *Detroit*? Who were they, really? I bowed humbly, thanked the interpreter politely, who relayed my thanks into the ear of the chief, and left."

"What did you tell your client?"

"Whatever they were doing with the chickens could not possibly be worse, under any circumstances, than what they were doing to me."

Pat told us about Queen Quet, professed queen of the entire Gullah-Geechee nation in the Lowcountry. Had she too, like the Yoruba villagers, been featured on national television? Not that he knew of, but she had been given special recognition and been honored by the United Nations.

"Really?" John asked. "Was she from Detroit too?"

"Through her emissary," Pat told us, "she asked me to appear on the dais with her and to speak, along with her, at some kind of event having to do with the 'Gullah-Geechee Nation.' I can't remember exactly what it was. What I do remember is that, yes, John, she was from Detroit, which did strike me at the time as odd, but I was ready to show up and help—I certainly wanted to support Gullah-Geechee culture—until the emissary informed me that the invitation was conditional, something that always raises the alarm for me, the condition being that, just as you, Scott, had to address the Yoruba chief as Chief, I had to address Queen Quet as *Queen* Quet, which I thought was the most ridiculous thing I'd ever heard."

"I told him to tell her that I would be delighted to address her as Queen Quet if I could address her as 'Queen Quet from Detroit' and if she would agree in her speech to address, however briefly, the problems of the auto industry in Detroit."

"Did no one ever question this stuff?" I wondered aloud.

"Of course not, Bernie. Political correctness: if a white guy questions it, he's a racist. If a black person questions it, he's accused by his own people of making them look like a bunch of hustlers. It's just bullshit, that's all. At Penn, Scott, when you were working there? You were working your ass off on the 'heir's property' issue: did anyone address this there? You had standing."

"If you remember, Bernie, Agnes was there."

Often we'd join my brother Aaron for lunch at Steamers on Lady's Island, where Aaron liked the mussels, Pat liked shucking oysters, John and I liked the gumbo, and Scott liked watching Pat so politely and graciously pausing, dabbing at his mouth, for photos with tourists.

Afterwards, Pat and I would lounge about on my front porch, where we'd smoke Saint Luis Rey cigars, which Pat always bought because he was rich and I wasn't, and talk until twilight, at which point he'd head back to Fripp.

The women's shelter was a few houses down and across the street from my home. We'd imagine what it might have been like had it existed in the forties and fifties and his mother, Peg, had walked in with Pat and his siblings trailing behind. Might that that changed their lives? For better or worse? Would they have ended up on the streets, ultimately without financial support? Would they have survived and come out in better shape? "Not without a sugar daddy," Pat concluded.

A friend of ours who really didn't like us all that much once told us in the nicest way, right before she walked off in a huff, that she preferred talking about "ideas, not people." There is just no question that we truly, especially if Sandra or Martha were with us, got off on gossip. We loved talking about people, especially about people we knew, including ourselves. My brother Aaron, as I said, often stopped by and joined us on the porch to give us the latest on the quality or lack thereof of any new food on the menu at the local restaurants and also, for a while at least, a report on how I was faring under his tutelage in the intricacies of finance.

Since Martha was so busy with her psychology practice and I had finished *If Holden Caulfield Were in My Classroom*, a book of stories mostly written in Atlanta about my time at Paideia (for which Pat offered to write the introduction), and I was only teaching creative writing here and there, I figured it was time for me to grow up, become a man, and take over the handling of our finances. A retired banker, Aaron began teaching me. We'd often work together over at Mom's house while she cooked or played the piano for us. At ninety-five she could still enchant us with Liszt's Second Hungarian Rhapsody or the Warsaw Concerto. Mom and Aaron and Pat and Martha all knew that dealing with numbers was not my forte. My tutor in math in high school fired me as her pupil, her only dismissal of a pupil ever. Mom was therefore watching my progress with interest, I'd explained to Pat, which caused him to erupt into laughter, not that he was any good at it either. At one point, he was so broke, with his house on Fripp in such need of repair, that Aaron and his wife, Nancy, had to go ski in Colorado so he and Sandra could live for a few months in their condo. They liked it there, particularly when through the picture window a full moon showed over the Beaufort River.

So, Aaron drops over one afternoon, plops down on the porch, and Pat asks him about my progress.

"Well, just today while I was in the grocery store with Mom, she gave *her* progress report. She said to me, 'After all your work with him, how come Bernie still doesn't know a thing about finances?'"

"'Well, Mom,' I explained, 'he doesn't have the mind for it.'"

"To which she said: 'You mean he's stupid?'"

"'Exactly.'"

"'Well now,' she said, thinking about it, 'that makes sense, it sure does.'"

Sometimes Mom would drop over. She was almost completely deaf now, though it didn't seem to affect her piano playing. Pat liked watching us yell at each other. She'd come over and watch the Westerns on Turner cable. The sound was muted, but it didn't matter. She followed the story, not missing a thing because she was raised on silent movies. When Pat and I watched them with her, we discovered we didn't need the sound either. The dialogue, Pat noted, having worked on the screenplay for *Prince of Tides*, was the least important thing in a screenplay.

Pat was the most generous book supplier imaginable. Sometimes we'd read passages we loved (or brief ones we hated) aloud to each other, sometimes we'd talk about new books, often we'd return to the classics, especially great beginnings: *The Adventures of Augie March, 100 Years of Solitude, Look Homeward, Angel*; and great endings: Andre

Schwartz-Bart's *The Last of the Just*, *You Can't Go Home Again*, *Tender Is the Night.*

We often talked about *South of Broad* at that particular time, with Pat trying out story and plot lines in which his alter ego, Leo Bloom, Leo's lifelong friend, Molly Rutledge, and their childhood friend who has become a major movie star, the beautiful Sheba Poe, are major characters. Their friendship has persevered through their adult lives. Hurricane Hugo and a porpoise, Pat explains, also play major parts.

A friend of ours, a military brat from Beaufort who had become something of a minor actress, inspired Pat's Sheba. Sheba's mother is based on a woman we both knew living in Charleston with her daughter, with whom Pat had become very close. In an advanced state of Alzheimer's, oblivious to all but a hallucinatory threat, she stabbed her daughter to death.

Pat had been talking about this for quite a while, so it was interesting to see him turn our military brat-cum-actress into Sheba only to have Sheba become his friend from Charleston stabbed to death by her mother, who becomes Sheba's mother who in the advanced stages of Alzheimer's stabs her daughter Sheba to death.

He'd also been talking a lot about the details surrounding Hurricane Hugo, which attacked Charleston mercilessly back in 1989. Hurricane Hugo, he now tells me, at this point in the manuscript of *South of Broad* has utterly destroyed Charleston and Sullivan's Island, where in the wake of the storm Leo and Molly are going through the debris in her family's devastated beach house.

"Wasn't the bridge out? How'd they get out there?"

"Molly rounds up a motorboat. So they're going through the debris, looking for Molly's family photograph albums, anything they can find, when they stumble across a porpoise barely alive, stranded on some stray cushions."

"Snowball?" Snowball was a white porpoise around here Pat had made legendary in his writings.

"No. They manage to wrap the porpoise in blankets, Molly cleans out his blow hole, they get him to the beach where a school of porpoises happily await him as he dives into the ocean as alive as he's ever been."

"Keep going."

"I can't. I can't figure out who that porpoise is, why it's there."

"It's Sheba!"

And Sheba the porpoise became. It brings her back. Molly and Leo later visit her out in the ocean when they're boating where she so happily greets them, frolicking and leaping about. Now we know why.

Often particular books mirrored us in ways we didn't realize until we began talking about them, or even much later. Pat was particularly interested in his discovery of David Herbert Donald's biography of Thomas Wolfe, in which Donald exposes as myth the idea that Wolfe's renowned editor, Maxwell Perkins, had so brilliantly transformed Wolfe's work into a cohesive narrative. Delighted—for a reason I was unaware of at the time—he reported that Donald presents Perkins's cuts and, after reading them, Pat went back to Wolfe's work and concluded that Perkins had been wrong and that Wolfe's work would have been better without him. Interesting.

If Pat got hungry or thirsty, he'd rummage through the refrigerator and join me on the porch with a glass of tomato juice or a Diet Coke. I'd have gotten it for him, but I was too lazy. He did teach me to make jugo, that Italian pasta, and by phone how to cook crabs, but by the time the water started boiling they were screaming like banshees, which I hadn't expected, and were crawling out of the pot, into the living room, and ended up all over the neighborhood, a parade of crabs.

Pat never drank liquor during this time, when he would be driving. He stayed on my front porch as long as possible, so he wouldn't drink. He knew it was waiting for him at home.

He was suffering, and it wasn't because of Santini, and it wasn't because of Lenore. It was because of Nan Talese, he told me, his editor at Doubleday. Her criticism of his work, in manuscript form, on his novel *South of Broad*, was confusing, didn't make sense to him, just as the cuts she'd made on *My Losing Season* had hurt that book, he felt.

I hadn't been aware of any of this. Nor was I aware, until he told me, why he'd been so delighted with David Herbert Donald's takedown, at least in his mind, of Maxwell Perkins. Who of all editors had recently won the Maxwell Perkins Award? None other than Pat's own, Nan Talese.

XVI

PAT LOSES CONFIDENCE IN HIS WRITING

When you're the artist Pat was, everything you write, everything you experience in order to write, is new. In Dylan Thomas's words, "the sun, born over and over." The vulnerability you have about your work, therefore, no matter how successful you've become, is inescapable. It's all new, every time the first time.

This is why, at least after becoming successful, Pat never read reviews and rarely read about himself. Fear of failure in him was compounded with Santini's dictum that pride not only goeth before the fall, it comes with a fist in the face.

With an artistic endeavor, it's easy to be reduced to a child, not the one who needs to speak but the one who needs to withdraw. So it was with Pat in reaction to Nan's comments as he began revising *South of Broad*.

Not only did he doubt himself, he was now doubting Nan, who had been honored with the Maxwell Perkins Award in no small part due to Pat's support, at least according to him. The award had meant a lot to Pat, since Maxwell Perkins had been Thomas Wolfe's editor at Scribner's, and Thomas Wolfe, a writer so exuberant and unrestrained that he, like Pat, couldn't have survived without an editor, was his literary hero.

Now, however, he was disillusioned. When Pat first began complaining about Nan's critique, I entertained doubts about *him*. Pat had considered Nan's work on *The Prince of Tides* masterful. He'd been totally enthusiastic, totally high on her then, but now, twenty years later, in 2008, he's suddenly souring on her?

Actually, because of our fifteen-year rift, I'd missed out on all her editing after *The Prince of Tides*. On *Beach Music*, published in 1995, she'd also done a great job, he said. She'd advised him to switch from third to first person, and in doing so he realized that first person was indeed his most natural and effective voice, so much so that he wrote all his subsequent books in the first person. She'd also done a fine job on his cookbook with stories, *The Pat Conroy Cookbook*, from 1999.

But with *My Losing Season*, published in 2002, his doubts about her editing began. *My Losing Season* was Pat's memoir about the losing season of the Citadel basketball team on which he had played point guard, about the players, the coach, and the Citadel itself. Pat confessed that, after receiving Nan's editorial comments, he'd had to hire a freelance editor to help him revise the manuscript and had never told Nan about it. He'd wanted her to think the final editing was his work. Perhaps he didn't want to offend her. That sounds like Pat. Or perhaps his confidence in his work then was much like it was now, when he was telling me this, in which case it's just as likely he was worried about undermining her confidence in him. She'd never liked the memoir, he felt, because she cared nothing for basketball. But one of the major scenes she wanted cut was of his father humiliating him after a game, slapping him and telling him he'd never be the player he, his father, was, a scene that Pat felt would have helped explain his character and would have deepened the book considerably. Coincidentally, Pat at the time in real life was reconciling with the Citadel, which was reflected in the memoir.

Skeptical of Nan's reactions to *South of Broad*, Pat turned to Sandra, our dear friend Janis Owens, Maggie, and me. Janis worked on the manuscript from her home in Florida, Maggie from Chicago where she was still in graduate school, and Sandra and I worked on it here in Beaufort. We'd all do our best to help, then Sandra filtered out our work while doing her own editing, and when she figured she had it all right she'd show it to Pat. Particularly demoralizing for him was when Nan, according to him, told him that the work was lacking "description, a sense of place." Well, the place was Charleston, his home for four years when he went to the Citadel, for Pat the most glorious city in the world, a place he'd celebrated in his writings before. In addition, description, he'd always felt, was his strength as a writer. Now he was forced to defend that?

The first chapter he had then is pretty much the first chapter of the published version, the protagonist's paper route south of Broad Street in Charleston. As he delivers the newspapers, we see what he sees, hear what he hears, breathe in what he breathes in: the Federalist and Colonial homes, the flora and fauna, the voices of folk who live there, dogs barking, birdsong, the sea oats and salt air, the pluff mud, the marsh, the river, the Colonial Lake, the bustling downtown, the great churches.

Yet Nan, apparently to better establish a sense of place, Pat said, wanted him to add a prologue, purely descriptive. None of us could fathom her reasoning. What she wanted, in our minds, was already there, and it was presented not as isolated description sticking out in the front of the book but through the narrative, the action of the story, with the reader taking it in as the protagonist does.

What was going on with her? She was getting up there in age, but weren't we all, and like I told Pat, none of us, especially Nan, looked as old as he did. That did give Pat pause. Nan's husband, the journalist Gay Talese, would later tell him, Pat told us, that Nan felt the protagonist's mother—cold, Catholic, and intellectual—was based on none other than Nan herself or at least inspired by her, and that's why Nan was so turned off by the book. Cold? That was hardly the Nan with whom I briefly communicated after Pat passed away. Her grief over the span of just a few emails was so soulful, so expansive, so palpable, I felt I could almost touch it. Cold? I don't think so. Certainly not towards Pat. Her heart was broken.

But that was later. For now, Pat was dissolving into a vulnerable puddle of fear and insecurity, drinking way too much. In one late-night phone call, his voice grew so small: "Description, Bernie, I always thought was my forte, what people liked most about my writing."

Daily, I'd phone him and read beautiful descriptive excerpts about Charleston from his manuscript. The first time I did it, I read passages from the prologue, then from chapter one.

"I carry the delicate porcelain beauty of Charleston like the hinged shell of some soft-tissued mollusk. . . . I grow calm when I see the ranks of palmetto trees pulling guard duty on the banks of Colonial Lake or hear the bells of St. Michael's calling cadence in the cicada-filled trees along Meeting Street. Deep in my bones, I knew early on I was one of those incorrigible creatures known as Charlestonians. It comes to me as a surprising form of knowledge that my time in the city is more vocation than gift; it is my destiny, not my choice. I consider it a high privilege to be a native to one of the loveliest American cities, not a high-kicking, glossy, or lipsticked city, not a city with bells on its fingers or brightly painted toenails, but a ruffled, low-slung city, understated and tolerant of nothing mismade or ostentatious. Though Charleston feels a seersuckered, tuxedoed view of itself, it approves of restraint far more than vainglory."

"I love those last two sentences in particular, Pat. They're really something."

This also from the prologue, in which Pat depicts himself as a boy who "in his own backyard could catch a basket of blue crabs, a string of flounder, a dozen redfish, or a net of white shrimp . . . in a city enchanting enough to charm cobras out of baskets, one so corniced and filigreed and elaborate that it leaves strangers awed and natives self-satisfied. In its shadows you can find metalwork as delicate as lace and spiral staircases as elaborate as yachts. In the secrecy of its gardens you can discover jasmine and camellias and hundreds of plants that look embroidered and stolen from the Garden of Eden for the sheer richness and the joy of stealing from the gods. In its kitchens the stoves are lit up in happiness as the lamb is marinating in red wine sauce, vinaigrette is prepared for the salad, crabmeat is anointed with sherry, custards are baked in the oven, and buttermilk biscuits cool on the counter."

"Hmm . . ."

Finally, this from chapter one:

"The gardens of Charleston were mysteries walled away in ivied jewel boxes emitting their special fragrances over high walls. The summer had proven good for the magnolias that had bloomed late. . . . One forty-foot tree . . . looked as though a hundred white doves had gathered there in search of mates. My sense of smell lit up as the temperature rose and the dew started to burn off the tea olive and the jasmine."

There was a pause, after which: "Bernie, all that, that's description. Right?"

"Of course, Pat, that's why I'm reading it to you. It's great. It's there. Your sense of place."

Still: "You want to go to Charleston with me tomorrow? I'm thinking I might need to take one of those carriage rides, the ones tourists take."

He was totally serious.

"We'll have lunch at Husk."

Then his voice grew even smaller, like a child's.

"Bernie, I'm afraid I won't get published."

That was an easy one.

"Pat, you could write your name all the way down three hundred fifty pages and they'd publish you. Are you kidding? You've made them a fortune."

Reading to him every day helped, I believe. Certainly, Sandra's uncanny editorial work on the manuscript pleased and delighted him. She rewrote an early scene for him, and I couldn't tell where her writing began and his ended.

But by then he wanted to have nothing more to do with the book. Even when Nan and Doubleday flew him to New York and put him up in the Surrey Hotel, he refused to see her. He phoned, miserable, drinking himself into a stew, I could tell, ignoring Nan's persistent knocking on his door. His agent, Marly Rusoff, also in New York, tried to intervene. He wouldn't see her either.

Once he'd returned to Fripp, Nan acknowledged their differences in an email to him. "This sometimes happens, Pat," she wrote. "It's not that unusual." Then she flew a well-known editor down to Charleston to take her place and meet with Pat. He had read her written editorial recommendations beforehand. They seemed to him, if not officious, pedestrian. He didn't meet with her either.

Ultimately, as we know, Pat's a fighter. As he always said, no matter how down he gets, he rallies. *South of Broad* was published. I think he pretty much held out till he got his way.

Sandra and I and my brother Aaron and Pat's old Citadel friends John Warley and Scott Graber were just worried as hell about his drinking. It calmed him down, he said: his anxiety, his rage. Any timely crisis—his divorces, his relationship with his children, with friends, his hatred of Lenore, his loss of Susannah, even briefly his tiff with Nan—could trigger it. But what triggered those crises? From what open wound had they surfaced, formed, and spread, one giving rise to another, throughout his life?

He knew the answer. He could tell you. And he did, unhesitatingly. It was his father's rage, the progenitor of his own fear and anxiety. This wounded little boy, Pat had yet to surrender to him, had yet to speak in his voice. He was still speaking for him. If that little boy, that child in diapers—who feared and hated his father even then, as he'd said— could speak for himself, might that offer salve to the wound so tender, so prone to inflammation, in the adult?

The high correlation between abuse and addiction is reflected as much in Pat as anyone I've ever known. It's why he understood it so well, how he wrote about it so well, and how he helped heal so many. According to those with whom I've spoken or whom I've heard from, particularly since he passed away, what he so courageously revealed in his writings and public speeches gave them the permission and the courage to speak for themselves.

Which is exactly what he gave to the students in my classroom back when he was working on *The Great Santini*.

In October 2009, *If Holden Caulfield Were in My Classroom* came out with Pat's introduction. We both spoke at the Pulpwood Queens and Timber Guys Book Club in Jefferson, Texas, one of the largest book clubs in the world at the time. Its founder, Kathy Patrick, a cosmetologist snubbed by the local book club, formed her own, which was so inspiring it spread all over the United States and Europe. It was a lot of fun while Pat and I were onstage speaking together—it was a pretty risqué audience of Rebel Yell–drinkin' Texans—but afterwards, sitting beside each other, with Pat signing *South of Broad* and me signing *If Holden Caulfield Were in My Classroom*, it should have been a lot more fun for Pat than for me. Unsurprisingly, if you knew Pat, it wasn't.

His signing line was the equivalent of several blocks long, as it usually was; mine was little more than six or seven people. So how does Pat handle this? He stands up, gets everyone's attention, holds up my book, and says, "Folks, this is the worst fucking book I've ever read!"

My books are next to his on the signing table. They've been there so he can sign the introduction. Now almost everyone's buying mine as they're buying his. I'd never signed so many books in my life, except for maybe at Paideia where we also spoke together, or in the Beaufort Book Store, where we signed together.

Pat was usually a happy, gregarious drunk. Most of the time, you could hardly tell he'd been drinking at all.

That's the way he was in Texas, I reported back to Sandra.

She'd been concerned, because earlier in the year when he'd been elected to the South Carolina Hall of Fame and was to present his speech at a luncheon in Myrtle Beach, he was so drunk when he got up that morning that he fell on the way to the event, and once there, stumbled onto the stage. We were both there.

But you know what? She reminded me: "Once he got on that stage, he gave an incredible speech, didn't he?"

He did. You couldn't even tell he'd been drunk.

Also appearing onstage at the Pulpwood Queens and Timber Guys Book Club was Pat's daughter Melissa ("Woo") Conroy with her highly praised children's book, *Poppy's Pants*, featuring Pat's khakis, the only color he ever wore, and a postscript from Pat.

Pat was the proud father, no question. It was a great story with fantastic illustrations, and the reviews confirmed that. However, not to be presumptuous, but when Melissa was asked if Pat taught her to write, she couldn't help but smile. "No," she said. "Bernie did." So not only was a proud father there, but a proud teacher.

That kid was smart as hell. Thirty years earlier, in my literature class at Paideia, some of her classmates were complaining that in Harper Lee's *To Kill a Mockingbird* Atticus Finch is idealized. This really frustrated Melissa. She raised her hand and shouted, "Of course he is. The whole story's told from the point of view of his daughter Scout, who's only five years old. What five-year-old doesn't idealize their dad?"

Several months after our book tour, in the spring of 2009, my daughter Maggie and her fiancé Jonathan Hannah moved to Beaufort, where she could work on her book of meditative fables for adults, *Lost Cantos of the Ouroboros Caves*, which Pat not only titled and passionately critiqued but eventually published under his own imprint, Story River Books, at University of South Carolina Press, about which more later. She also worked part-time as what Pat called his "gatekeeper," daily astonished and reduced to tears over emails from his readers thanking him for changing their lives through the telling of his own story. "I hate to sound corny," Maggie told me, "but they're thanking him for *healing* them."

Pat was always compelled by the issue of cruelty, whether it was a personal holocaust such as he went through or a greater one, such as Germany's or Rwanda's or Sarajevo's. Who is Man? Can he be saved? Maggie's doctoral dissertation had been about cruelty in all its manifestations. She was so immersed in the subject that at the University of Chicago the writer J. M. Coetzee referred to Maggie, along with himself, as "professors of cruelty." Clearly, it was a topic Maggie was intensely exploring as well as one Pat in his own way had been exploring all his life. Neither could let go of it, and when they were supposed to be "taking care of business," as Maggie put it, they'd end up spending so much time talking about it that they almost never got to "business." Pat thought her book on the subject, which she was also working on at the time, was important, and later when they would be on tour together with Story River Books authors (along with me), he talked about her work on cruelty as much as he did *Lost Cantos of the Ouroboros Caves.*

Nietzsche, Primo Levi, Jean Améry, Montaigne, Sartre, Jankélévitch, Camus: all had suffered, as Pat had, great trauma and had sought to "manage" it (Maggie's term) by turning it into fiction and memoir or exposition, as Pat had and would. This in and of itself fascinated Pat— how does an artist, an intellectual, deal with unbearable pain and suffering? Maggie was impressed by the breadth and depth of Pat's reading on the subject. She'd studied all these writers and philosophers with great interest for almost twenty years; it was her work. Pat had read them all on his own, with an astonishingly clear and profound understanding of them. Their conversations were electrifying. Some I was lucky enough to be a part of.

Maggie shared Pat's understanding that abuse had certainly shaped his life and writing but felt that even if he hadn't been abused, he'd still have these same questions, and he'd still be compelled by them. His life and writing might be different, but the questions are there to varying degrees in everyone, especially someone like Pat, who was born into the world with such imagination and curiosity. He was born with those characteristics as sure, she told him, as he was born without an aptitude for charging a battery or adjusting the breaker box. Everyone has suffered, in one way or another.

When did the questions begin for you? Pat asked her.

"I was three years old. Mom and Dad and I were taking a walk around the neighborhood in Atlanta."

"On the street where I was born," Pat reminded her.

"Rosedale Road. I had just had tubes removed from my ears, my hearing was ultra-sensitive. I hear a kitten. It's coming from a trash can. We walk over to it. Dad opens it. The purring and whining grows louder. It's coming from the bottom, under a bag stuffed with trash.

Mom pulls out the trash bag. Underneath it is the kitten. Remember Tigger-Tiger?"

"I think I do."

"Mom lifted the kitten out of the trash can, handed him to me, and we took him home. 'Why,' I wondered aloud, asking Mom and Dad, 'would anyone throw away a kitten?'"

"They didn't have an answer."

"I've been asking ever since."

XVII

THE GRIFFIN MARKET LUNCH GROUP

Griffin Market opened in 2011. By that time our usual lunch group of Pat, John Warley, Scott Graber, Aaron, and now Maggie's husband, Jonathan Hannah—having dined everywhere in town many times over and even at Husk in Charleston—were more than ready for a permanent home. Griffin Market featured classic Piedmont Italian cooking, which none of us, including Pat, had ever tasted before, very different from traditional Italian restaurants. In fact, no bread: Ricardo, the wine sommelier and co-owner with his wife Laura, who was the chef, was born and raised in the Piedmont, and he said his mother wouldn't allow it.

So who gives a shit? This was Jonathan Hannah, my embarrassing son-in-law.

His mother, replied Ricardo. The entire menu was his mother's. Wild boar, baby octopus, cuttlefish, tagliatelle with Italian sausage or chanterelles and sweet corn, sablefish, tuna and caper sauce over pork tenderloin, panna cotta, local shrimp in a lemon and caper brown butter sauce over polenta, carnaroli rice risotto with wild boar sausage, Amarone wine and borlotti beans, pickled anchovies in tarragon and capers vinaigrette, so many unique flavors and distinctly compelling tastes, and homemade pasta made daily. For most of us, it became addictive. If we missed a Wednesday lunch, we'd have withdrawal pains.

Pat loved it all. That they changed their menu daily, he noted early on, was a good sign. I began growing heirloom tomatoes for them, and before you knew it, their new tomato sandwich appeared as "Bernie's Best" on the menu.

I knew little about wines, but both Pat and Aaron knew more, and they relished Ricardo's selections, though Pat would only allow himself half a glass. No problem, said Aaron, who downed the rest, then inevitably ordered another bottle, one for lunch, then another to take home.

Pat, of course, put Griffin Market on the map, writing about it gloriously for the *Lowcountry Weekly*, getting us all to review it online, giving them advertising copy. Locals, guests, and tourists would come for the food, most certainly, but word spread that Pat sightings were there for the having at our Wednesday lunches.

We worried about the cost. Pat insisted on paying for everything, the bill for which was usually over three hundred bucks. I know because I served as interim head of a new school forming in Beaufort, so for a brief period I was loaded, Pat knew it, and without barking about it, let me pay for a lunch. I began asking Sandra about the wisdom of Pat weekly footing such a big bill. Sandra was famous for her frugality, but she insisted that we let Pat do it. "It's the only time he gets out at all. His only social event. He loves it, looks forward to it, it makes him happy, let's let him do it."

Pat loved conversation, as long as it wasn't about practical things, which the rest of us weren't that interested in talking about over lunch anyway. We talked about anything and everything of interest to us. Saul Bellow's take on what made a good story: It had to be "interesting; above all else, interesting."

"Did you know that the old Gold Eagle Hotel was also a whorehouse?" I asked once.

"Context, Bernie," admonished Jonathan. "What the hell is the Gold Eagle Hotel?"

"Right, Jonathan, sorry. The Gold Eagle Hotel, since torn down and replaced with the ugliest house I've ever seen, was as stately and elegant as any place in the Lowcountry. My aunts stayed there when they'd visit from up north. Very high end, tasteful, just east of downtown on the Point, overlooking the bay."

"It was majestic," Pat said. "Everything about it. It spoke of elegance."

"Yes, my point exactly, Pat. It was a hotel that actually spoke, like Francis 'the talking mule' on television."

Pat: "He's trying to be funny, boys, at my expense, but can he pull it off? No."

"What neither Pat nor I knew," I continued, "is that it was also a whorehouse."

Pat: "You're kidding."

"Only the top floor, the third floor. Very, very high-end escort service. The girls were from Atlanta."

Aaron: "Who were they servicing? We know what Beaufort meant to marines back then: 'bars, broads, and booze.' Wasn't that the catch-phrase? There were all these little whorehouses back then around Beaufort."

"Oh, these girls were hardly servicing noncoms. Think generals, top brass, the head honchos coming to Parris Island from Washington. Think," I added, "of the most prominent men in town, like for example, Al Martin's dad."

"Al Martin's dad?" asked Aaron. "He cut our hair when we were kids."

"Right, just like Al does now."

Pat: "Can you imagine the money Al's dad made back then? Just about the only barber shop in town, servicing all those marines? Al must have died a million deaths when Parris Island brought in their own barbers."

"Pat, can you imagine the Gold Eagle as a whorehouse?"

John Warley: "Did Al tell you this, Bernie? I'm going to have to forego Great Clips and get my hair cut at Al's. How'd Al know about it?"

"Because his dad told him 'in no uncertain terms,' once he got in high school, that if he ever found out Al was anywhere near the vicinity of the place, he'd 'beat the living shit' out of him."

"Jonathan, your face," Pat said. "We've let you sit there in peace. Now, it's time. Tell us just what a cruel motherfucker you were." Though Jonathan was a fourth-degree black belt, you wouldn't know it because he was an artist and musician and computer guy and could nerd out on you in the blink of an eye.

"For Christ's sake, Pat, I was sparring, a long time ago. I was still learning. The guy was like Mr. New York of the karate world. He's spinning, jumping, wheel kicks. My elbow's too low, so I get kicked right in the face, a few bones broken, no big deal. It was an accident, what can I say?"

"Well now, Jonathan," said Aaron, "was it really what you'd call an 'accident'? I mean, if I saw a foot heading straight for my face, no stops on the way, no pause for refreshment, I think I would probably have lifted that elbow and covered said target, as they say. Just one man's take on it, thank you very much."

"My take on it is whatever yours is, Jonathan," said Pat, "so you won't beat me up. I love you."

"Thank you, Pat. What I meant was he certainly didn't mean to do it."

"I know that, Jonathan. You don't have to explain anything to me. Ever. Aaron's the one you need to beat up."

Scott: "Has anyone read Nicole Krauss? I think she just won the National Book Award—"

Aaron: "Pass the antipasto this way. Pat, how about another glass of your wine? This time I'll just go ahead and drink the whole thing."

After which, when we're all full and in absolutely no shape whatever to work, Chef Laura steps out to a healthy round of applause. Ricardo is ready with a bottle of wine for Aaron to take home. On the way out, Pat turns to Scott: "She's great, Scott. Terrific."

Scott: "Ah, and who might that be?"

"Nicole Krauss."

Scott seemed suddenly lost, confused, scouring his brain for . . . something. "And who, if I may be so bold as to ask, is Nicole Krauss?"

"Very funny, Scott. Jesus."

"Why, thank you, Pat," Scott said, throwing his arm around him. "Thank you."

Sometimes Sandra or Martha or Maggie joined us for lunch at Griffin Market. When Pat's kids Jessica, Melissa, and Megan, or my step-daughter, Lara, were in Beaufort, they too usually joined us. So did Pat's brothers and his sister Kathy, as well as old friends who were visiting. Lynn Selden, an old writer friend of Pat's was in Beaufort so often he became a regular.

For dinner, we'd all gather over at Pat and Sandra's with Pat's brothers if they were in town and Pat's sister Kathy, her husband, Bobby Joe, and their son, Willie, who played in a band with Craig Washington. Old friends also dined with us, including Mike and George and some of Pat's old teammates at the Citadel. Annually, that included Tim Belk flying in from San Francisco. With Sandra in charge of the cooking, the food was always great. Pat's grandkids were entertaining as hell. I loved teasing Jessica's daughter, Stella, who loved acting like she hated it. Sometimes Barbara, Pat's ex, joined us. It was all easy and fun and very Irish and loud; Pat loved it. I certainly did. He was great with his grandkids. They loved being around him. Jessica's oldest, Elyse, marveled that he could talk about things most adults generally didn't talk about with kids. They knew him well. They knew he talked in opposites, saying precisely the opposite of what he meant. So, when he'd scream, "Go, go, get out of here! Awful kids! Awful kids! The worst of all possible kids! Go! Go!" he knew they'd swarm all over him, which they always did. When little Katie, Megan's daughter, was about three years old, she actually got in a fight with the evil dragon on television, taking a small broom and beating it over the head. Pat thought that was funny as hell. Melissa's kids, Lila and Wester, acted out plays for him. He talked basketball with Jack, Megan's middle one, who was going to be a monster on the court. Molly Jean, Megan's oldest, he worshipped.

Like his father, Pat was becoming a terrific grandfather.

XVIII

THE INTERVENTION

The Griffin Market Lunch Group, with the intentional exception of Pat, was summoned to a meeting one afternoon in Scott Graber's law office in downtown Beaufort. John Warley, another member of the group, couldn't attend in person because he was in Virginia closing out his law practice so he could live in Beaufort and devote all his time to writing. Though present only on Scott's speakerphone, he was the one who had called the meeting. He'd talked to Pat by phone the night before, and Pat was drunker than he'd ever heard him. He was afraid, as were we all, that Pat was killing himself with booze. An intervention, he said, was now necessary, though he couldn't get back to Beaufort for it.

"So necessary," said my brother Aaron, "that you can't get back in time for it?"

"Yes, I must confess," admitted John, "not something I'd look forward to, but boys, he sounded awful."

We called Sandra, who also, by this time, was desperate for some kind of intervention.

Pat respected Aaron. Unlike Pat and me, Aaron had perspective, an easygoing take on life, even though he was a Jew. He'd been a banker in Houston and discreetly advised Pat and Sandra on their finances.

Aaron was a soothing, calming influence on all things Pat and I were too impatient and emotional about. He was patient and entirely unpretentious, and his favorite phrase about a problematic issue was, "Let's just chew on it for a while, in the cool of the evening." Or: "Let's give it some time, see where we are then." Because with some time, if we weren't over it, we at least had some perspective.

But about this matter Aaron was pretty definitive. There was no time to give it time. Pat didn't have any.

"I think you're right," Scott said. And Scott, unlike Pat and me, was a thinker.

Our strategy was for Aaron, Scott, and me to drive out to Fripp Island, drop in on Pat, and with Sandra's help get him to allow her to call EMS to come get him and transport him to the hospital. If he refused help, Sandra would call EMS anyway. The hospital, we felt, would get him into the Recovery Center. Since we wanted him to agree, we were prepared to be honest.

Well, *they* were. Upon pulling up in Pat and Sandra's driveway, I magnanimously offered to remain in the car. As intellectually intimidating as I already was to Pat, I explained, why compound the threat with my presence?

"Well," Aaron said, considering the possibility, "John did remain in Virginia."

"In all candor," offered Scott, "Virginia is a large state. Perhaps John could make room for me?"

"*Intellectually* intimidating to Pat?" Aaron said, looking at Scott. Clearly, I had him thinking, further considering my offer. "*Bernie?* Until he said that, I'd always thought Pat was pretty smart."

"Look, I'm serious. I'll wait here. But I'll have my cell phone. Call me if you need me. How's that?"

"An excellent idea," said Scott. "I wouldn't mind making the ultimate sacrifice and waiting with you. Aaron?"

"Now that I think about it, I believe I'm too intellectually intimidating also. You know, like Bernie."

We sat there a good ten minutes, contemplating the idea of poor, sweet Sandra confronting him all by herself. What was so frightening was that Pat had never acknowledged he was an alcoholic. So, we hadn't confronted him, though we all knew about it.

Our plan for the intervention, particularly with Sandra's wholehearted collusion and cooperation, had given us all reason to hope. By the time we finally dragged ourselves out of the car, entered the house, and settled into the living room, however, it was clearer than ever that our intervention was destined to fail.

None of us had the balls to begin. Pat just sat there, looking embarrassed, preparing himself for humiliation, it seemed to me, and we all sat there, in silence that was growing more and more uncomfortable.

Scott explained that John had called. We waited for more. That was it. John had called.

What I am about to tell you, Pat, I will pay for for the rest of our lives.

Only with wit, Bernie, I promise. He knew what was coming.

We're worried, I managed to say, about your drinking.

Aaron told him that John had gotten us together because, when he and Pat were talking on the phone the previous night, Pat had seemed dangerously drunk to him, drunker than John had ever heard him before.

Then Sandra told him she'd call EMS. He needed to go to a treatment center, dry out, sober up, and learn to quit drinking. EMS would take him to Beaufort Memorial Hospital. From there the doctors would commit him if he wouldn't go voluntarily.

"EMS?" Pat said. "The neighbors will see. The story will get out."

"If you're dead," Sandra told him, "what difference will it make? You're killing yourself, Pat. Your insides are in such bad shape you can hardly eat."

Sandra was great, but the whole business was awful. Pat looked helpless, trying to rationalize this new confrontation, a little like he felt exposed, perhaps betrayed, though not necessarily by us.

It was all so tense and embarrassing and humiliating that Aaron ended up blaming the whole thing on John Warley, since he wasn't there to defend himself. For himself, Aaron added, he'd had no problem with Pat's drinking. He just hoped it wasn't affecting his health—which it was; that's why we were there. Actually, truth be told, I told Pat, I liked him better when he was drunk. Scott even apologized to him for unnecessarily alarming him, then pulled out an entirely irrelevant legal form for Pat to sign, explaining that "in all honesty" he was here as Pat's lawyer; he needed Pat's signature.

Only Sandra had any balls. She flat out told him that unless he stopped he was going to die, and that that prospect pissed her off, at which time she shooed us out to let in the EMS people she'd called.

Aaron, Scott, and I crept around the yard to the side of the house and peered into the living room window. We wanted to be certain he wasn't somehow hurt or humiliated when they applied force to get him to the ambulance. Who knows, we might have been needed, at least for that. Realizing he had to go, he might want one of us to accompany him. We were anxious, worried, sad for him, no question. Now things were really getting serious, but this had to happen, it had to.

Unfortunately, it didn't.

The EMS guys were all but having a drink with him. They sat around the living room as comfortable and congenial as Pat appeared to be. It was as if the neighbors had come calling and Pat had welcomed them inside. Come on in, have a seat. Can I get you anything? Whatever story Pat had concocted, they completely bought into. What was he telling them? By the time he'd signed books for them, they were still laughing as they headed out the front door.

I intercepted them.

"Please, Pat has somehow lied to you. I don't know what he told you, but if he doesn't get to the hospital, something terrible is going to happen to him. He's an alcoholic. He gets so drunk he can't stand up. He falls. There's no way any human being's constitution can stand the amount of liquor he drinks daily. That's why Sandra called you. You've got to go back in there and get him to the hospital."

I thought about Sandra's worry over his falling. He could kill himself falling, she'd told me. And who was going to be there to pick him up, she'd worried, when she was on her own book tour?

But the EMS guys looked at me as if something might be wrong with me. What had Pat told them?

"He needs to be in the hospital," I repeated, following them as they carried their newly autographed books to the ambulance.

Clearly, Pat had fooled them, charming the pants off them with stories, probably about the Three Stooges peering in the window outside.

Sandra told me later that as soon as Pat saw them come in, he appeared as sober as she'd ever seen him. In that brief period of time, she said, Pat had made friends with the EMS people. He'd probably be having drinks and dinner with them that weekend.

One evening several weeks later Sandra grew alarmed at how much blood Pat was coughing up. She drove him over to Beaufort Memorial Hospital. The doctors told her X-rays showed that the blood vessels in Pat's esophagus were not only swollen but bleeding out, erupting. The surgeon at Beaufort Memorial patched him up temporarily, enough so that they could helicopter him over to the Medical University at the College of Charleston.

The next morning in the hospital was when Pat confided to me that he had been drinking a quart of liquor a day since he was twenty-six years old. He'd admitted to the doctors, he said, that he was an alcoholic. The doctors told him that if Sandra hadn't gotten him to the hospital in time, he would have bled to death.

"The doctors told me that if I have another drink it'll kill me."

Was he exaggerating? Probably. The greater truth underneath that exaggeration, however, was that for his own survival he needed to quit, and he was going to give it a go.

XIX

ONCE MORE INTO THE WRECKAGE

Pat quit drinking, at least for a while. I don't even think he was drinking on the sly, at least not very much, because Sandra wasn't finding hidden liquor bottles. He began going to the local YMCA again with Aaron, and they would work out with Mina Truong, who pushed them so hard Pat began bragging about it. Sometimes I'd be there too, exercising mostly on my own, shooting baskets and stretching, and Pat would join me after his workout. Where before he admired my stretching when I showed off for him, now he'd start barking out instructions: "Higher, Bernie, higher, lift the leg higher." "Can't you do more? Do more." It made me want to do more by lifting my leg higher and peeing on him. He was serious.

Once I saw Mina sparring with a guy you could tell was experienced. She hit him so fast and so often he looked as if he was being lassoed. She was thin and muscular and quick-witted, spoke English energetically but haphazardly, and soon periodically began joining us for lunch at Griffin Market. She had a terrific personality. And Pat genuinely took to her. "She's saving my life," he told me.

He was working pretty regularly and pretty hard in the mornings and afternoons on *The Death of Santini*, his autobiography.

"When I was thirty years old," he tells us in his introduction, "*The Great Santini* was published, and there were many things in that book I was afraid to write or feared no one would believe. But this year I turned sixty-five, the official starting date of old age and the beginning countdown to my inevitable death. I've come to realize I still carry the bruised freight of that childhood every day. I can't run away, hide, or pretend it never happened. I wear it on my back like the carapace of a tortoise, except my shell burdens and does not protect." He grew up, he writes, in a "house of pain," concluding his introduction by saying that he must once again enter it, "a final time."

And so he does. We get, with no holds barred this time around, the full force of the violence, both physical and mental, that traumatized Pat and his siblings. As Pat promises, he leaves nothing out, even a family trauma so horrifying it completely wipes out his memory of the rest of that year. All seems undeniably true to me, in the voice of a man who must tell his story humbly and realistically in order to survive the "house of pain" in which he grew up and to save himself.

This is a story told by a man who wants to live. And the only way to escape the hold it had on him, to survive it, to somehow transcend it, was to tell it. And remember, as Pat would say, there's always more. So this was a story about what he hadn't said. The problem is that, at Pat's age then, if you're going to tell the story, you better tell all of it. And if not, you'd better just shut up about it in public, especially if it's about your daughter Susannah's mother, Lenore, whom Susannah was still living with at the time, that same daughter you're yearning more and more to reconnect with the older you get.

After the breakup of his marriage to Barbara, he married Lenore "on the rebound." He writes that she "would teach me everything about life and love I didn't want to know." Everything?

He does supply a few examples from his years with her in San Francisco. He had terrible back pain for two months and Lenore, he

writes, basically ignored him. One of his kids would bring him breakfast, the maid his lunch, and another of his kids his dinner. "I've always
hated sickrooms and invalids," Lenore tells him. "I just can't stand it,
and it's nothing I can help." So, Pat concludes, "I inhabited a loveless
home, and one where I couldn't depend on my wife to take care of me."

Well, I guess that's something, but "loveless"? Personally, as his
friend and reader, I need more here.

Lenore, he writes, got caught up in "the whirlpool of high society, a
place I had no desire to be part of." He mentions the "dozen Fancy-
Dan parties" he attended because of her, but that he hadn't come to
San Francisco "to grow shallow." Knowing Pat, I certainly believe that.
But why *did* he go to San Francisco? Why did he marry Lenore? "On
the rebound" doesn't quite cut it.

"In San Francisco, except for Tim Belk," he writes, "I found myself
cut off from the stimulating conversation of friends. As I thought about
this painful isolation and incurable solitude, I finally figured out that
Lenore had isolated me from all the friends I had brought to our marriage. Because she was merciless and conniving, I found myself in my
late forties facing a loneliness that cut like a horse's bite."

When I was going through an early draft of the manuscript for him,
I asked Pat exactly how she was "merciless and conniving." "Dad was
leaving messages for me," he told me. "She hid those from me. I never
knew until I left."

"Did you ever entertain the idea of picking up the phone and calling him?"

"It was hard."

At a party, he writes, a lovely woman tells him, "Pat, you are aware
that your wife hates you, aren't you? If not, everyone else in this room
knows it."

Does Pat not know that's a pick-up line? Even after their affair
begins?

Was Lenore a social climber, materialistic, selfish, possessive, dividing Pat from his friends so she could have him all to herself? She may well have been—I have no idea. What's the rest of the story? Where's Pat? Has he completely absolved himself of free will? He leaves his friends, and all we get is the villain Lenore? He left his wife and daughter, and all we get is the villain Lenore? Pat refers to Lenore's "unadulterated hatred" of Emily. He medicated himself long before he married Lenore. His father abused him. Then like Emily, to survive he learned to lie, to cover up. That's what Pat has done here.

Don't get me wrong. I love *The Death of Santini*. It's strong and humble and incredibly loving and beautiful, to say nothing of funny as hell. It's so painful it moves me even now. But as Pat said, "There's always more." And with Pat, once again, you can't really separate the personal from the professional, certainly not the artist from the man.

As far as Susannah's concerned, I couldn't help but imagine, he didn't just leave, he left *her*. Was he cruel on the way out? Was there a "Santini-lash" to his comments beyond what Sandra heard him tell her about her writing the last time he saw her? He can't just absolve himself of all responsibility. At some point, he needed to tell the rest of the story, both to uncensor himself and to get his daughter back, which he was talking about more and more.

XX

PAT RALLIES AGAIN

Martha began noticing that Pat's belly was swelling. Sandra began worrying about it. Also, Sandra noticed he was eating less. His belly, Martha said, was now looking like the belly of an alcoholic. Sandra worried that his organs weren't properly ridding him of fluids. They weren't.

This time—three years before death finally cornered him, taking him away from us forever—was as bad as the first one. One night he fell in the bathroom. Sandra heard him. He was bleeding profusely. She drove him to Beaufort Memorial Hospital, and they had him helicoptered to the Medical University of South Carolina in Charleston. Again, the doctors told him that if he continued to drink he would die, which he in turn told us.

He'd fallen off the wagon. Sandra had found the hidden vodka bottles.

He fucked up, he told me.

Upon his return from the hospital, Pat began working out every day with Mina, who with his support and encouragement opened her own private fitness center, the Mina & Conroy Fitness Studio. He stretched, lifted weights, boxed, and worked out with ropes. She massaged him, working different muscles at different times. Once again, he quit drinking.

And what really got his juices flowing was joining forces in 2013 with the young Jonathan Haupt, the gifted editor who had also become publisher of the University of South Carolina Press, to form Story River Books as Pat's imprint, for which Pat's title would be editor-at-large. It would publish only fiction. Jonathan would go through the manuscripts and offer comments and suggestions not only on those he deemed worthy of publication but on those he didn't. Pat loved him for this; it was consistent with Pat's desire to support potential writers in general. In the process of editing those he felt were worthy of publication, Jonathan would give them to Pat for his approval, reaction, and comments. Once the prospective authors' revisions met Jonathan's approval, he would send them a contract, after which Pat would help promote them once published.

This, all who knew and loved him down here agree, was the happiest time of his life. As I've said before, Pat never did anything he didn't want to do. And he did want to do this. He loved reading the manuscripts, reacting to them, and appearing onstage, as he once told me, facetiously of course, "in his kingly fashion," speaking and moderating panels with Story River authors.

When he wasn't touring with Story River writers, he'd be up on his porch overlooking Battery Creek in Beaufort, where he and Sandra had moved from Fripp Island. Every afternoon, he'd be happily going through manuscripts, commenting in the margins, making notes, offering perspective. He had always been a stickler for logistics, what he referred to as "getting people through doors" in a fluid way. He was insightful about finding where in the story the drama lay: for example, an emphasis less where the protagonist might be going in the narrative and more on where he was coming from and why he was leaving.

The drama, Pat felt, was in the trauma. Don't emphasize your escape at the expense of your motive. Place, he felt, was highly personal. Don't be coy. Don't cheat yourself by leaving it too early, or you cheat the reader of the satisfaction and catharsis that can come later. Don't give us a tour on a road trip. We want to know why you're taking it. And if therein lies the drama, exploit it; the more personal, the better. If you're leaving because your boyfriend beat you, for example, that may be your story. Go deeper, to find the story leading up it. And don't use the same word over and over, like "beautiful." Be precise in your details and descriptions: we should "see" them, as if we're watching a movie. Go just beyond the obvious to get that prized shock of recognition.

Catharsis: Pat loved it. Not just as a reader but as the son of a warrior.

A novel we both loved and admired was Chaim Potok's *My Name Is Asher Lev*. When I taught it at Paideia back in the eighties, I thought he would like it and showed it to him. I mention it here because there is a particular scene that hooked him and that he never forgot and would forever use to illustrate what he felt was a perfect example of catharsis. I can't tell you how many times I heard Pat quoting it to potential writers, including, of course, Story River writers.

My Name Is Asher Lev is about a sensitive, artistic boy in an ultraorthodox Hasidic community in Crown Heights, Brooklyn. Totally devoted to his painting and drawing at the expense of his culture and religion, he's obviously a misfit, alien to his family and his community. One kid in particular regularly taunts him in school, shouting and screaming that he's a blasphemer when he catches Asher unconsciously, without even realizing it at the time, drawing in a sacred text. Asher's shy, but when soon afterwards he draws a picture of his antagonist for his mentor, a man as alienated as he from the Hasidic community, his mentor looks at the picture for a long time. Finally, he says, "I would not like to be hated by you, Asher Lev."

Now there's a warrior, Pat would say: "'I would not like to be hated by you, Asher Lev.'"

There's catharsis.

Story River writers were so grateful to Pat they would have killed for him. He genuinely thought that Story River books were good books. Pat knew he'd discovered in Jonathan Haupt a publisher and editor who was magnificently gifted. He also understood that traditional publishing, i.e., New York publishing, was approaching its demise. The traditional houses had been gobbled up by superconglomerates. To them, the bottom line—funded by celebrity writing, franchise writing—was all that mattered. Editors no longer edited. The traditional houses downsized, shedding experienced editors and staff. Phillip Roth predicted that literature would become as rarified as philosophy and, like philosophy, like textbooks, would be read mostly in colleges and universities. Pat's former editor, Jonathan Galassi, now the distinguished publisher of Farrar, Straus and Giroux, wrote in *Muse*, his own novel about publishing, which would come out in 2015, that if today's major publishers did publish a good book, it would never get out of the warehouse. I knew bestselling writers who, when their next books proved less successful, could no longer get published in New York, much less low-level writers such as I and many of the Story River authors.

Pat was so confident in his perspective that he told me that eventually he would end up publishing his own books with Story River, where, he felt, he'd make more money from them.

Money, however, wasn't what was driving Pat. He just loved helping. He loved the work. He'd finished *The Death of Santini*, which was coming out in October of this same year, 2013. That book was done. However, he was doing all this work for Story River at the expense of his next novel, *The Storms of Aquarius*, which he was supposed to be working on for Nan and Doubleday and for which he was under contract for around a million dollars, the balance of a multimillion dollar, multibook contract he'd signed before publishing began gasping its last breath—a contract, he told me, he'd never get today. In 2013, he figured he'd get about half that. "Old publishing" was failing. What he meant by that in his own respect I'm uncertain. No movie had been made of his books since *The Prince of Tides*. I know he had concluded that that would be the biggest windfall of his career. In the matter of his literary career, disappointment was always just around the corner.

At the time, Sandra and Maggie told me that Nan Talese and Marly Rusoff, Pat's agent, were worried about whether he'd finish *The Storms of Aquarius* even somewhere within sight of the vicinity of the delivery date in his contract. I didn't know when it was due contractually. For some reason, I never thought to ask. I just took it for granted, knowing Pat, and hearing what I'd heard, that he'd be late. So, I worried about it too. His livelihood, to say nothing of his career, depended on Doubleday. I said to him Story River Books could wait. Sandra and Maggie were concerned, too. All of us were. In retrospect, of course, we should have been worried about whether he would finish it at all.

As for my own novel, *Famous All Over Town*, I'd been working on it forever, as far back as my last few years in Atlanta. Pat and I began talking about it well before Story River Books came to fruition. He had read the first thirty-five pages or so of an early draft, in which I was introducing major characters and through them hinting at the action to come in the storyline. He didn't like that approach and suggested the reverse, going straight into the action, which I then did, the characters introduced as they appeared.

The book opens with the daughter of the sheriff's former mistress, who is black, accusing the white sheriff of raping her mother—who is present in the room, her back turned to both of them—throughout their entire decade-long affair back in the fifties and sixties, though in fact it was consensual; then the story heads across the river to Parris

Island, where a drill sergeant marches his platoon, rifles over their heads, into Oyster Creek, where three of them drown. Dramatic, Pat said. I thought so too.

Once Story River Books began, Pat, for reasons of appearances and propriety, recused himself from considering or editing *Famous All Over Town*. Pat had introduced me to Jonathan Haupt at the 2010 South Carolina Book Festival in Columbia, where at that time I was plugging *If Holden Caulfield Were in My Classroom*, and he had encouraged me to tell Jonathan about *Famous All Over Town*. At the time, Jonathan was an editor and not the publisher at USC Press, but he appeared interested. He took over as publisher in 2012. By the time Story River was in the works, the novel was way too long, about 750 pages, and I'd asked my readers, Sandra, Janis, and Maggie, to just go through and cut whatever stopped them in the reading, whatever bored them. They were helpful, but it wasn't enough. The book was still way too long. Janis Owens talked about helping me cut a few characters and subplots just to shorten it, but the problem, I realized, was that the novel was about a town, with multiple narrators and interweaving stories all somehow connected, like *Spoon River Anthology* or Sherwood Anderson's *Winesburg, Ohio* or Robert Altman's movie *Nashville*.

Jonathan's gift as an editor was this: he knew what to do, understood what the writer wanted done, discovered for the writer what he wanted done even if the writer didn't yet know it, and just as importantly knew what not to do. He himself likened the novel, structurally, that is, to all the works named above. Yes, he emailed me, you have multiple narrators, all of whom are major characters—Jews, Gentiles, blacks, whites, journalists, politicians, aristocrats, marines, civilians, sane, insane, young, old, male, female, gay, and straight—but your main character, your "central" character, is the town itself, the small Lowcountry town of Somerset, South Carolina, your stand-in for Beaufort. Cut, he said, all that is not directly pertinent to Somerset.

I cut 250 pages in no time.

I showed his email to Pat, for whom it was another confirmation of the man's gifts. He was thrilled.

Jonathan began editing. My biggest problem was the absence of "signposts" for the reader. I had become so immersed in the story that I needed to surface periodically to let the reader know where I was and when I was there. "You're not only leaving the reader behind," Jonathan said, "you're leaving him confused."

Some of what I'd thought were my most powerful sentences now appeared to both Jonathan and me as incomprehensible; without question, according to Jonathan, worthy of repair but in dire need of it. For some reason, I thought of "The Perils of Pauline."

Famous All Over Town was scheduled to come out in September 2014.

During this period, strangely enough, Pat encouraged me to continue drinking bourbon when we would smoke cigars together on his back porch. I had refused, because he wasn't imbibing and I didn't want him to be tempted. Besides, it wasn't much of a sacrifice if I was the only one drinking; I was a social drinker, and even then, not much of one. Pat, however, insisted. He'd go downstairs to pour me a glass of Woodford, which he knew I really enjoyed, my favorite bourbon. He enjoyed my drinking vicariously. Was I, in his mind, doing it for him?

"I love smelling it," he said.

So I'd hold it up and let him sniff it. He got a kick out of that too, especially if I overdid it, waving it tantalizingly under his nose.

Maggie was with us one afternoon observing this ritual when she asked him what he missed most about drinking.

"That warm feeling in my belly," he told her.

The book launch for *Famous All Over Town* took place at the old Arsenal. I couldn't believe how many people showed up: locals, old friends from college and high school, writer friends, old students and colleagues, my kids and grandkids—it was pretty amazing. Lots of out-of-towners, but Beaufortonians all over the place. Supportive friends of writers really got the word out. Facebook helped bring in out-of-towners. Wilson Macintosh, the owner of the Beaufort Book Store who handled the sales, announced that we'd sold 350 books, not counting another 150 people who grew restless waiting in line and chose to order from Wilson instead.

Pat just loved it. It was great. My hometown turned out.

John Warley's novel *A Southern Girl*, published six months before mine, was the first book Story River Books published; ultimately, it proved to be their best seller. Pat, John, and I and Mark Sibley-Jones attended the Nashville Book Festival, where Ann Patchett introduced Pat, who introduced each Story River writer, so we could talk about our books. Speaking to that crowd was a whole lot of fun, but with the lineup of famous and well-regarded writers present, I certainly didn't expect to hit the jackpot.

I was on my way home, only about an hour from Beaufort. It was about one o'clock in the morning, when my cell phone rang. It was Pat. He couldn't have been prouder, couldn't have been more excited.

"Bernie, pull over to the curb. Take your time. Savor this: you sold out. Jonathan Haupt had fifty of your books there. They sold them all. Who'd have thought he needed more? He went out scrounging up books from any place he could find them, including Anne Patchett's bookstore here. Let it register, Bernie, this doesn't happen often. Congratulations. Jesus Christ. Can you hear me? You fucking sold out! They ran out of your books!"

I couldn't believe it. All I could say was "Wow!"

"Thanks, Pat."

"You're welcome, Bernie. Isn't this great?"

It was.

Of course, I showed up at a signing at the bookstore in Seaside, Florida, a few days later only to find out they didn't even know I was coming. The owner was out of town that day and forgot to tell them. If there's not at least a poster in the window, I learned, you might as well turn around and go home.

There were places I went, like the Litchfield Book Store in Pawley's Island, South Carolina, where the owners would fit the size of the place where the writer would speak to the size of the crowd he might draw. Those people and their employees were so thoughtful. They advertised, they knew in advance who might be interested in coming. They planned carefully. For a writer as well-known as Pat or Sandra or Dottie Frank, they'd procure an auditorium; for a writer like me, it would be a large, pretty much soundproof back room in a restaurant, with a podium, lectern, and microphone perfectly set up, and an introduction by someone who'd actually read the book and done the research, filled with sixty wonderful people, just about all of whom bought books. I couldn't have asked for more.

Often, they'd ask me if stories Pat had told about me were true. No, they were not, I'd say, then retell them casting myself as the hero and Pat as the dunce. It was all in good humor and fun. Sometimes I'd just volunteer stories about Pat—what he was like in high school, how writing the way he did not only saved his life but countless others', then I'd usually end by explaining how I taught him everything he knew and how I ended up writing most of his books for him.

He was a beautiful teacher, and he's a teacher in *Famous All Over Town*. So, I could segue into the story about the last class he ever taught, a story about censorship not from some radical-right rube but from the progressive left, about Paideia and how the fight against censorship is a fight for freedom, therefore always personal: *Who* gets to decide what goes public? The story he fought for at Paideia, I would explain, was his student's story about an attempted suicide, a theme, along with mental illness and death, that permeated his own books, the banning of which he fought with equal fervor.

We toured together with Story River authors, including Maggie when her *Lost Cantos of the Ouroboros Caves* came out. Pat would inevitably tell about the night Maggie was born, when I rushed out of the hospital room just like most new fathers, overcome with a love and joy and excitement I'd never even imagined, much less known. "Is it a boy or a girl?" he asks me. Then: "'Wait a second,'" Bernie says, "'I'll be right back!'"

Sometimes, when we were touring by ourselves, I could make him laugh anytime I wanted to just by introducing him to our audience as an alcoholic, just as I'd done back in Beaufort at social occasions.

"Welcome, everyone. Hi," I would offer from the podium, pointing to Pat. "His name is Pat Conroy, and he is an alcoholic."

To which audiences began responding: "Hi, Pat."

"Hi, everyone," he would say, pointing to me. "His name is Bernie Schein, and he is a study in abnormal psychology."

"Hi, Bernie."

Alcoholism—his own, that is—just the mention of it, never failed to make him all but collapse with laughter.

In Atlanta, we were speaking together at the Jewish Community Center, and before we began, I spotted some old Paideia friends in the audience and pointed and waved at them, only to look over and see Pat imitating me, after which he introduced me as Bill Clinton.

We were having fun.

XXI

A RECONCILIATION

Story River Books was flourishing. Jonathan Haupt set up author talks and panels all over the Southeast. By 2015, twenty books were on the market, several garnering the Independent Book Publishers Award, the Bronze Medal for Contemporary Fiction, the Bronze Medal for General Fiction, the Southern Independent Booksellers' Alliance Award, and the Florida and Georgia Book Awards. (Bren McClain's *One Good Mama Bone* in 2017 would win the Willie Morris Award for Southern Fiction, which unfortunately Pat would not be here to see.) Pat was more judiciously dividing his time between helping edit the books and writing *The Storms of Aquarius*.

I couldn't help but wonder whether somehow Story River Books was, among other things—and like liquor—a way to escape pain that perhaps his own writing didn't allow him to do.

In any case, he was writing about the friendships back in the late sixties that included George Garbade, Mike Jones, Pat, of course, and me, transporting the setting from Beaufort to Charleston. He didn't seem to need to talk about this book as much as the previous ones. I think he pretty much knew, or thought he knew, what he wanted to say, and he got whatever he may have needed out of me just through reminiscing, like we always did: George in the summer of '68 when we all went to Europe showing Pat how to pick up a girl and then what to do when he did; Pat and I both still in disbelief over his Daufuskie kids staying in white homes in Beaufort; and of course, Agnes Sherman, who if complicit in destroying Pat's teaching career was instrumental to his success as a writer. Pat's take on it now was without Agnes *The Water is Wide*, as well the excerpt from it in *Life* magazine that helped bring it national attention, would never have been written, the movie *Conrack* never made. Hell, he'd probably still be teaching on Daufuskie.

Susannah, however, remained his obsession. He was still hoping, still knocking on Lenore's front door whenever he happened to be in Atlanta, still sending over intermediaries, still writing her letters, still getting no response. The way he wrote about Lenore in *The Death of Santini* couldn't have helped. Also, his going on and on publicly and privately about what an all-around horrible person Lenore was and how she had all by herself ruined his life no doubt didn't help either.

That nagging question persisted: was it true? What's disturbing to me about this question is that countless readers and fans and even friends of Pat ask this same question about Pat's dad. Could he have been as monstrous as Pat depicted him?

Our friend, the writer and novelist Terry Kay: "Pat's father told me after the publication of *The Great Santini* that a hero always needs a villain, that since Pat always made himself the hero it followed naturally that he would make his father the villain."

That was true, no question about it. As Pat had told me, he always wanted to be the hero not only in his fiction but in real life. However, he also said that Santini as villain was ready-made. Was that true? According not only to Pat but his mother, his brothers, and his sisters, indeed it was true. I was working with Tim, a poet—the youngest now of Pat's siblings since their brother Tommy had committed suicide— on his poetry. We were going over several of his poems, and I was marveling at the beauty and intelligence of his language, his gift for description, for metaphor even if I didn't know what the hell he was talking about, when Tim realized that his dazzling display of language was a way to avoid the childhood fear that he and younger brother Tommy would experience nightly, the fear of his father's cruelty, of being hit. His sister Kathy with a poetic, Borges-like quality of her own avoided it all: "I went to bed at 6 o'clock every evening." Their father backhanded their brother Jim when he was still in his high chair.

Besides, I'd witnessed the flashbacks, heard the voice of the Navigator when Pat got so confused about the directions on our way to Janis's house.

I could go on and on, but Pat already did. Contrary to what Pat's father had told Terry, Pat as the oldest child in the family needed to be a hero because his father, the Great Santini to him, required it; it was from him Pat had to protect his siblings and mother, which he did. Pat was a hero. That's who he was, and his heroism continued throughout his life. He took the blows. He herded his family away from them. He was protective of everyone in his life, even if he never before had met them. A man is screaming, verbally assaulting his wife in San Francisco: Pat to the rescue. A man is on fire after a terrorist attack in Paris: Pat to the rescue. A buddy is broke: Pat to the rescue.

Even on the basketball court Pat was great in the clutch. Why? He told me, remember? "I wanted to be a hero."

No one, however, is a hero in a vacuum. The need has to be there. Throughout Pat's childhood, Santini, for better and for worse, created that need, the need for Pat to protect his mother and his siblings; and from his mother came the need metaphorically to "hide Jews," literally to fight against segregation, for civil rights, against the tyranny of authority, against brutality, and for the underdog. Pat was gracious in victory. "Thank you, Santini," as he has expressed in interviews. "Thank you, Santini, for this feast of drama you have so bountifully placed upon my literary table."

Pat's father was a hero in wartime, a villain in peacetime, in his most terrible moments making war on his family. Pat was a hero in peacetime. But like his father, was he also a villain, in his worst moments, in peacetime? Was Lenore? As Pat says, there's always more to the story. Can you imagine Susannah having to read and hear about this? If he continued in this vein, would he alienate her forever?

Pat had all but given up hope for any reconciliation with Susannah when he found out, probably from Emily, perhaps through Megan— she and Emily still talked—that Susannah, at about age thirty now, had moved out of her mother's home in Atlanta into her own apartment in our old neighborhood near the Emory University Hospital, where she was working at the Emory Cancer Center.

As far as Pat knew, until then Susannah had lived with her mother all her life. Had she ever dated, finished college, made friends? All he could do was wonder.

She was living alone, and Pat was looking for any opportunity he might have. So, he drove to Atlanta and pinned a note to the door of her apartment. When he arrived back in Beaufort at his home on Battery Creek, he discovered an email from Susannah. "Wanna have lunch?"

And so, the reconnection began. He just didn't want to come on too strong, to act desperate. He didn't want to fuck it up. Little did he know he already had.

They met for lunch in Atlanta, and when he returned home Sandra said he was the most depressed she'd ever seen him. Ever. Pat had hoped for a more openhearted, a more welcoming and inviting Susannah, but throughout lunch, he told Sandra, though Susannah was polite, she seemed distant, guarded. "How's Gregory doing?" "Fine." "Your job sounds great. Do you like it?" "Yes, I do." "You still writing poetry?"

"No." "What are you reading now?" "Nothing much." Pat offered to publish anything she wrote. She wasn't interested.

Finally, as he drove her back to work after their lunch, according to Pat, she let it all out. She told him she was furious about what he'd written about her mother in *The Death of Santini*; that he'd been mean to her aunt Carol Ann in *The Prince of Tides*. He confessed to her—he had to, he didn't want her to be surprised, she'd certainly find out sooner or later—that he'd been talking openly to biographers, and that talking "openly" was the only way he could do it. He invited both Susannah, as well as her mother, he told her, to be interviewed and to have their say without any censorship whatever, just as he was doing.

Never, she insisted, she would never talk to his biographers, she resented the invasion of her privacy, and already she was upset that he'd told everyone they were estranged. Further, unlike him, she told him, she'd never do anything to hurt her family. When she got out of the car, Pat said "I love you," to which her response was, "Thank you."

Right or wrong, Pat could no more refrain from writing or talking about Lenore than he could live without breathing. Katherine Clark, a Story River author, was interviewing Pat via phone every evening for her oral history of him, and Catherine Seltzer, his biographer, was not only interviewing him but touring with him.

Pat wanted the whole truth out there, but he wanted it coming from him, from his family and friends, from writers he trusted, so damned if the stupid son of a bitch didn't tell them everything, I mean, everything. He wanted no makeup covering up his life.

"No matter," I asked him, "how shitty and sordid it's been?"

He wasn't a hypocrite, you have to give him that, and yes, I can't blame him for wanting to beat biographers he didn't trust to the punch, and yes, he was Catholic, but did he really want to turn the whole world into a confessional?

After telling me about his lunch with her, Pat continued forwarding me their subsequent email exchanges. He received a very nice email from Susannah, a hopeful sign for him, but Sandra warned him to tread lightly in his response.

Did he? Yes, but in his own way. He said he wanted her to understand that if he didn't tell the whole truth to Katherine Clark and Catherine Seltzer, he couldn't help but feel his whole life was a lie. He'd lived carelessly, he told her, and he was filled with shame over his affairs and his drinking. All he had basically was the truth as he discovered and saw it. He knew it was incomplete, which is why he wanted Susannah and Lenore to tell their version of it to his biographers. The oral history and the biography were unauthorized. He neither wanted nor had any control over the contents in either of them.

He had begun this process before her "glorious"—his term—return to his life. Katherine Clark's book was already at the publisher. He confided Sandra's "tread lightly" warning and wanted badly to follow her advice but said he just couldn't. He'd been walking on eggshells, terrified of saying the wrong things to her, of losing her, and he just couldn't continue that way. He didn't want their relationship to be tense and unnerving, to be a lie, and if he was wrong to be telling her all this and she chose to discontinue their relationship, he would spend the rest of his life doing all he could to get her back. If he had to camp out at her front door, he would. He was ready to outlove anyone in her life, he'd show her. He was basically pleading, Please, Susannah, let me show you who I am and what I stand for.

Her response essentially was that she was glad he was looking for openness and honesty between them, and that she too wanted him to know who she was and what she stood for. Neither she nor her mother would participate in either of the biographies. However, she told him, like him, she did not want their relationship to become unhealable. So, for now she would drop the subject of the biographies, assuming he would show her that he respected their decision, which he did.

She was on her way to Rome, she told him, for a visit. Ah yes, Pat responded, the city where you were born, where I got to partake in your childhood. When she sent him a photograph of the two of them in Rome, Pat told her he would treasure it for the rest of his life. Susannah was excited about the upcoming Conroy@70 Festival in Beaufort where his "fat ass," as Pat had put it, would be celebrated, and she said she would be there.

And so, the reconciliation began.

Susannah was coming to Beaufort. None of us had seen her in more than a decade. Maggie and I and Martha hadn't seen her since she was five years old.

Meanwhile, throughout their email exchanges Pat had been on the phone every night with Katherine Clark and Catherine Seltzer, talking about Susannah's mother, and you can bet your ass he was spilling the beans like he never had before. He couldn't help it, and in her heart and soul, Susannah must have known it. No matter how I look at it, she's caught in a hellish cross fire in the war between Mom and Dad. It's been public, it's going to be public, and either way, Susannah can't help but feel like a traitor to the people she loves most in her life. No child deserves this, even a child of thirty. My heart goes out to her.

Pat did what he had to do, but he better, for both their sakes, have done it right. That is what we talked about in the fall of 2015 as he worked out daily at Mina's, worked on *The Storms of Aquarius* and Story River manuscripts, toured with Story River authors, talked with Katherine Clark and Catherine Seltzer at night, breathed in my Woodford, smoked Saint Luis Rey cigars with me on his back porch, and watched the sunset every evening with Sandra.

He was happy Susannah was coming, but, like Susannah I imagine, deep in his heart he was also worried. Was Truth really worth all this?

XXII

CONROY@70, HIS LAST HURRAH

Conroy@70, we were all there, at least it felt that way; even Peg and Pat's brother Tommy, both long dead, appeared to us onscreen in a showing of *The Great Santini*, Peg in the stands right behind her alter ego, the actress Blythe Danner, both of them cheering like crazy as Michael O'Keefe, playing Ben Meecham, Pat's alter ego, puts the ball on the floor and, risking it all, drives with abandon to the basket, albeit a bit stiffly. Blythe Danner and Michael O'Keefe are in the audience. So is David Keith, whose younger self is playing so insightfully onscreen the mean racist redneck Red Pettus, particularly the shock and dismay he registers when he realizes he's actually killed a black man, Toomer, whom he'd been scapegoating publicly, shamelessly, without conscience for years. Suddenly, all that hate disappears. You see not only fright, but in that moment of realization, love; one human being shocked at what he'd done to another human being. Underneath all that venom and hatred and condescension we'd seen earlier, we discover, if only briefly, before he runs for his life, that it wasn't Toomer's inhumanity that had so threatened Red Pettus but his humanity. He says. "Toomer, oh God, I didn't mean to."

And damn if we don't believe him. He shows us his humanity when he shows us that finally he sees Toomer's. I asked David how he was able to do that. "I'm a Southerner," he told me. "I grew up in Tennessee, I saw it."

Nan Talese is there, Jonathan Galassi, Marly Rusoff and her husband along with her assistant, the always embraceable Romanian immigrant Mihai Radulescu—Pat loved Mihai. Story River Books writers, whom Pat so generously and joyfully supported during the last several years of his life, were there: Ellen Malphrus; Eric Morris; Mark Powell; Ray Hirsch; Pam Durban; Katherine Clark; his biographer at the time, Catherine Seltzer; John Warley; Maggie and her illustrator, and her husband, Jonathan Hannah. The editor and publisher of Story River Books, Jonathan Haupt, and his wife, Lorene, were there. Nationally recognized, bestselling novelists Ron Rash, Patty Callahan Henry, Mary Alice Munroe, and the inimitable Janice Owens, all of whom Pat had also so generously and lovingly supported over the years, were there. Local former journalist-cum-novelist Scott Graber, also Pat's lawyer, and his wife, Susan, were there. And here is something I'll never forget: the Gullah cookbook author and former Daufuskie student Sallie Anne Robinson, and the critically acclaimed novelist and director of the Creative Writing Program at Notre Dame, his former Beaufort High School student Valerie Sayers. Pat's brothers and sisters and kids and grandkids, who number in the millions, were there. All of Beaufort was there, everyone in praise of Pat Conroy. Bronwen Dickey, James Dickey's daughter and a professor and writer in her own right, read with the ferocity and menace of the master himself Pat's favorite Dickey poem, "For the Last Wolverine," with Pat onstage behind her reciting every word to himself as she did. "Lord, let me die," she concludes, "but not die out."

Pat was dying at the time, though neither he nor we knew it. Like Dickey himself, however, he would never die out.

Pat had arrived, like Dylan Thomas's horses in "Fern Hill," another of Pat's all-time favorite poems, onto the "fields of praise," but instead of absorbing and basking in the magnificence and glory of it all, he was merely, to me, doing the job he'd always done. He was working, doing his duty, with all his usual gregariousness, graciousness, humor, and good will, but he was *working*.

When his fellow writers were on stage, he enjoyed it as he always did; he was thrilled, never missed a session the entire weekend. But he was impatient, I could tell, for it to end. He was tired, not because he was sick, but because he was giving so much, his mere presence a social draw.

On Sunday night, in the final session on the final evening of the festival, his biographer Catherine Seltzer was to interview Pat onstage. Billy Keyserling, our mayor and lifelong friend, would introduce him, reading a letter from Barbara Streisand, who couldn't attend. The letter was lovely, beautiful, and heartfelt, but it wasn't short. Then Billy had to run on with all the announcements the hosts had instructed him to make, which you could tell was becoming even painful for him they were so long. Finally, Billy arrived at his introduction to Pat, which you could tell from his smile he was quite pleased with and couldn't wait to begin. Billy was pretty interesting, but the night was growing long, I could tell that Pat was really getting impatient, especially when Billy began to get serious—he wanted to get everything in—and immediately after Billy offered a celebratory nod to the occasion, "Pat's seventieth birthday," Pat, sitting onstage with Catherine Seltzer for the upcoming interview, raised his hand, interrupting: "No, Billy, it's not. It was. I'm now seventy-one."

Catherine Seltzer is pretty amazing. She is naturally, even as an interviewer, unthreatening, disarming. Her body language suggests she's with you, behind you all the way, supportive, in your corner, wants to be helpful. Her questions reveal a subtle, deceptively astute intelligence, as if she might be thinking it all through *with* you, and with her natural humility, grace, and charm, the overall effect is compassion.

Clearly, she adores Pat. She has faith in him. She knows he is behind *her*, that he has faith in her. Like just about everyone, she can't help but forget herself momentarily and fall apart at his verbal antics, but she knows him, and that however slippery and evasive he might appear, such appearances in Pat are deceiving. At this stage of his life, he wants what he needs, and what he needs is the truth to, in his words, "go deeper," to openly express gratitude, warmth, love, and appreciation so as to truly feel it himself. The "little boy" he struggled with every morning of his writing life must be fully present for the wisdom of this truly great man to be openly and fully expressed.

I was just sick that he couldn't enjoy himself, that he couldn't let all this in. Couldn't accept, acknowledge, and enjoy that people loved him.

I had run across Catherine that afternoon and had become so frustrated over all this that I found myself presumptively blurting out to her about the interview coming up that night, "Break him, Catherine. Please. Just risk it all. Break the son of a bitch. That's what he'd do. That's what he's always done. Break him. Maybe he'll open up and let all this in."

What I meant by that, of course, was not the breaking down of Pat himself but of his defenses, so that he could open up more truly.

"Batter them," I said, after which immediately I thought, *Jesus, I sound like a real asshole*, but she didn't react that way at all, only, as you might expect if you know her, with attentiveness.

For whatever reasons—her own, I'm certain—she *did* in her own way, the only way always—as Pat himself would say—which happened to be the nicest way you might imagine. Pat completely opened up, talking about his mother, who always told him to help others, to listen to what they had to say, to be kind, polite, and generous. And he had done what she had asked. He had been a good little boy, I thought to myself, and so he was a good man. His mom was with him now, he told Catherine, touching his heart, and the child spoke, rising from his chair to the front of the stage, standing stubbornly, unwaveringly on diabetic legs, quieting as best he could the standing ovation. I was overcome with adoration. It was all I could do not to leap onto the stage and kiss him and hold him in my arms, love him openly, nakedly, without humor, without qualification. "Thank you," he said. "Thank you. All of you. I never dreamed any of this would happen. I always thought I'd teach high school and write on the side. I am grateful to all of you."

He was.

"Hey, grandkids, all of you out there, am I not something?"

Thank you, sweet Catherine Seltzer. Thank you.

The child spoke.

Pat spoke.

None of us knew it at the Conroy@70 Festival, but it was even more important than I could have ever have imagined that the little boy he once was, that he struggled with every morning at his writing desk, the little boy so eager to please, could become the man finally expressing his love, his appreciation, his gratitude.

He meant it! He meant it!

It wasn't "five faces" between Pat and us, his audience. The "five faces" he had told Martha about were now only one. It was Pat's true face, innocence now tempered and matured by wisdom. He saw us truly. He felt us truly. We saw him, we felt him.

It was important because only five months later he would die from pancreatic cancer, and he told me shortly before he ascended from this world pain-free that it was at the festival that he'd first felt the stirrings of his murderous blood cells. At the time, naturally, he didn't know it was cancer, but once he was told he had it, he realized that it had announced itself five months earlier at the Conroy@70 Festival. What he knew then, he said, was that he'd felt "weird." He thought at first he'd had the flu.

That Susannah was there was so important to him. She certainly is a Conroy, we all realized, so much like him. Gregarious, friendly, knew everyone's name from her past, remembered everybody, in my case even recounting a story about my rescuing her from a bully when she was in kindergarten at Paideia, a story I couldn't recall. She was so attentive, so gracious and kind, so like her dad in this way that you would have thought she'd been eavesdropping when Pat was but a child himself listening to Peg as she told him how to conduct himself socially.

She renewed her relationship with the other Conroy daughters, with Megan and Melissa and Jessica, in the same way Pat had so often renewed old friendships and loyalties, without any mention at all of whatever might have caused them to deteriorate in the first place.

I still find this strange as hell. Were the Conroys Jews, I once told Pat, they'd be incapable of renewing a relationship gone sour without discussing ad nauseum the reason for it. The Irish, he said, are too terrified.

So are the Jews. That's why we can't shut up about it. As long as we're talking, we're not fighting.

Which is why the Irish, he said, talk about everything *but* that.

I did ask Susannah about her mom, to please tell her that I'd asked about her and to give her my regards, which she genuinely and openly appreciated. Still, I did it for her, for Susannah, out of concern and politeness, probably much like Pat had in his emails to her. Whether Irish or Jewish, whoever you are, unfinished business is always sad. For her and for Pat, it was.

XXIII

PAT'S LAST NIGHT ON EARTH

"We've had great conversations," he said. It was his last night on Earth, we were all certain. Sandra had made all the funeral plans, fulfilling Pat's wishes. She and I were in his hospital room at the Medical University of South Carolina in Charleston. He'd said goodbye to his children, his brothers and sisters, all but Carol Ann, whom he couldn't bring himself to see. He feared, he told me, the drama she would bring. It would be too much. In the waiting room were his brother Tim, his biographer Catherine Seltzer, and if I remember correctly, his sister Kathy.

"We'll have more, Pat," I said, desperately. "We'll have more."

But he knew better.

"Who will I talk to?"

I was so broken, it's a wonder I even made it back to Beaufort that night. The Angel of Death, however, had given Pat a brief reprieve. The next morning, with only Sandra in the hospital room with him, all prepared to travel with his body back to Beaufort, he woke up, surprised as anyone else.

"What the fuck am I still doing here?" he wondered aloud.

Sandra told me he began, all on his own, getting out of bed, undoing the million wires and intravenous fluids to which he'd been connected, and proceeded to get dressed.

She was shocked.

"Pat, what on earth are you doing, baby?"

"I'm going to Beaufort," he told her. "Bernie doesn't have anyone to talk to."

The following evening, his last on Earth, back in Beaufort in his bed facing the sunset in Sandra's study, we talked about Susannah and Carol Ann.

"Take care of everybody, Bernie."

He showed me a postcard from Carol Ann, an overture in which she offered to donate her kidney to him. He didn't need a kidney, needless to say, but she volunteered it nonetheless.

"She's wounded," he said at the time, handing me the postcard. "Take it with you."

Then he said, "Susannah gave all she could. She too is wounded."

So was he.

The next day, with his brother Tim applying the morphine and his family and friends gathered around him, he passed away, and after leaning over to kiss him, all I could think was, "His life was so painful." Maggie remembers me saying it aloud.

It was sad, so sad, but as he passed away, in his ascension, as I felt and imagined it, the pain fell away.

XIV

MY FAREWELL LETTER TO PAT

Sandra asked me to "write up something" to be read at the reception for close friends and family immediately following Pat's funeral service. My daughter Maggie braved reading it for me.

Maggie's introduction:

"My father, Bernie Schein, asked me to read his farewell letter to Pat, his best friend and soulmate, to you all. Wish me luck.

"I am not sure his heart would have survived his reading this himself.

"Let it be his proof to naysayers and skeptics of love, that time, enough salted tears, hearty hugs, fierce fights, and life lived truly together forges of elements a connection that can't be destroyed by anything. Not even death.

"Bernie's letter:"

My dearest Pat,

I know we've said goodbye to each other more times in the last several weeks than either one of us might have imagined only a short time ago. Such is the nature of the obsessive-compulsive Jew who can't let go and an Irish Catholic blowhard with a heart so big I imagine it now dwarfing the universe. They'll love you up there: Peg and Don, Stannie, Mom and Dad, Gene, Doug, Tommy, Nancy Jane, all your loved ones. You're regaling all of them right now, I have no doubt; they're so happy to see you.

You had to have been dying to see them, since you did.

Frankly, my guess is your arrival on the scene at St. Peter's has even God opening his arms with a grin to match yours and a heart-felt embrace. If he hadn't needed a good laugh and some personality up there, you'd probably still be here driving all of us crazy.

When we last said goodbye to each other, I told you my heart and soul will always be with you, as yours will always be inside me. The advantage there, as I've reminded you on countless occasions, is yours. Needless to say, mine will make you a better person.

Your love, so inspired, so generous and warm and such a pain in the ass, that's what I'll miss, Bubba. That's what I'll miss. Your humor, which is so pathetic. Please, some new material, you've got time up there, mentally telegraph it to my imagination. God, did we laugh.

And Lord, did we cry. My friend, my friend. My soulmate, my inspiration, my muse, my devil's advocate. You care so much, I feel it. Yes, you could be a jerk, we all know that, but in the final analysis, when all is said and done . . . I remember we were talking to James Dickey's sister, Pat Dickey, in your study in Atlanta, about "character," about seeing people accurately. At that moment, you challenged me to look around your library and tell you the most important book of your youth. (*Famous All Over Town* had not yet been written.) You're laughing at that last comment right now, from heaven. Yes, heaven, where the dead come alive and have a great time laughing at us all, mere mortals, stupid people, fretting over nothing, right? Tell me, are we endlessly, over the long haul, fretting over trivia? You'll tell me when I see you, which I hope and pray is a fucking long, long time from now. I don't miss you *that* much. This whole thing scares the hell out of me. As for the book that most influenced you, let's let that hang for a while. We'll come back to that.

We had great conversations, you said, during our goodbye. We did, we did. Except when you wanted to talk too.

I know, you can't help it. I'm funny. But indeed we did, profoundly deep ones in our shallow age: we talked about everything, about ideas, yes, but they could bore us if disconnected from people. Boy, did we talk about people, about who we are, about what motivates us, about Beaufort, our country, our society, friends, enemies, your stupid relationship with the Citadel, your stupid relationships with everyone, even your relationships with old friends, some still alive and well here in Beaufort, you hadn't seen in forty years. All played even until the end a prominent role in your mind.

Truth is all that mattered to you, which I found sometimes a pain in the ass. But we discovered that ignorance is not bliss, that What you don't know *can* hurt you, and that sometimes you had to do unto others *BEFORE* they did unto you. And though we created our own reality, that reality made us both a bit paranoid. God, did we hate critics of all types. Unless we were doing the criticizing, which we did all the time.

We visited Dachau in the summer of '68, when we assured ourselves with great authority—our own—that we'd change the world. Your conclusion: People were basically evil. Mine: No, their leaders were, but people were generally basically good. We had no idea back then that our views were reflected not so much by Dachau but by the way we felt about our fathers.

Your life has been as painful as it has been joyful. I know that. Back then I didn't believe you when you talked about your father. No one did. Because you lied all the time, hell, you began lying for a living. Pat's exaggerating, like always, I told everyone. Until you painfully and relentlessly simultaneously sacrificed, discovered, and realized yourself with the Truth, the only way you could do it, publicly, through your art, and when you did, you saved and warmed the hearts of the lives of so many people—Yes, eventually, even your father's, the Great Santini's. You taught your father to love. Let me correct that. He always loved you, the only way life would let him, the only way he knew how. But you taught him to love *with* love, with humor, with warmth and tenderness. Pat, you taught your *father* to love. Your *father*. The Great Santini. And you think *he* was a war hero? He was, but you, Pat, became his. You had to, it was a matter of survival, and you did it with relentless love. You made him *see*. You made us all see, Pat, and what you and I discovered was that indeed we were both wrong, after Dachau, weren't we? The history of the world, all the emotions of every human being who ever lived, is in the heart and soul of each of us. Not either good or bad, but good and bad, and thank God for that. To look the other way, to deny, that is what makes us evil. The Truth does liberate.

Let us return now to your study, your library, in Atlanta, where we are talking with Pat Dickey about "character." The most important book of your young life?

Standing right there in front of me, third shelf down. Remember?

Lives of the Saints. Subtitle: *The Autobiography of Bernie Schein.*

Come on, you know that was funny. You can never keep a straight face with me. No one can. Right?

Your mom's love poured out of you your entire life. And the love of so many . . . I think, Pat, in all honesty, you are a saint. A shithead sometimes, but overall, a saint.

I love you, Pat. My heart, my soul, forever.

God's getting a kick out of you now, probably even more so as you tell him stories about me. Please, resist that urge. I can hear Him now: *"When's Bernie coming, Pat? We need Bernie here!"*

Please explain that patience is needed here, Pat. That *no*, we don't need Bernie, not for a long, long, long time, thank you. And don't encourage Him just to piss me off.

I speak now to you, family, friends, admirers:

Pat asked me, knowing what was coming, to "take care of everybody." He loved so much, so expansively, which is why he was loved so much. He cared so much. He cared for us all, but of course, no one did he care for like his beloved Sandra, his truly beautiful daughters, so beautiful, in every way. Jessica, Melissa, Megan, and Susannah. He was so proud of you. When he was sick in the hospital and back at home, and I was entertaining everyone with my formidable wit, you girls thought: Oh, good, he's enjoying Bernie's humor so much, but that wasn't entirely accurate. He was enjoying *your* enjoying my humor. While you were enjoying me, looking at me, he was enjoying you, looking at you. He loved so much. And like you, I love him so much. Pat will always be with us, inside us. And I promise you, as I promised him, I will take care of you. In fact, I can assure you, I will probably be a monotonous pain in the ass because even though it no doubt leaves you cringing in despair, it reassures him and makes him happy. So, up yours.

Kathy, Tim, Mike, Jim, Carol . . . I'm here, and I'm here for you to take me out to dinner as often as you like. Too bad we no longer have his credit card, but, hey, Mike just sold a house. What a brother is Pat, what a brother. I adore all of you, all of you. You're the best, far better, I used to tell him, than he was. He liked that.

I want to close by saying to everyone whose heart he has touched, whose soul he has comforted, and whose mind he has expanded, to all he has understood, inspired, and loved through words and his actions, to all his family, friends, and readers . . .

You have been in the presence of greatness, you have been in the presence of one who *dared* to be great.

Pat, you will live forever in our hearts, souls, minds. And I pray we are worthy to live now in yours.

He was a great artist—a great writer, a great teacher, a great friend—because he was a great audience. Writing, teaching, being a good friend is truly listening, turning your attention on a person so vividly it expands their image and vision of themselves. He made *me* feel great, not that I didn't already. Still, that's what love is, isn't it?

Eternally, I love you, Pat, always and forever, wherever you are, my beautiful, beautiful friend. I'm with you, my friend, inside you, of you, your heart, your soul, as you are with me and in mine. Forever.

XV

THE AFTERLIFE:
THE CONVERSATION CONTINUES

Catherine Seltzer, as she interviewed Pat for her biography of him in his last years, confided that he had told her over and over, as he'd always suggested to writers, to go deeper with her questions, as he had tried to do with his own every time he put pen to paper; indeed, to get more and more personal, to ask him what she was most uneasy about asking, what she was most afraid of, most uncomfortable asking; the hardest, the most difficult questions, admonishing her when she didn't, educating her as she was interviewing him, enlightening her, inspiring her, opening her up to greater possibilities. He loved to make people squirm. He was mischievous that way, and he delighted when what he did unto others she did unto him. Pat told me this too, wincing and grimacing in his self-deprecating way, on the one hand wondering what the hell he was doing opening himself up to her so much and on the other thrilled with himself, loving every minute of it. It was as if he was intent on scaring himself, playing peekaboo with it all, proving to himself and everyone else he could forsake all for truth, regardless whether it was clean-shaven, well groomed, and dressed appropriately. He trusted and liked her sensitivity, her sincerity, her innate goodness, her sense of humor, her appreciation of his humor—in short, her all-around loveliness—so hit me hard, he told her, as hard as you can. Do your job. That's what a writer does.

It is probably facile to judge that as a power play on Pat's part, but it did come to mind when she told me about it in an interview with me a few months following his passing. *How clever*, I thought at the time, smiling. By reducing her to the role of student, of protégée, his role becomes the teacher, and the teacher, however open and inviting he might be, is in charge.

Pat smiled too, above it all now, above us all now, at the thought. "Very good, Bernie. Interesting, in fact. Yes," he said. "Being in charge, no matter how much I tried to hide it, was my sanctuary, though of course I had no idea of it at the time, my shield, my safety zone. It was my protective coloration, behind which I could allow myself to be encouraging, supportive, inspiring. Remember, it was dangerous for me, Bernie. I needed a kingdom, a throne from which to issue my decrees. But I just wanted to help. I wanted everyone to be great. You didn't need that zone of protection like I did. You were brought up differently."

"But I also ended up naive, Pat." I know this might seem weird, if not absolutely nutty, but since he passed away, we talk like this all the time. "You fortified yourself against disappointment that at least in my life turned out to be a perfectly reasonable expectation."

In fact, we talk now as much as when he was alive.

"I miss you, Pat, but I'm with you, always, forever. I'll never figure out how we weren't gay."

Power play or not, clever and seductive though it may have been, his need to be powerful came from a wounded, frightened heart, that necessary distance providing him a buffer zone from which to support her getting him to get to the truths he needed and wanted to get to: his true face, that nice "little boy," his mother's child, that Catherine brought out in him at the Conroy@70 Literary Festival. That lessens neither his sincerity in the interviews nor his gratitude toward

Catherine; rather it reveals even more his fears, the strength of his ambition, his humanity. More than just about any of us, he knew the difficulty, the dangers involved, in finding and telling the truth, the one he needed to survive, the one that mattered. Throughout his childhood, he was taught not to. And let us not judge his mother, Peg, here: back then, divorce was unthinkable, a scandal, like being an unwed mother. She'd had little formal education, and her survival and the survival of her children were at stake. Unlike later, she had no choice.

Pat was not just her little boy but her little man.

XXVI

PAT'S LEGACY

Grief makes of us all narcissists. And with Pat's death, there are so many of us: close friends, family, readers and admirers, acquaintances drawn to his generous, expansive personality. If openness and honesty, expressing what you're most afraid to somehow express and talk about, is the hallmark of an intimate friendship, Pat was on intimate terms with half the world. He was a walking, talking suicide hot line. Through his own self-evisceration and the public exposure of his own wounds, he saved lives, thousands of lives. I know, I have read emails, listened to his readers, heard the stories. I call him Saint Patrick to amuse him, yes, but he spent his life performing psychological open-heart surgery on himself, the wound from which poured such a powerful empathy it's a wonder he didn't drown in his own blood. It's a miracle he even managed when nature called to pry out the nails, extricate himself from the cross and climb down just to take a piss.

That last line's for Pat. "I know, Pat, I'm funny. I see you."

The other half of the world, just as naturally, probably just thought he was an ass.

"They did," he tells me. "They did, they do, and they're right."

"Heavenly wisdom?"

Pat looks thoughtful, smiling. "I don't think so. The possibility that I was an asshole was never exactly alien to me."

"Nor to anyone else not comatose."

That just breaks Pat up. He was always so self-deprecating, so ready to abandon whatever might have been on his mind, to laugh at himself. He might require a little stimulus here and there, but laughing at himself and his flaws was more than anything else a gift he gave to himself. Comic relief, he was so susceptible to it, so easy, most of the time. There were those occasions in which I'd offer up something promising, something I thought might be hilarious, that ended up just hanging in the air, evoking nothing more than a grimace from Pat, after which it would fall flat. It was hard to get it off the ground after that, not that I didn't try. Jesus, Bernie, he'd say, forget it. I'm sorry, it's not funny, it's a corpse, bury it. I often disappointed him like that. He needed the comic relief. But hey, as I regularly informed him, I wasn't selling tickets, if you catch my drift.

"I'm still here."

"I was just thinking about what a willing audience you were."

"Like I said, I'm still here. Heavenly wisdom," he reminded me. "We were talking about heavenly wisdom." I'd often go flying off on some tangent, even if only in my own mind; his reminding me was nothing new.

"Right, how do I get that as a mere earthling?"

"You can't," he said. "You have to be above it all, where I am, with God, with the angels, with everyone in your life you've ever loved and hated."

"Hated? You're up there with Alan Fleischer?"

"I'm up here with Don Conroy. Up here it's all the same. If you come wounded, it's open, nothing to be ashamed of, something only to be healed. Up here, you're past shame, past judgment. That part happens before you get up here, when you did to others what was done to you. As a mere earthling, like you, a dumb fuck, I knew I was perfectly capable of being an asshole and was one on countless occasions with countless people, sometimes with people I loved, sometimes in defense of them. I could also be good, and I was, on countless occasions with countless people. I was human. So were they. To the degree we were hurt, we hurt; to the degree we were loved, we loved. Heavenly wisdom, Bernie, is knowing that, understanding it, seeing it. Understanding is a universe of its own, it just doesn't leave any room for judgment.

"I confessed, sought atonement. Voilà! Here I am."

"Is that why you persisted in telling Katherine Clark and Catherine Seltzer every feeling and thought you'd ever had in your life, every sordid act you'd ever committed? You felt you had to *earn* heavenly wisdom, peace of mind, an afterlife without the lash of judgment."

"Yes, though I wasn't as conscious of it then as I am now. Remember, right before I passed away I had serious regrets."

He had, I remembered, particularly about Katherine Clark's oral history, *My Exaggerated Life*. He hadn't checked his impulse to divulge, he'd realized. He'd just run his mouth about everybody and everything while she wrote it down and recorded it. Just because you're uncensored doesn't mean you're telling the truth. Had it been a book he was writing, I think he would have revised and rewritten it. Still, though at the time it was too late for him to go over it with Katherine Clark, he did ask Scott Graber to go over it for him, as his lawyer and friend.

"The regrets I remember. Once you realized what you'd done, who you might have hurt, you were pained. That's how you 'earned' it. Still, that makes me sad. As soon as you passed away, all I could think of was that your life was just so painful. But right after I thought it or said it, I could imagine, could feel, in your ascension your pain slipping away. There was peace for me in that. I didn't want you to suffer anymore. I just didn't."

"I know. I knew it would be very difficult for you. But that pain, just like you said, was in the past tense. You did say it. I heard you. 'His life *was* so painful.' It was, but it was also filled with joy, as you know. Think of that too. But: I told the truth as I felt it, and I did hurt people I loved."

"Pat, you told the truth as you *felt* it." I was about to bring up Lenore and all that he'd said about her, but he stopped me.

"Heavenly wisdom," he smiled, "comes slowly, when it's ready."

"Like any good story."

"Like any good story."

Old friends, new friends, writers, editors, family members, readers, fans, admirers, many often rightly assuming an intimate relationship with him if only having read his books and talked with him at a signing, so many, all asking in the aftermath of his death the same question: What would Pat want? What can we do to ensure his legacy?

Did he himself not do enough? For all of us? I thought he did. What more could we want? In remembering, however, grief makes us forget.

What we want is *him*, back again, walking the earth among us. I want him back with me, smoking those great cigars and drinking Woodford on his back porch overlooking Battery Creek, Sandra coming up with her white wine and one of her patented sweet mischievous smiles and some juicy gossip. I want Pat footing the bill as we, all friends, make fun of each other at our weekly lunches at Griffin Market. I want Martha once again annoyed with me because I'm late coming home for dinner after spending too much time talking with Pat. I want his fucking excitement, his inspiration, the depth of his feeling, the breadth of his joy, his uncommon stupidity.

Early on there was talk about a statue. He'd have hated it. About a museum. Maybe, but only if it contained programs that could really help people, as he had. And then his agent Marly Rusoff came up with the idea of the Pat Conroy Literary Center—a center to inspire and enrich stories, a place to hear and to tell stories that is now smack dab in the middle of downtown Beaufort, just where Pat would want it, accessible, as he was.

So hell, come see us.

The truth is, everyone who loved Pat has his or her own agenda. Everyone wants to contribute. But many also want to contribute so as to be *part* of his legacy; others use it to channel or project their own grief. Really, it has little to do with him and everything to do with us. That does not lessen its importance. Pat, however, is *dead*. Let's let him be at peace with the universe.

"They're projecting," he tells me. "Remember, you taught me that word, though I taught you everything else. But you were right, Bernie. It's so true. Everybody does it. It's a way of handling pain, feelings. Deny them in yourself, displace them elsewhere, and project them onto someone else. At some point, they'll forget about all this shit and everything will calm down. Just stay away from it all, try to get Sandra and the rest to do the same thing, and write your book. Everyone should. That's my legacy. I told my story, now you tell yours, or just shut the fuck up. Why do you think I was so involved with Story River Books? So people could tell their stories. A statue? Please. A literary center? A place that inspires and nurtures great stories? Sure, tell 'em to contribute to that. You should too, you cheap bastard."

A place that nurtures and inspires great stories.

Indeed, it has become that, no question. The theme, in Pat's own words: *Tell me a story.*

"And look, Bernie, if a museum brings people to Beaufort, fine, I don't mind that. With your huge ego, you'd love something like that. Me, I'm modest—a character trait beyond your limited imagination—I couldn't care less. Why do you think I picked a black Baptist cemetery to be buried in? That could be part of my legacy, if you want to call it that. But it's not up to me, is it? And Bernie, it's not up to you, so don't worry about it. No one should be worrying about it. I've already done all that. Pat Conroy's legacy, tell the living, Bernie, is to get as many people as possible to create their own. My name is not James Dickey. It is not Thomas Wolfe. It's certainly not Hemingway. It is Pat Conroy. Their names are their own. Otherwise, there is no truth to be told, no beauty to behold, no love to lose. I just thank God every day my name is not Bernie Schein. That's the silliest name I've ever heard. You should be ashamed of it. Hey, Bernie, I'm still me! Isn't that great?"

This is why, too, I think, he was so dedicated to telling Catherine Seltzer and Katherine Clark everything that mattered, everything he had not yet told in his books, anything he might have left hidden under the makeup his mother had applied to cover the wounds of his childhood.

He knew above all, however, that no matter how hard he tried, telling everything is impossible, and therein lies his legacy. Too bad he couldn't, even to his biographers, because his credo was the truth. Truth is what he needed to survive; not what he wanted, but what he needed. The truth he did tell, the beauty of the language in which he told it, the passion of the drama in which he expressed it will survive in his readers, in all those whose lives he touched, far beyond the concrete plans and limited imaginations of those of us left among the living.

And the living? What then of us? Pat loved our misery. He had to, in order to embrace his own. Who else does that?

I drive down Bay Street, the great antebellum homes with their discreet interior gardens and grand verandahs overlooking the oak trees draped in Spanish moss that stand sentry over the Beaufort River, as beautiful today as Pat told me it was more than fifty years ago. I drive through downtown, dominated largely by tourists and retirees now, the only place for the locals to shop back when Pat and I were kids, the only place they don't shop now, what with the malls and shopping centers and chain stores on the outskirts of Beaufort. I wave at the bridge man, whose leisurely job and daily view of Beaufort and the barrier islands I envy as I cross the bridge onto Lady's Island, which soon gives way to St. Helena Island and Penn Community Center, after which I pass the oldest church in Beaufort County, the Brick Baptist Church, then turn left on Club Road toward the Brick Baptist Church cemetery in which Pat is buried.

I love it out here. It's home, this cemetery. The sunlight, filtered through the oaks and Spanish moss, allow for just enough shade. It's simple, it's comfortable, it's necessary, it's perfect. Countless visitors have left everything from bottles of Rebel Yell to vivid hibiscus and lilies to a basketball at his gravesite. His daughter Jessica, when she's in town, sits here and reads the *New York Times* to him. Maggie has placed a mailbox here, which overflows with letters and cards.

Sandra told me that recently an elderly black man expressed his disapproval to her that a man who wasn't one of their own was buried here. Sandra was appalled. Aren't we beyond that? she wondered aloud. By "that," naturally, she was referring to race.

"This cemetery for Baptists," he said.

Standing now at the foot of Pat's grave, I smile at him, remembering.

"I was here," he says. "I'm everywhere. I heard it. I'm ahead of the game, Bernie, above it all. It's great. Don, Peg, Doug, Nancy Jane, Stannie, Tommy, they're all here. I saw your parents the other day. I can see them whenever I want. They get such a kick out of you. Isn't it great out here?"

I look around the graveyard that would now bring the world to Penn Community Center, but I can't get past the gravesite right next to him, only a few feet away, directly to his left.

"Jesus, Pat . . . You stupid son of a bitch."

While I can't get beyond it, he can see only beyond it, perhaps the story or our lives.

"Look to your left, Pat, directly to your left."

Buried right next to him, sleeping right next to him for all eternity, is Agnes Sherman.

Agnes?

Like Pat said, there's always more to the story.

ACKNOWLEDGMENTS

Thanks goes to my agent Peter Riva for his indefatigable support and tenacity, to my editor at Skyhorse, Cal Barksdale, for his equally indefatigable editing and his editorial gifts. That guy doesn't miss a thing.

Thanks to Maggie Schein for her great help, encouragement, criticism, and perceptiveness throughout the writing of this book. Thanks to Janis Owens and Cassandra King Conroy for not only their help and support and encouragement but for their pure and loyal friendship. Thanks to Tim Conroy for his passionate critique and enthusiasm.

Many thanks to Jonathan Hannah not only for his website and design but also for so many things having to do with this book they're impossible to list here, also for allowing me to chronically interrupt his work that pays.

I also cannot thank Scott Graber enough for his friendship, his expertise, and his support. Thanks to John Warley. Thanks to John Swensson for his love of Pat, his teaching of Pat's books, and his incredible support out on the West Coast.

Many thanks to Lara Williams for her great love and unwavering support. And also to Vanessa Schein for her openness and interest. Thanks to Charlotte Reid.

Thanks to Catherine Seltzer, also to Marly Rusoff, Mihai Radulescu, Billy Keyserling.

Thanks to Amy and Frank Lesesne at the Anchorage Inn.

Thanks to Jessica Crouch and the University of South Carolina Archives.

Thanks to Jonathan Haupt and the Pat Conroy Literary Center.

Thanks to the University of South Carolina's Story River Books for giving Pat the time of his life.

Thanks to my brother Stanley Schein for his unflagging support and for his research, and his wife Isabelle for adding some humor to the process. Thanks to my brother Aaron Schein and my sister-in-law Nancy.

Thanks to "the boys": Cliff Graubart, Terry Kay, Frank Orrin Smith, and Daniel Sklar.

Thanks to the Griffin Market lunch group: John Warley, Scott Graber, Jonathan Hannah, Aaron Schein, Lynn Seldon, and Pat for footing the bill. With his passing, we eat at McDonald's.

Thanks to Kathy Harvey and Mike and Jim Conroy.

A very special thanks to Jessica, Melissa, and Megan Conroy, to all your beautiful children, and to your great mom and my friend Barbara Conroy.

And thanks to you, Pat, my love always and forever.